Let Coincraft help you in three ways...

COINS MARKET VALUES

Editor:
David Jinks

Consultant Editor:
Richard West

Advertisement Manager:
Lawrence Brown

Advertising Executive:
Matthew Clifton

Production:
Gina Mitchell
Joanna Usher

Associate Publisher:
Paul Cheal

A IPC Media annual published by IPC Country & Leisure Media Focus Network (part of the IPC Media Group of Companies) from:
IPC Media
Network Focus
Dingwall Avenue
Croydon CR9 2TA.
Tel: 020 8686 2599
Fax: 020 877 0939

Distributed by:
MarketForce,
247 Tottenham Court Road, London,
W1P 0AU.
Tel: 020 7261 5555

Pre-press by CTT; printed by Millennium Offset Ltd, Penryn, Cornwall

British
COINS
Market Values 2001
CONTENTS

Pattern half-crown of Oliver Cromwell, featured on the cover (see page 38 for details of all cover illustrations)

7

Market Trends

THE British coin market continues to be firm, but not spectacular, with prices in most series rising in a steady and controlled manner.

Price levels in many series continue to be attractive, certainly compared with some levels reached in the past, and may have deterred the uncommitted collector from putting material back on the market. The lack of readily available material continues to be a drawback but collectors have bought intelligently when coins are offered and rarely reacted by buying at any price.

During the last year only one major collection has come to auction, the Millennial Collection of Irish coins sold by Whyte's of Dublin on April 29, 2000. Otherwise Spink have conducted two useful sales of English silver coins, the Hughes Collection of shillings and sixpences on November 16, 1999, and the Ashby Collection on July 14, 2000, the second containing material largely acquired in the 1950s.

Glendining's sold the well-known Bell Collection of Commonwealth Coins on February 9, 2000, while Baldwin's Auctions offered the Gorefield Hoard of Edward I and Continental pennies on October 12, 1999. Some of the finest Saxon and hammered gold coins were contained in the Triton III sale, held in New York on November 30, 1999, mainly from the Collection of Marion Sinton.

Celtic Coinage
Ten years ago the Celtic market was flooded with new material and collectors could have their pick at low prices. Now the series is one of the strongest in the British coinage with unprecedented prices for coins in really top grade or for significant unpublished pieces. In Sotheby's sale of October 14, 1999, an uninscribed silver unit attributed to the Belgae with a facing head of 'the

Above left: A splendid Testoon of Henry VIII which sold in the Hughes sale at Spinks for £7,150.
Right: A superb Elizabeth I Gold Ship Ryal which sold in the Triton III sale in New York for £20,800.

Cernunnos', the second recorded – but chipped and only very fine, was fought up to the astonishing price of £2,420.

English Hammered Gold
The popularity of hammered gold is not surprising, in no other field but coinage can one obtain an intricate gold item from the reign of Richard II or an official portrait in gold of Elizabeth I for such a modest outlay. Unfortunately the shortage of material on the market is making it difficult to collect. Nobles and quarters of Edward III and Henry VI, ryals of Edward IV, angels of Edward IV and Henry VII and VIII and the unites and fractions of James I and Charles I appear in most auctions but little else is seen.

The Triton III sale contained the best recent group: a very fine Henry IV heavy noble sold for £8,600, an Edward V angel for £15,000, a George-Noble for £10,400 and an attractive Elizabeth I Ryal for £20,800. These prices are good but not

Below left: An excessively rare Edward V Angel, one of five known, which sold in Triton III for £15,000.
Right: An historic and extremely rare George-Noble of Henry VIII which sold in Triton III for £10,400.

Above left: A magnificent Edward IV double groat of Dublin in the Millennial Collection which sold for £5,100.
Right: Ireland's only issued gold coin – Duke of Ormonde's Gold Pistole of 1646 – sold in the Millennial Collection for £74,000.

exceptional and though hammered gold prices are rising steadily, many items still sell for no more than they would have fetched 25 years ago.

Hammered Silver
This is an enormous series ranging from early Saxon to the first coinage of Charles II. Few in-depth collectors can cover its whole range.

Most serious collectors in the field are specialists, by reign (perhaps Stephen or Elizabeth I), by denomination (say sceats or groats), or by time period (for instance, Saxon or Charles I Civil War). This means that, at any one time, some series are popular while others are out of favour and it is quite possible for the canny collector to acquire unique coins in currently unpopular series for less than £100.

At the moment the value of the earlier series – sceats, Saxon and Norman, short and long-cross – has been somewhat diluted by the huge quantity of new material which has come onto the market in recent years.

By contrast the demand for coins of the latter series, particularly for denominations of groat size upwards and for portrait issues of the Tudor period, is very strong, and common but attractive pieces such as Henry VIII groats continue to reach new levels.

The hammered coins in the Hughes sale sold well, the cover coin – a Henry VIII testoon which had cost £3,080 at auction in 1995 – sold for £76,150, and a Bristol testoon of the same reign which had realised £935 in the famous Norweb Collection in 1985, went for £2,530. The Ashby Collection, although lacking the rarities present in Hughes, realised over high estimate with less than 1 per cent unsold.

Milled Gold
For many years milled gold was more the province of the investor than the collector and prices were expensive compared with other coins of similar rarity. This legacy lingers and the collector upsurge of the last decade has largely passed milled gold by. Guineas are popular, like shillings they are a very convenient and attractive denomination to collect, but prices for Five Guineas and Two Guineas remain flat and are certainly now cheap in the higher grades. Milled gold is particularly susceptible to edge knocks and damage and pieces without flaws are most desirable. Curiously there is a much lower price premium for the rare dates in early milled gold than there is in almost any other dated series, possibly because the starting price for a common date is higher.

This year saw the long-awaited publication of *English Pattern, Trial and Proof Coins in Gold 1547-1968* by Alex Wilson and Mark Rasmussen. This covers a fascinating series which has for many years been referenced only by the 1974 auction catalogue of the Douglas-Morris Collection. The publication of a new standard work often creates enhanced interest.

Below left: An irregular shilling struck in Cork in the Great Rebellion, 1647, made a record £3,000 in the Millennial Collection sale.
Right: An unusually fine Hiberno-Manx silver penny, circa 1025, which sold for £5,000 in the Millennial Collection.

Milled Silver

In the last few years determined bidding in the saleroom by individual collectors has pushed the price of choice milled silver up sharply.

It is possible that the top grade coins are now expensive compared with sound very fine specimens and it was noticeable that several pieces in the Hughes sale did not make the extravagant levels which had been paid for them – the 1666 shilling bought at the Kaufman sale in 1997 for £7,150 sold for £4,400 and the 1724 WCC shilling bought in 1998 for £2,640 sold for £1,650.

It is curious that the rarity of quite key coins in the series continues to fluctuate. Over the last few years a number of new specimens of the Dorrien and Magens shilling have turned up and it is now nowhere near as rare as it once was. In contrast some types regarded as only very rare are hardly ever seen. Market prices can take years to adjust to such revised rarity.

Interest has focused recently on engraving and legend errors on milled silver coins, and many new examples have been added to the classic varieties of the old ESC. It is difficult to established quite how rare or important some of these variants will turn out to be and it may take some time for the market to clarify itself.

Copper and Bronze

Condition is more important to this series than virtually any other and the lack of good old collections coming onto the market is sorely felt.

There was a buzz when it was learnt that the Ashby Collection was to be sold at auction, but it appears that the copper coins were disposed of many years ago. When top quality currency copper and bronze does appear it sells extremely well, though the market for patterns and proofs is a little less certain.

Scottish Coins

Journalists have often asked whether Scottish devolution has encouraged

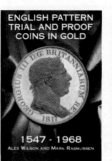 

Above left: An important new publication on English Pattern Gold.
Right: The Millennial Collection sold by Whytes of Dublin on April 29, 2000.

interest and pushed up prices in Scottish coins. The answer is 'yes and no'. Interest continues to rise but it comes from a keen new generation of collectors and there has not yet been the interest from national buyers such as Scottish banks which has been seen in the past.

Silver and billon coins continue to be a strong market and examples sell very readily but many coins may still be had for a very modest outlay and, unlike some other series, are regarded as collectable in almost any grade.

The gold market could be poised for a major uplift. The Horace Hird sale in 1974 pushed gold prices to undreamed of levels which the market has been struggling to regain ever since. The supply of the best coins, having whetted collectors' appetites, has now dried up. The Marion Sinton collection saw some record prices, including £1,750 for a James V Crown and £3,300 for a Mary 44 Shillings, though the first was water worn and the second double-struck.

Irish Coins

The highlight of the year was the sale by auction of the Millennial Collection by Whyte's of Dublin. One of the finest private collections ever formed, this was originated in the late 1960s and contained such rarities as the only specimen of the Gold Pistole in private hands, acquired at the Bridgewater House sale in 1972. The Irish series has a strong domestic market,

Coin News continues to bring the latest information to collectors.

fuelled by a booming economy, but British, European and particularly North American collectors were well represented.

The gold pistole is the pre-eminent Irish coin and it realised a hammer price of I£100,000 or £74,000, compared with the Bridgewater House £9,500 in 1972. Many other records were set: £5,000 for an excellent Hiberno-Manx penny; £5,500 for a Lord Justices annulet groat; £6,400 for an Ormonde crown in the name of Charles II. The strongest interest was in the irregular issues of the Civil War with a Cork shilling realising £3,000, and in rare and quality copper and pewter, a St Patrick's farthing selling for £760 and a 1687 James II halfpenny also making £760. This catalogue will long be a standard reference for the Irish coinage.

The current strength of the Irish market can be seen by an astonishing price of £4,025 paid at Glendining's on July 19, 2000 for an Edward IV Cross on rose groat. This coin has been broken into at least three pieces and repaired.

Anglo-Gallic Coins

More than any other series Anglo-Gallic is divided into sub-sections, common silver and billon, rare silver and billon, and gold. Until recently it was possible for a dealer to make a steady return by buying the common Anglo-Gallic in Paris and selling it in Britain and North America. This is no longer possible, the demand for common pieces priced at under £100 had risen and now outstrips supply.

The market for rare pieces remains more uneven. By definition they are not often available and so difficult to collect, and when they do appear their lack of eye-appeal contrasts with their undoubted historical appearance.

How to Collect

A few words of advice for those who have recently discovered coin collecting.

How much is it worth?

There was a time when newcomers to coin collecting would ask the question 'What is it?'. Nowadays certainly the most common question dealers hear 'What is it worth?'. It is a sign of the times that history takes second place to value. The object of COINS MARKET VALUES is to try to place a value on all the coins produced in what is known geographically as the British Isles, in other words England, Wales, Scotland and Ireland, and the Channel Islands,

as well as the Anglo-Gallic series.

This is a difficult task because many coins do not turn up in auctions or lists every year even though they are not really rare. However, we make a stab at a figure so that you the collector can at least have an idea of what you will have to pay.

How to sell your coins
Auction

In England we are well served with a number of auction houses, giving the potential seller considerable choice. In

Price lists and auction catalogues will prove invaluable.

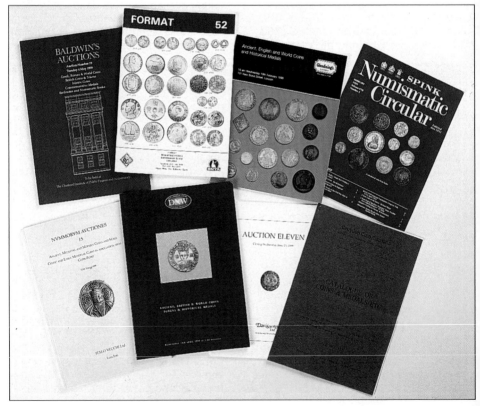

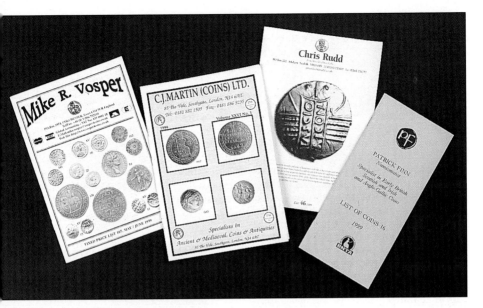

London alone we have, in alphabetical order, Baldwins, Dix Noonan Webb, Glendinings, Sothebys and Spink; while there are smaller companies up and down the country, such as Croydon Coin Auctions. In Ireland Whyte's of Dublin hold the pole position.

The best approach for the seller is first of all to compare all their catalogues and if possible attend the auctions so that you can see how well they are conducted. Talk it over with their experts, for you may have special cataloguing requirements and you could find that one of the firms might look after them better than the others.

An obvious coin, like say an 1887 £5, requires little expertise and will probably sell at a certain price in almost any auction; however, if you require expert cataloguing of counter-marked coins or early medieval, then you need to know what the company is capable of before you discuss a rate for the job.

You should remember though that while it is not complicated to sell by auction you may have to wait at least three or four months from the time

you consign the coins to the auction-eers before you receive any money. There are times when auctions manage to achieve very high prices, and other times when, for some inexplicable reason, they fail to reach even a modest reserve.

You should also bear in mind that the best deal in the long term is not always the lowest commission rate. Finally, auctioneers will usually charge you at least 10 per cent of the knock-down price, and you should remember that some buyers may also be inhibited from paying a top price by a buyer's premium, also of 10 per cent (indeed, some firms are now charging 15%).

Dealers

The function of a dealer is to have a stock of coins for sale at marked prices. However, they will naturally only wish to buy according to the ebb and flow of their stocks. It is also true to say that dealers infinitely prefer fresh material, and if you strike at the right time it is possible that you could achieve a better price than by waiting for auction, since of course you will receive the money immediately. Generally speaking, both dealers and auctioneers will not make any charge for a verbal valuation, but you should allow for the dealer to be making a profit of at least 20 per cent.

Bullion coins
Relating to Kruggerands, sovereigns, and so on, most newspapers carry the price of gold, which is fixed twice daily by a group of leading banks. Anyone can buy sovereigns, and Krugerrands and other bullion coins, and it is better these days now that there is no VAT on top. Normally, when you sell the bullion coin you expect the coin dealer to make a few pounds profit on each coin, but don't expect a good price for a mounted coin attached to grandfather's watch chain, which will not be worth anything like the same price as an undamaged item.

How to collect coins
You should obviously purchase your coins only from a reputable dealer. How can you decide on a reputable dealer? You can be sure of some protection if you choose one who is a member of the British Numismatic Trade Association or the International Association of Professional Numismatists. Membership lists of these organisations can be obtained from the respective secretaries: Mrs Carol Carter, PO Box 474A, Thames Ditton, Surrey KT7 0WJ (tel: 020 8398 4290; fax: 020 8398 4291) and Jean-Luc Van Der Schueren, 14 Rue de la Bourse, B 1000 Brussels.

However, many dealers are not members of either organisation, and it does not mean that they are not honest and professional. The best approach is simply to find one who will unconditionally guarantee that the coins you buy from him are genuine and accurately graded.

As a general rule you should only buy coins in the best condition available, and on this subject you will at first have to rely on the judgement of the dealer you choose. However remember it will not always be possible to find pieces in Extremely Fine condition, for example, and it can sometimes be worth buying coins which are not quite Very Fine.

In the case of great rarities, of course, you might well have to make do with a coin that is only Fine, or even Poor. If there are only six known specimens of a particular piece, and four are in museums, it seems pointless to wait for 20 years for another

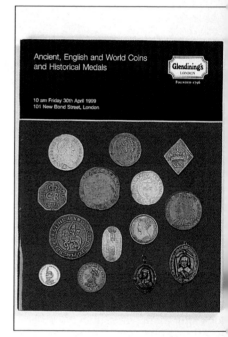

one to be found in the ground. Over the last few years condition has become too important in many ways, and has driven away collectors, because obviously you cannot buy coins only in top condition, since in certain series that would rule out at least 50 per cent of the available specimens. It depends on the type of coin, the reign and so on, so be realistic.

It is worth taking out subscriptions with auction houses so that you can receive copies of all their catalogues, because this is an excellent way to keep up with prices as well as the collections that are being offered.

However, one should not overlook the fact that a number of dealers produce price lists, which in many ways are most useful to the collector, because coins can then be chosen at leisure by mail order. It is also easier to work out what can be afforded to buy than when in the hot-house atmosphere of the auction room.

The most famous list is Spink's

Numismatic Circular first published in 1892, and still going strong with six issues a year. It is more than a price list being an important forum for numismatic debate and the reporting of new finds, etc (annual subscription £18).

There are also many expert dealers who produce excellent lists; many of them advertise in this publication and obviously we cannot mention them all here, but a good cross section of those who list domestic coins, and not listed

in any order of preference, is as follows:

Lloyd Bennett, PO Box 2, Monmouth, Gwent NP5 3YE. Hammered, Milled, Tokens.
B. J. Dawson, 52 St Helens Road, Bolton, Lancashire BL3 3NH. Hammered, Milled, Tokens, Medals.
Dolphin Coins & Medals Ltd, 22 High Street, Leighton Buzzard, Bedfordshire LU7 7EB. All British.
Patrick Finn, PO Box 26, Kendal, Cumbria LA9 7AB. Hammered English, Irish, Scottish.
Format, 18 and 19 Bennetts Hill, Birmingham B2 5QJ. All British.
Grantham Coins, PO Box 60, Grantham, Lincolnshire. Milled, good on Maundy.
K. B. Coins, 50 Lingfield Road, Martins Wood, Stevenage, Hertfordshire SG1 5SL. Hammered and Milled.
C. J. Martin, 85 The Vale, Southgate, London N14 6AT. Celtic and Hammered.
Peter Morris, PO Box 223, Bromley, Kent BR1 4EQ. Hammered, Milled, Tokens.
S. R. Porter, 18 Trinity Road, Headington Quarry, Oxford OX3 8QL. Milled and Hammered.
Chris Rudd, PO Box 222, Aylsham, Norfolk NR11 6TY. The only specialist dealer in Celtic Coins.
Seaby Coins, 14 Old Bond Street, London W1X 4JL. Hammered, some Milled.
Simmons & Simmons, PO Box 104, Leytonstone, London E11 1ND.

Also don't forget there are specialist dealers who do not produce lists, for example, Chelsea Coins (Dimitri Loulakakis, 020 8879 5501) who, although a prominent dealer in European and world coins, is also the man for Maundy money.

Societies
You should consider joining your local numismatic society, there being quite a number of these throughout the country. To find out if there is one near

you, contact the British Association of Numismatic Societies, Mr P. H. Mernick, c/o Bush, Boake, Allen Ltd, Blackhorse Lane, London E17 5QP (tel: 020 8523 6531). The BANS organises annual congresses and seminars, and it is a good idea for the serious collector to consider attending one of these. Details are usually well publicised in the numismatic press.

Those collectors who wish to go a little further can apply for membership of the British Numismatic Society, and for their annual membership fee they will receive a copy of the *British Numismatic Journal* which incorporates details of current research and many important articles, as well as book reviews.

Another useful facet of membership of this society is that you can borrow books from its library in the Warburg Institute. The secretary of the British Numismatic Society is C. R. S.

Farthing, 10 Greenbanks Gardens, Wallington, Fareham, Hants PO16 8SF.

Londoners might like to consider joining the London Numismatic Club, which is the best society after the Royal and the British, and is always looking for new members. Newcomers will be sure of a very friendly reception. The secretary is Robert Hatch, c/o P. Rueff, 2 King's Bench Walk, The Temple, London EC4Y 7DE.

Coin Fairs

Whilst it is always important to visit museums to see coins, it is worth remembering that there is often a fine array on show at coin fairs around the country, and most dealers do not mind showing coins to would-be collectors, even if they cannot afford to buy them on the spot.

The BNTA have been very successful with the COINEX shows, and the annual event at the Marriott Hotel should not be missed (October 6 and 7, 2000). Likewise COINEX North held each Spring (in 2000 in Harrogate: for further details contact BNTA Secretary 020 8398 4290).

Howard and Frances Simmons are the popular organisers of the Cumberland Coin shows, held at the Cumberland Hotel, London, since the late 1960s (for details ring 020 7831 2080).

The Croydon team of Davidson/Monk organise the monthly shows at the Commonwealth Institute, Kensington, London W8 (ring 020 8656 4583).

David Fletcher organises the monthly Midland Coin and Stamp Fair, second Sunday every month (enquiries 01203 716160).

There are also fairs held at York racecourse in January and August. For information ring 01268 726687.

Finally for details of the successful Irish coin shows in Dublin ring Peter Sheen (003531 496 4390); and for the annual shows in conjunction with the Irish Numismatic Society ring Ian Whyte (003531 874 6161).

Keeping your Coins

ONCE you have started to collect coins make sure you know how to look after them properly.

Storage
Careful thought should be given to the storing of coins, for a collection which is carelessly or inadequately housed can suffer irreparable damage. Corrosion depends essentially on the presence of water vapour, and therefore coins should not be stored in damp attics or spare bedrooms, but where possible in evenly heated warm rooms.

We should also point out here that one must be very careful only to pick up coins by the edges, for sweaty finger prints contain corrosive salt. The following are suitable methods of storage.

Wooden cabinets
A collection carefully laid out in a wood cabinet is seen at its most impressive. Unfortunately, though, the modern wooden cabinets which are custom built especially for coins are not cheap. Their main advantages are the choice of tray and hole sizes, and the fact that because the manufacturer is often himself a collector, he takes

Coins cabinet produced by Peter Nichols of St Leonards-on-Sea.

care to use only well matured woods, which have no adverse reactions on coins.

Among the makers of wood cabinets are H.S. Swann, of Newcastle (tel: 01661 853129) and Peter Nichols of St. Leonards, East Sussex (tel: 01424 436682).

Safe Albums offer a wooden cabinet with six trays for £140 (tel: 01189 328976).

If one cannot afford a new cabinet, then a second-hand version may be the answer. These can sometimes be purchased at coin auctions, or from dealers, and can be very good value. However, it is not always easy to find one with the tray hole sizes to suit your coins.

Do-it-yourself cabinet makers should also be careful not to use new wood, which will contain corrosive moisture. In this case the best method would be to use wood from an old piece of furniture.

Albums, plastic cases and carrying cases

There are many of these on the market, and some of them are both handsome and inexpensive. There are also very attractive Italian and

Coin boxes produced by Lindner.

German-made attache type carrying cases for collectors, with velvet lining and different sizes of trays, and so on. These can be obtained from a number of dealers, but Collectors Gallery, Castle Hall, Castle Gates, Shrewsbury SY1 2AD (tel: 01743 272140) makes a speciality of them.

We would also recommend the coin album, which claims to prevent oxidization. The coins are contained in cards with crystal clear film windows enabling the collector to see both sides of the coins. The cards then slide into pages in an album, and might be a convenient method of storage, especially for the new collector.

Coins International of 1-2 Melbourne Street, Leeds LS2 7PS (tel: 0113 2468855) also offer a large range of albums, envelopes, plastic boxes and capsules, etc.

Lindner Publications Ltd, 26 Queen Street, Cubbington, Leamington Spa CV32 7NA (tel: 01296 425026) supply very useful coin and collecting boxes as well as albums.

A new extended range of Lighthouse coin accessories is available from the Duncannon Partnership, 4 Beaufort Road, Reigate, RH2 9DJ (tel: 01737 244222). Phone them for a brochure.

In Central London, probably the best place to visit is Vera Trinder, 38 Bedford Street, London WC2 (tel: 020 8836 2365/6) who does appear to keep a very good stock. Stanley Gibbons, 399 Strand, London WC2 (tel: 0800 611622) also produce large size coin albums. Phone them for a free brochure.

W. H. Smith (larger branches) offer a very good coin album and collecting system.

Envelopes

Plastic envelopes, being transparent, are very useful for exhibition, but we never recommend them for long-term storage purposes. They tend to make the coins 'sweat', which with copper and bronze in particular can lead to corrosion.

Manilla envelopes are much more suitable, since the paper is dry, unlike ordinary paper, and consequently they are

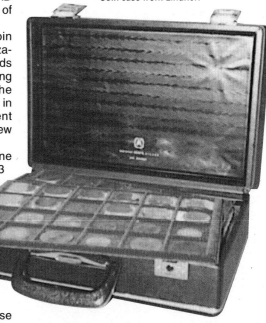

Coin case from Lindner.

ideal for the storage of coins. Most collectors use them in conjunction with a cardboard box, which makes for simple unobtrusive storage. This is the most inexpensive method of storing coins.

Still the best article we have seen on the storage of coins and medals, which deals with all the materials which are used, was by Mr L. R. Green, who is Higher Conservation Officer at the Department of Coins and Medals at the British Museum. This appeared in the May 1991 issue of *Spink's Numismatic Circular*.

Magnifiers

New collectors will need to have a good magnifying glass to examine coins, and these can be obtained from W. H. Smith or most other stationers; many opticians also offer very good magnifying glasses.

There is now also an excellent and inexpensive binocular microscope on the market, manufactured in the USA and available for less than £200 from Allan Davisson of Cold Spring, MN (fax: 001 320 685 8636).

Cleaning coins

In the course of each week dealers examine many coins which some poor unfortunates have unwittingly totally ruined by cleaning. They are, therefore, usually the best people to ask about the subject.

One dealer tells of a bright-eyed expectant gentleman who offered his late father's very useful collection of copper coins, which he proudly said he had 'brightened up' the previous day, so as to be certain of a good offer. The dealer did not enjoy his customer's sad disappointment when he found himself unable to make any offers, but then the coins had been cleaned with harsh metal polish and looked like soldiers' buttons.

We always advise people never to clean coins unless they are very dirty or corroded. Also by 'dirt' we do not mean oxide which, on silver coins, can give a pleasing bluish tone favoured by many collectors.

The following simple instructions may be of some help, but do not, of course, apply to extremely corroded coins which have been found in the ground, for if important they are the province of a museum conservationist.

Safe Albums (tel: 01189 328976) offer coin cleaning fluid for gold, silver and copper coins at £7.50 each.

Gold coins

Gold should cause collectors few problems, since it is subject to corrosion only in extreme conditions. For example, a gold coin recovered from a long spell in the sea might have a dull, rusty appearance. However, in the normal course of events a little bath in methylated spirits will improve a dirty gold coin. A word of warning, gold coins should not be rubbed in any way.

Silver coins

Silver will discolour easily, and is particularly susceptible to damp or chemicals in the atmosphere. A gentle brushing with a soft non-nylon bristle brush will clear loose surface dirty, but if the dirt is deep and greasy, a dip in ammonia and careful drying on cotton wool should do the trick. We should once again stress that there is no need to clean a coin which simply has a darkish tone.

Copper and bronze coins

There is no safe method of cleaning copper or bronze coins without actually harming them, and we would only recommend the use of a non-nylon, pure bristle brush to deal with dirt.

There is no way of curing the ailments peculiar to these metals, namely verdigris (green spots) or bronze disease (blackish spots) permanently, and we would advise collectors not to buy pieces in such condition, unless they are very inexpensive.

Museums

ONE of the best places to see and admire coins is in museums. Many have coin collections, but here are the museums which keep the major collections.

London
The British Museum.
The HSBC Money Gallery illustrates the development, management and production of the coins, banknotes and electronic money in use today. The display ranges over an enormous number of coins and other objects which have been used as money over the last four and a half thousand years. There are 19 specially designed cases displaying many choice pieces, beautifully presented and making the best use of modern lighting techniques.

The Keeper of Coins is:
Dr Andrew Burnett,
British Museum,
Great Russell Street,
London WC1B 3DG.
Tel: 020 7636 1555
Fax: 020 7323 8171
E-mail: coins@british-museum.ac.uk

A superb £20 piece of 1576 in the National Museum of Scotland (copyright: National Museums, Scotland).

Edinburgh
National Museums of Scotland.
The National Museums house the premier collection of Scottish coins and tokens, but also possess significant collections of English, British, ancient and foreign material. The Scottish coins include the Coats collection, on which Edward Burns based his three-volume standard work, *The Coinage of Scotland.*

Many coins of all periods and of types made or used in Scotland are included in various thematic displays in the Museum of Scotland, opened in 1998.

There is currently no numismatic exhibition in the adjoining Royal Museum, but anyone wishing to view or study specific coins or series is welcome to visit the Coin Room by appointment.

The Curator of Numismatics is:
Mr Nick Holmes,
Royal Museum,
Chambers Street,
Edinburgh, EH1 1JF.
Tel: 0131 247 4061
E-mail: nmmh@nms.ac.uk

Glasgow
Hunterian Museum.
A new permanent gallery devoted to numismatics has

Some of the attractive showcases in the exhibition at Cardiff (copyright: National Museum of Wales).

been opened at the Hunterian Museum. It is situated in an upstairs mezzanine gallery off the main hall and features over 2,000 items.

The Hunter Coin Cabinet contains the important 18th century collection of the eminent Scot and royal physician Dr William Hunter, and in the new gallery there are many of the choice specimens from this collection.

The curator of coins is:
Dr Donal Bateson,
Hunterian Museum,
University of Glasgow,
Glasgow, G12 8QQ.
Tel: 0141 339 8855

Cardiff
National Museum and Gallery.
There is an excellent general exhibition of coins, medals, decorations and tokens in the National Museum and Gallery, Cardiff. The displays include many superb and rare pieces, presented with excellent lighting in good showcases. The Tregwynt (Pembs) Civil War hoard of gold and silver coins, found in 1996, provides a spectacular centrepiece.

The exhibition is supported by an entertaining guide by Edward Besly entitled Loose Change, a guide to common coins and medals.

The assistant keeper in charge of coins is:

The famous Charles I Oxford crown showing a view of the city. One of the important pieces at the Ashmolean (reproduced with permission of the Ashmolean Museum).

Mr E. M. Besly,
Department of Archaeology and Numismatics,
National Museum and Gallery,
Cathays Park,
Cardiff, CF10 3NP.
Tel: 02920 573291
E-mail: Eward.Besly@nmgw.ac.uk

Birmingham
Birmingham Museum and Art Gallery.
Birmingham Museum has one of the largest regional coin collections in England. Although it is very diverse there are important groups of British Celtic, Saxon/Norman and Medieval coins. The collection is also particularly noteworthy for the products of local mints such as Matthew Boulton's Soho and its successors, including today's Birmingham Mint. There is also a fine collection of commemorative medals.

At present there are no numismatic displays on show, but a new gallery is planned as part of a major re-display programme.

The curator of coins is:
David Symons,
Birmingham Museum and Art Gallery,
Chamberlain Square,
Birmingham B3 3DH.
Tel: 0121 303 4201

Cambridge
The Fitzwilliam Museum.
The Fitzwilliam in Cambridge houses the famous Grierson collection of European Medieval

A view of the new display area at the Ashmolean (reproduced with permission of the Ashmolean Museum).

The Numismatics Gallery in the Ulster Museum (reproduced with the permission of the Trustees).

Coins currently being catalogued in a series of 13 volumes (Volume 1, now available, consists of 674 pages and 65 plates - so you can appreciate the magnitude of the task).

In recent years the Museum has acquired the important collection of Christopher Blunt, which will also be published in due course. There is also a very good exhibition.

The curator of coins is:
Dr Mark Blackburn,
Fitzwilliam Museum,
Trumpinton Street,
Cambridge, CB2 1RB.
Tel: 01223 332900

Oxford
The Ashmolean Museum.
The Ashmolean Museum contains the oldest public collection in Great Britain; it was designed to serve the purposes of teaching. It is a very large and all embracing collection and like Cambridge, very important for serious students.

The curator is
Nick Mayhew,
The Ashmolean Museum,
Heberden Coin Room,
University of Oxford,
Oxford, OX1 2PH.
Tel: 01865 278058

York
Yorkshire Museum.
The Yorkshire Museum holds one of the most important coin collections in the United Kingdom, being particularly strong in the fields of Roman coinage, Northumbrian stycas, English hammered silver and trade tokens. Hoards and single finds from Yorkshire are particularly well represented.

Many of the finest coins in the collection are featured in bright, modern displays, and the museum also stages regular temporary exhibitions of coins and medals.

The Keeper of Numismatics is:
Craig Barclay,
Yorkshire Museum,
Museum Gardens,
York YO1 7FR.
Tel: 01904 629745
E-mail: craig.barclay@york.gov.uk

Belfast
Ulster Museum.
The Ulster Museum has some very interesting display techniques and certainly makes the most of a relatively small collection. The museum acquired many of its important Irish pieces from the Carlyon-Britton collection and the enthusiastic directorship of Bill Seaby in the 1970s put it on the map numismatically.

The curator of coins is:
Mr Robert Heslip,
Ulster Museum,
Botanic Gardens,
Belfast,
Northern Ireland,
BT9 5AB.
Tel: 01232 381251

Dublin
National Museum of Ireland.
The National Museum has the most important collection of Irish coins and houses the former collection of the Royal Irish Academy. The museum is

currently undergoing reorganisation and there is now a small exhibition at Collins Barracks in Benburb Street; however coins can also be seen if an appointment is made.

The curator of coins is:
Mr Michael Kenny,
National Museum of Ireland,
Kildare Street,
Dublin 2,
Eire.
Tel: 003531 6618811

Other important museums

There are many other museums up and down the country which have excellent collections of British coins. The following are well worth a visit:

Blackburn Museum, Museum Street, **Blackburn**, Lancashire (01254 867170) has a good reputation for numismatics.

City Museum, Queen's Road, **Bristol** BS8 1RL (01179 223571). Especially good on coins of the Bristol mint.

Royal Albert Memorial Museum, Queen Street, **Exeter** EX4 3RX (01392 265858) has a very good collection of Exeter mint coins.

Manx Museum, Douglas, Isle of Man (01624 675522). Particularly excellent for students of Viking and Hiberno-Norse.

A view of the Yorkshire Museum.

City Museum, Municipal Buildings, The Headrow, **Leed**s, West Yorkshire (01132 478279). An excellent all round collection.

Manchester Museum, The University, **Manchester** M13 (0161 275634). Another excellent all round collection.

Reading Museum and Art Gallery, Blagrave Street, **Reading**, Berkshire (01735 399809). Good medieval and interesting local finds.

Many of our museums have co-operated with the British Academy to produce a wonderful series of books under the heading of *Sylloge of coins of the British Isles* which now runs to 50 volumes. Some of these volumes refer to coins held in Museums overseas, but we list here the ones which deal with coins in these islands, and this will give students a better idea of some of the material they have for study.

1. Fitzwilliam Museum, Cambridge. Ancient British and Anglo-Saxon Coins by P. Grierson.
2. Hunterian Museum, Glasgow. Anglo-Saxon Coins, by A.S. Robertson.
5. Grosvenor Museum, Chester. Coins with the Chester Mint-Signature, by E.J.E. Pirie.
6. National Museum of Antiquities of Scotland, Edinburgh. Anglo-Saxon Coins, by R.B.K. Stevenson.
8. British Museum. Hiberno-Norse Coins, by R.H.M. Dolley.
9. Ashmolean Museum, Oxford, Part I, Anglo-Irish Coins, John-Edward III, by M. Dolley and W. Seaby.
10. Ulster Museum. Belfast. Part I, Anglo-Irish Coins, John-Edward III by M. Dolley and W. Seaby.
11. Reading University, Anglo-Saxon and Norman Coins, by C.E. Blunt and M. Dolley.
12. Ashmolean Museum, Oxford, Part II. English Coins

1066-1279, by D.M. Metcalf.

17. Midland Museums, Ancient British Coins, and Coins of the British and Gloucestershire Mints, by L.V. Grinsell, C.E. Blunt and M. Dolley.

21. Yorkshire Collections. Coins from Northumbrian Mints c.895-1279; Ancient British and Later Coins from other Mints to 1279, by E.J.E.Pirie.

23. Ashmolean Museum, Oxford, Part III. Coins of Henry VII, by D.M. Metcalf.

24. West Country Museums. Ancient British, Anglo-Saxon and Anglo-Norman Coins, by A.J.H. Gunstone.

26. Museums in East Anglia. Morley St Peter Hoard, and Anglo-Saxon, Norman and Angevin Coins, and Later

Coins of the Norwich Mint by T.H. McK. Clough.

27. Lincolnshire Collections. Coins from Lincolnshire Mints and Ancient British and Later Coins to 1272, by A.J.H. Gunstone.

29. Mersey Country Museums. Ancient British and Later Coins to 1279, by M. Warhurst.

32. Ulster Museum, Belfast, Part II. Hiberno-Norse Coins, by W. Seaby.

34. British Museum, Anglo-Saxon Coins, Part V. Athelstan to Edgar's Reform, by M.M. Archibald and C.E. Blunt.

35. Ashmolean and Hunterian Museums. Scottish Coins, by J.D. Bateson and N.J. Mayhew.

42. South-Eastern Museums. Ancient British, Anglo-Saxon and Later Coins to 1279, by A.J.H. Gunstone, with V. Smart and others.

43. Thompson, R.H. and Dickinson, M. Part 3. Hampshire to Lincolnshire. 1992. liv, 216(2) including 51 plates with descriptive text (Sylloge of Coins of the British Isles. Volume 43.) Cloth. £25.

* - - Part 4. Norfolk to Somerset. 1993. Including 50 plates, with text. Cloth. In preparation. Prices to be announced.

44. Stockholm Part V. Forthcoming.

46. Tokens 1575-1750. Part V. Staffordshire to Westmorland by R.H. Thompson and M.J. Dickinson.

47. Schneider Collection. Part 1. English Gold Coins 1257-1603 by Peter Woodhead.

48. Northern Museums - Ancient British, Anglo-Saxon, Norman and Plantagenet Coins to 1279 by J. Booth. 1997.

Useful Books

HERE is a small selection of books dealing with the coins that are covered in COINS MARKET VALUES. Books are the tools of the trade and an investment in a small library will be money well spent. The more you can teach yourself the better.

We have included the prices you can expect to pay, but since some of the books are long out of print they can only be obtained second-hand (indicated in the list by SH).

Bateson, J.D. *Coinage in Scotland*. 1997. 175pp. and well illustrated. £20. The most up to date narrative account of the coins, and the only currently in print.

Bateson, J.D. *Scottish Coins*. 1987. Shire Publications no.189. 32pp. and illustrated. £2. A useful little 'taster' to the subject. The Shire Publications are always good value.

Besly, E. *Coins and Medals of the English Civil War*. 1990. 121pp. and beautifully illustrated. (SH)

Besly, E. *Loose Change, a guide to common coins and medals*. Cardiff 1997. 57pp, beautifully illustrated. £6.95.

Blunt, C.E. Stewart, B.H.I.H., Lyon, C.S.S. *Coinage in Tenth Century England*. 1989. 372pp. 27 plates. £60.

Byatt, D. *Promises to Pay. The First Three Hundred Years of Bank of England Notes*. 1994. 246pp., beautifully illustrated. £35.

British Academy (publisher) *Sylloge of Coins of the British Isles* 48 volumes many still in print available individually. (See list under Museums.)

Brooke, G.C. *English Coins*, Reprint Edition. London 1966. 300pp., 72 plates. (SH). An important one volume account of English coinage.

Challis, C. *A new History of the Royal Mint*. 1992. 806pp., 70 figures and maps. £95. A very substantial volume.

Coincraft's Standard Catalogue of English and UK Coins, 1999. 741pp., 5000+ photographs. £19.50.

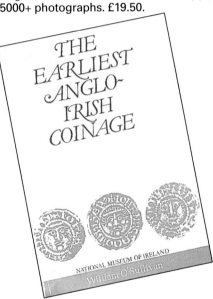

Coincraft's Standard Catalogue of the coins of Scotland, Ireland, Channel Islands and Isle of Man 1999. 439pp., fully illustrated. A new volume £34.50.

Cooper, D. *Coins and Minting*. 1996. Shire Publications 106. 32pp. and illustrated. £2.25. An excellent account of minting through the ages.

Cooper, D. *The Art and Craft of Coinmaking*. 1988. 264pp. fully illustrated. £2.25. An excellent account of minting through the ages.

Dolley, M. *Viking Coins in the Danelaw and Dublin*. 1965. 32pp., 16 plates. (SH). This and the next two are excellent little introductory handbooks.

Dolley, M. *Anglo-Saxon Pennies* - Reprint, 1970. 32pp., 16 plates. (SH).

Dolley, M. *The Norman Conquest and English Coinage*. 1966. 40pp., illustrated. (SH).

Dowle, A. and Finn, P. *The Guide Book to the Coinage of Ireland*. 1969. (SH). The first standard catalogue of Irish, useful still for information on patterns and proofs and good bibliography.

Dyer, G.P. (Editor). *Royal Sovereign 1489-1989*. 1989. 99pp., fully illustrated. £30. An attractive book published by the Royal Mint to coincide with the 500 anniversary of the Sovereign.

Elias, E.R.D. *The Anglo-Gallic coins*. 1984. 262pp., fully illustrated. £20. Essential for collectors of this series.

Freeman, A. *The Moneyer and Mint in the Reign of Edward the Confessor 1042-1066*. 2 parts, 1985. £40. A complete survey of the coinage of one reign.

Frey, A.R. *Dictionary of Numismatic Names*. Reprinted 1973. 311pp., and an additional 94pp. of glossary of numismatic terms. (SH). The best numismatic dictionary, well worth searching for a second hand copy.

Grinsell, L.V. *The history and Coinage of the Bristol Mint*. Bristol Museum and Art Gallery publication. 1986. 60pp., fully illustrated. £5.

Grueber, H.A. *Handbook of the Coins of Great Britain and Ireland*, revised edition London 1970. 272pp., 64 plates. (SH). A superb book, full of information, and well worth searching for.

Hobbs, Richard. *British Iron Age Coins in the British Museum*. 1996. 246pp., 137 plates. £40. Invaluable. The British Museum Catalogue listing over 4,500 pieces.

Holmes, Richard. *Scottish Coins, a history of small change in Scotland*. An invaluable guide to the identification of 'historic' small change. Edinburgh 1998. 112pp, many illustrations. £5.99.

de Jersey, P. *Celtic Coinage in Britain*. Shire Publications 1996. 56pp., illustrated. £4.99.

Linecar, H.W.A. *British Coin Designs and Designers*. 1977. 146pp., fully illustrated. (SH).

Linecar, H.W.A. *The Crown Pieces of Great Britain and the Commonwealth of Nations*. 1969. 102pp., fully illustrated. (SH). The only book dealing solely with all British crowns.

Lincecar, H.W.A. and Stone, A.G. *English proof and pattern crown-size pieces, 1658-1960*. 1968. 116pp., fully illustrated. (SH). An important book, full of useful information.

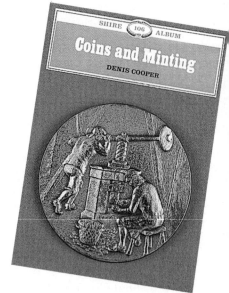

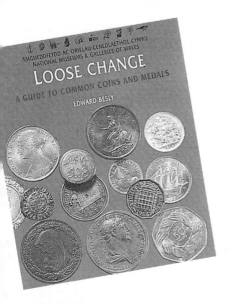

Manville, H.E. and Robertson, T.J. *Encyclopaedia of British Numismatics*: Vol.1 — British Numismatic Auction Catalogues from 1710 to the Present. 1986. 420pp., illustrated. £25.

Manville, H.E. Vol.2.1. *Numismatic Guide to British and Irish Periodicals 1731-1991*. 1993. 570pp., illustrated £60.

Manville, H.E. Vol.2.2. *Numismatic Guide to British and Irish Periodicals 1836-1995*. 1997. 634pp., 31 illustrations. £60. A highly important reference series.

McCammon, A.L.T. *Currencies of the Anglo-Norman Isles*. 1984. 358pp., 1000+ illustrations. £25. Essential for students and collectors.

North, J.J. *English Hammered Coins*. Volume 1. Early Anglo-Saxon to Henry III c.A.D.600-1272, 1994. 320pp., 20 plates. £35; Volume 2. Edward I to Charles II 1272-1662, 1993. 224pp., 11 plates. £30. Essential. The first point of reference for all serious collectors.
North, J.J. and Preston-Morley, P.J. *The John G. Brooker Collection - Coins of Charles 1*. (Sylloge of Coins of the British Isles, Number 33) £19.50.

O'Sullivan, W. *The Earliest Irish Coinage*. 1981. 47pp., 4 plates. (SH) Deals with the Hiberno-Norse Coinage.

O'Sullivan, W. *The earliest Anglo-Irish Coinage*. 1964. 88pp., 10 plates. (SH). Deals with the coinage from 1185-1216. (There is a reprint available at £5.)

Peck, C.W. *English Copper, Tin and Bronze Coins in the British Museum 1558-1958*. 1960. 648pp., 50 plates. (SH). Essential. The seminal work on the subject.

Rayner, P.A. *English Silver Coins Since 1649*. 254pp., illustrated, 3rd edition 1992. £19.95. Essential. 3000 coins listed, 400 illustrated. Deals with varieties, rarities, patterns and proofs and mintage figures.

Robinson, B. *Silver Pennies and Linden Towels: The Story of the Royal Maundy*. 1992. 274pp., 118 illustrations. £29.95. A very important work, entertainingly presented.

Seaby. *Standard Catalogue of British Coins*, 33rd edition, 1998. 411pp., fully illustrated. £15. After half a century still the first point of reference for most collectors of English coins. Now produced by Spink and Son Ltd.

Spink and Son (publishers, but edited by H.A. Linecar). *The Milled Coinage of England 1662-1946*. Reprinted 1976. 146pp., illustrated. (SH). A useful volume dealing with the gold and silver coinage and giving degrees of rarity; superseded on the silver by Rayner, but important for the gold.

Stewart, I.H. *The Scottish Coinage*, Second edition, 1967. 215pp., 22 plates. (SH). Long out of print but still essential for the serious collector.

Sutherland, C.H.V. *English Coinage 600-1900*. 1973. 232pp., 108 plates. (SH). Beautifully written and probably the best narrative account of coinage, worth a search.

Thompson, J.D.A. *Inventory of British Coin Hoards AD 600-1500*. 1956. 165pp., 24 plates. (SH)

Van Arsdell, R.D. *Celtic Coinage of Britain*. 1989. 584pp., 54 plates, 80 maps. SH. A pioneering work which sparked much debate; important for the number of illustrations alone.

Withers, P. and B. *British Coin Weights*. A corpus of the coin-weights made for use in England, Scotland and Ireland. 1993. 366pp., fully illustrated and with a price guide. £95. A labour of love for the authors; an essential volume for the serious student.

Woodhead, P. *The Herbert Schneider Collection of English Gold Coins*. Part 1. Henry III-Elizabeth I. 1996. 466pp., 83

ENGLISH PATTERN TRIAL AND PROOF COINS IN GOLD

1547 - 1968
ALEX WILSON AND MARK RASMUSSEN

plates each with descriptive text. £60. A wonderful catalogue of the finest collection in private hands. This first volume describes and illustrated 890 coins, most in superb condition.

Wren, C.R. *The Voided Long Cross Coinage 1247-1279*. 1993. 80pp., illustrated. £9.

Wren, C.R. *The Short Cross Coinage 1180-1247*. 1992. 90pp., illustrated. £8.75. Two very good guides to identification with excellent line drawings of the coins and lettering.

Williams, J. *Money, a history*. 1997. 256pp., fully illustrated. £25. A beautiful volume published to accompany the British Museum's HSBC Money Gallery opened in January 1997.

Wilson, A and Rasmussen, M, *English Pattern Trial and Proof Coins in Gold 1547-1968*. 2000 537pp, illustrated, £85. This long awaited publication covers a beautiful and fascinating series and is likely to enhance interest in these eminantly collectable non-currency gold issues.

Coins of England and the United Kingdom

36th Edition 2001

The only single volume work that features every major coin type from Celtic to the present day.

Features a survey of the market for English coins during the past 100 years, discussing the relative value of collectors' coins.

Revised and updated section on the coinages of Edward V and Richard III.

Expanded coverage of the shilling bust types of Edward VI.

Coins of the Commonwealth valued by date for the first time.

New illustrations added throughout, including new line drawings of the portrait types of Elizabeth I.

Comprehensive revision of the Milled copper and bronze coinages, with additional varieties included. In this section the introductions to each monarch have been expanded to include additional information on the designers and engravers.

Updated sales figures and edition limits for many of the Special Issues from the Royal Mint.

520 pages. Hardback ISBN 1 902040 36 8

Still remarkable value at only £15 plus postage and packing. Postage and packing: Inland £4; Europe Air £8; USA Air £12; Far East & Australasia Air £15; Worldwide surface £6.

To order by credit card Tel: 020 7563 4056 or fill in the form below.

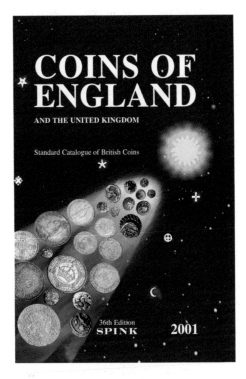

SPINK

FOUNDED 1666

COINS BANKNOTES MEDALS STAMPS

A MEMBER OF THE CHRISTIE'S GROUP

I would like to order_____ copy(ies) of 2001 Edition of the Spink Standard Catalogue of British Coins @ £15 per copy.

Preferred method of postage_____

Method of Payment: ☐ Visa   ☐ MasterCard

Card Number ___ ___ ___ ___ / ___ ___ ___ ___ / ___ ___ ___ ___ / ___ ___ ___ ___

Expiry Date ___ ___ / ___ ___   Card Member Signature_____

☐ I enclose a cheque for £_____ made payable to Spink

Name_____

Address_____

_____ Post code/Zip_____Tel_____

Return to: Book Department, Spink, 69 Southampton Row, Bloomsbury, London WC1B 4ET. Fax: 020 7563 4068

Coins at the British Museum

Richard West visits Bloomsbury to delve into the delights of the British Museum's Department of Coins and Medals.

At first sight, it is extremely difficult to gain any idea of the scope of the collection of coins, banknotes and medals housed at the British Museum. The Museum itself is, of course, justifiably a major attraction, situated in Great Russell Street in London (just off Tottenham Court Road).

Wandering around the galleries one is frequently confronted by displays of coins, for rightly the coinage is shown in its appropriate context, and not as a single, separate entity. There are also temporary exhibitions staged which focus on a particular aspect of coinage. Most notably, however, there is the HSBC Money Gallery, which puts all forms of money into the context of the demands of everyday life, rather than being just a collection of coins. In all, at any one time there might be about 10,000 coins and banknotes on display.

But these are just glimpses at the collection. Under the careful and knowledgeable custody of those in the Department of Coins and Medals, the Museum has around one million objects, making it one of the strongest collections in the world, noted for its quality and range.

The British Museum was established in 1753 when the collections and library of Sir Hans Sloane were acquired by the government. The collections included over 20,000 coins, including Greek, Roman, British and Islamic.

View of the new HSBC Money Gallery at the British Museum. It tells the story of money from all over the world and from the earliest times to the present day.

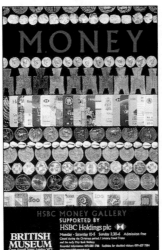

The poster for the HSBC Money Gallery. The lines of coins and other objects are drawn from different cultures and periods, symbolising the wealth and comprehensiveness of the Museum's collection.

A number of acquisitions were made during the late 18th and 19th centuries, which included the collection of King George III.

Today, there are fairly limited funds available to add to the collection. Acquisitions are often the result of gifts or bequests.

'Treasure'

Finds are very important, although these can take different forms. It might be a random selection of coins, scattered over a number of years, or it could be a hoard, a deliberate deposit of coins. The latter is more likely to be regarded as 'treasure' and, following the decision of a coroner, might be available for any museum (including the British Museum) to purchase at a fair price.

Even if no museum feels the coins will add to their particular collections, still a photographic record will be made of the hoard.

Hoards can be a good source of a range of coins from a particular period. More difficult for the Museum to acquire are the small, individual collections which might be useful in filling gaps in the collection.

The Department of Coins and Medals was established in 1860. Today it forms a significant section of the British Museum, with a staff of nearly 30, which includes no fewer than twelve curators, all experts in their own special fields. The aim is to be of maximum benefit to any student.

The collection is especially strong in Greek and Roman, but is equally wide-ranging, and covers both the Orient and Africa.

Edward VIII coinage

Naturally the collections of British coinage are very strong. Indeed, such collections are incomparable, including many fine and rare, and in some cases unique, pieces. For example, the collection has the unissued coinage of King Edward VIII, and the 1933 penny.

Those fascinated by British coinage will wish in particular to visit the following galleries.

Gallery 42 deals with 'Western Europe and the Byzantine World AD 500-1500' and shows the development of medieval coinage in Britain and Europe.

Gallery 49 is 'The Weston Gallery of Roman Britain' which includes late Roman gold and silver coins, in particularly those from the hoard found at Hoxne in Suffolk.

However, what is on general view is only the tip of the iceberg as far as the services offered by the Department of Coins and Medals.

Students are very welcome to visit the Museum and can have access to any part of the collection. Sensibly arranged, the collection is preserved in a multitude of cabinets. Of vital importance is the fact that alongside the cabinets appear the relevant books from the Department's magnificent library. Students have access to both the coins and the library.

Arranging access

If you would like to consult the collection, you will need a letter of recommendation, plus of course identification. You will also need to telephone in advance to book your appointment [(020) 7323 8404].

Students are able to conduct their research in a quiet, dedicated room, and are in no way encumbered by either the public or staff peering

A view of some trays in the Department of Coins and Medals. Objects which are not on display are housed in trays in wooden cabinets. Anyone who wants can see them in the Department.

over their shoulders. Last year alone students were able to examine some 100,000 coins from the collection.

The Department prides itself that it is easily and readily able to deal with enquiries. With a large and knowledgeable staff, questions posed can be answered within a matter of a day or two.

There is an identification service. Anyone can bring along up to ten coins for identification, either personally or by post (items should be sent by Special Delivery, with return postage by the same method enclosed). It is usually possible to identify the coins on the same day. This service is well used, and last year alone some 7,000 were brought in for identification. However, the Department is not able to value coins.

The Department is keen to educate about coins. Indeed, that was the principal rationale behind the HSBC Money Gallery. Situated close to the entrance to the Department, the aim of the gallery is to present coinage in the context that most will recognise; the development and use of money.

The display takes the visitor from the early ways of making payments using weighed amounts of silver, through the familiar coins and banknotes right up to today's electronic means of payment.

All can relate to what is on show, so it is not surprising that the material attracts a great deal of interest. Many other museums have shown interest in the project, which was opened in 1997: the British Museum co-operates fully with other museums. At the moment there is close co-operation with Manchester Museum which is planning its own Money Gallery.

The Department is fully aware that it is good to handle coins. Presentations are given at which participants can not only learn more about the coinage, but touch and feel it as well. Indeed, certain coins are

Crown and half-crown of Elizabeth I.

Gold £5 pattern of Queen Victoria.

kept especially for this purpose: in other words, an example is kept in the main collection, but other copies are retained simply for educational purposes. Groups are very welcome, including visits from numismatic societies. School groups are also very much encouraged.

Money Week

At the end of October 1999 a highly successful Money Week was held at the Museum. That success is certain to be repeated in 2000, and hopefully each October hereafter. The programme includes talks, storytellers, the chance to see banknote making, and to watch a moneyer making coins.

Highlight of the week is the open day (in 2000 on October 25) when there will be an identification service taking place in the coins gallery. It is a chance to meet not only those from the Department of Coins and Medals, but knowledgeable representatives from the Royal Mint as well.

A good opportunity to visit the Museum, and perhaps bring a friend along to introduce to numismatics.

However, the mention of handling coins should not give any false impressions about the willingness to look after these treasures. A full preservation and conservation programme is undertaken - but not in isolation. There is the nation's heritage to be maintained, but at the same time it should be there to be enjoyed.

The curators are all well versed with their own sections of the collection, so advice is readily available to students as to how they can be helped by the collection, its coins and library. The Roman coins are all fully catalogued. There is a programme to gradually put all the items in the collection on a database, but this is going to take a great deal of time. The database that is being created will give full information about each coin, including its weight, dimensions, and full history.

I can only add that I was amazed, pleasantly surprised and very impressed by what I saw at the British Museum. It is not only good to know that such a magnificent collection exists and is being well maintained, but that it is so accessible. I can fully recommend that you take the opportunity to use this wonderful resource for yourself - perhaps during Money Week.

The Department of Coins and Medals at the British Museum is open at the following times: Monday to Friday – 10am to 12.30pm; 2pm to 4.30pm (except Wednesday – 2pm to 4.30pm only Saturday – please telephone (020) 7323 8404.

Front cover illustrations

Shown on the front cover are three others coins from the collection at the Department of Coins and Medals:

Gold stater of the British Iron Age, 1st century AD. The discovery of this new coin in the Alton hoard in Hampshire showed that the correct name of the ruler whom had previously been called Tincommius was in fact Tincomarus ('Big Fish').

Gold coin of Offa, King of Mercia 757-99. The 'Offa dinar' combines his name and titles with designs based on the Islamic coins which came to Britain at the time.

Pattern half-crown of Oliver Cromwell.

COINS MARKET VALUES

An Invitation

TO JOIN THE ROYAL MINT COIN CLUB

In order to satisfy the demands of the modern collector, the Royal Mint has established its own Coin Club to provide its members with the latest information on new coins from both home and abroad. Recognised as the supreme examples of the minter's art, Royal Mint collector coins form a tangible record of our heritage.

Some of the benefits of becoming a Coin Club member are:

FREE
Coin Club Membership.

**No COMMITMENT
TO PURCHASE**
whatsoever.

ROYAL MINT GUARANTEE
return your coins within 30 days for
an immediate refund.

FREE
Quarterly
Coin Club Magazine.

INTEREST-FREE
Payments on selected
high-value products.

ROYAL MINT

ADVANCE NOTIFICATION
of rare and
limited-edition issues.
OPPORTUNITY
to purchase products
which are NOT offered
to the general public.
SPECIAL PRE-ISSUE PRICES
(subject to status).
The **confidence** that
you are dealing with
one of the most
prestigious and reputable
numismatic organisations
in the world with
a history spanning
over 1100 years.

A TRADITION OF EXCELLENCE

*To receive your free brochure, please telephone (01443 62 34 56)
or write to the address detailed below, quoting ref: MR99C
Royal Mint Coin Club, FREEPOST, PO Box 500, Cardiff, CF1 1YY.*

Coin Grading

IT IS MOST important that newcomers to collecting should get to know the various grades of condition before attempting to buy or sell coins.

The system of grading most commonly used in Britain recognises the following main classes in descending order of quality: Brilliant Uncirculated (B.Unc,BU), Uncirculated (Unc), Extremely Fine (EF), Very Fine (VF), Fine (F), Fair, Poor.

It is not surprising that beginners get confused at their first encounter with these grades. The word 'FINE' implies a coin of high quality, yet this grade turns out to be very near the bottom of the scale and is in fact about the lowest grade acceptable to most collectors of modern coinage in Britain.

American grading

It is not really necessary to go into the details of American grading here, since it is only on a very few occasions that a British collector will order the coins he wants directly from an American dealer. However, across the Atlantic their grading system is quite different from ours, and whilst it purports to be a lot more accurate, it is actually much more prone, in our opinion, to be abused, and we prefer the English dealers' more conservative methods of grading. American dealers use many more terms than we do, ranging from Mint State to About Good. The latter could be described as 'very heavily worn, with portions of lettering, date and legend worn smooth. The date may be partly legible'. In England we would simply say 'Poor'.

Numerical method

The other area which British collectors will find difficult to evaluate is the American numerical method of describing coins as, for example, MS 70, MS 65. The MS simply stands for Mint State and an MS 65 would be described as 'an above average Uncirculated coin which may be brilliant or lightly toned but has some surface marks'. The MS system seemed to be acceptable at first but there now appear to be two schools of thought in America and you will quite frequently see coins graded in the more traditional manner as well as the MS style in sale catalogues. Fortunately American grades have not come into use in this country, although dealers have followed the American manner of embellishing coin descriptions to make them more desirable, which is understandable and in many ways can be an improvement on the old method of saying simply that the coin is 'Fine', which, of course, might not do justice to it.

Full mint lustre

There are two schools of thought on the use of the terms Brilliant Uncirculated and Uncirculated. The former is often considered to be the most useful and descriptive term for coins of copper, bronze, nickel-brass or other base metals, which display what is known as 'full mint lustre'. When this term is being used it is often necessary in the same context to employ the grade Uncirculated to describe coins which have never been in circulation but have lost the original lustre of a newly minted coin. However, some dealers and collectors tend to classify as Uncirculated all coins which have not circulated, whether they are brilliant or toned, and do not use the term Brilliant Uncirculated.

Fleur de coin

Sometimes FDC (fleur de coin) is used to define top grade coins, but this really only applies to pieces in perfect mint state, having no flaws or surface scratches. With modern methods of minting, slight damage to the surface is inevitable, except in the case of proofs, and therefore Brilliant Uncirculated or Uncirculated best describe the highest grade of modern coins.

The word 'proof' should not be used to denote a coin's condition. Proofs are pieces struck on specially prepared blanks from highly polished dies and usually have a mirror-like finish.

Opinions differ

In all this matter of condition it might be said that the grade 'is in the eye of the beholder', and there are always likely to be differences of opinion as to the exact grade of a coin. Some collectors and dealers have tried to make the existing scale of definitions more exact by adding letters such as N (Nearly), G (Good, meaning slightly better than the grade to which the letter is added), A (About or Almost) and so on. To be still more accurate, in cases where a coin wears more on one side than the other, two grades are shown, the first for the obverse, the second for the reverse thus: GVF/EF.

Additional description

Any major faults not apparent from the use of a particular grade are often described separately. These include dents and noticeable scratches, discoloration, areas of corrosion, edge knocks, holes, on otherwise good quality pieces, and the like.

Middle range of grades

One should always look for wear on the highest points of the design, of course, but these vary from coin to coin. To present a comprehensive guide to exact grading one would have to illustrate every grade of every coin type in a given series, on the lines of the famous *Guide to the Grading of United States Coins*, by Brown and Dunn. This is a complete book in itself (over 200 pages) and obviously such a mammoth task could not be attempted in the space available here. Therefore, on the following page we present representative examples from three different periods in the British series, to illustrate the 'middle' range of coin conditions.

Still in mint state

We have already dealt with the grades BU and Unc; they both describe coins which are still in the state in which they left the Mint, and which have never passed into general circulation. They are likely to show minor scratches and edge knocks due to the mass handling processes of modern minting.

Fair and Poor

At the other end of the scale we have Fair, a grade that is applied to very worn coins which still have the main parts of the design distinguishable, and Poor which denotes a grade in which the design and rim are worn almost flat and few details are discernible.

Here we show (enlarged) examples of the grades EF, VF and F. On the left are hammered long cross pennies of Aethelred II; in the centre, from the later hammered series, are groats of Henry VIII; on the right are shillings of William IV.

Extremely Fine. This describes coins which have been put into circulation, but have received only the minimum of damage since. There may be a few slight marks or minute scratches in the field (flat area around the main design), but otherwise the coin should show very little sign of having been in circulation.

Very Fine. Coins in this condition show some amount of wear on the raised surfaces, but all other detail is still very clear. Here, all three coins have had a little wear as can be seen in the details of the hair and face. However, they are still in attractive condition from the collector's viewpoint.

Fine. In this grade coins show noticeable wear on the raised parts of the design; most other details should still be clear. The penny and the groat show a lot of wear over the whole surface. On the shilling the hair above the ear has worn flat.

Extremely Fine (EF)

Very Fine (VF)

Fine (F)

Abbreviations and Terms
used in the Market Price Guide Section

* – Asterisks against some dates indicate that no firm prices were available at the time of going to press.

2mm – P of PENNY is 2mm from trident. On other 1895 pennies the space between is only 1mm.

AE – numismatic symbol for copper or copper alloys.

Arabic 1, Roman I – varieties of the 1 in 1887.

Arcs – decorative border of arcs which vary in number.

B (on William III coins) – minted at Bristol.

1866 shilling lettered BBITANNIAR in error

BBITANNIAR – lettering error.

Bank of England – this issued overstruck Spanish dollars for currency use in Britain 1804-1811.

black – farthings 1897-1918, artificially darkened to avoid confusion with half sovereigns.

briit – lettering error.

B. Unc, BU – Brilliant Uncirculated condition.

C (on milled gold coins) – minted at Ottawa (Canada).

C (on William III coins) – minted at Chester.

close colon – colon close to DEF.

crosslet 4 – having upper and lower serifs to horizontal bar of 4 (see plain 4).

cu-ni – cupro-nickel.

dashes (thus –) following dates in the price list indicate that some particular characteristic of a coin is the same as that last described. Two dashes mean that two characters are repeated, and so on.

debased – in 1920 the silver fineness in British coins was debased from .925 to .500.

diag – diagonal.

'Dorrien and Magens' – issue of shillings by a group of bankers. Suppressed on the day of issue.

DRITANNIAR – lettering error.

E (on William III coins) – minted at Exeter.

E, E* (on Queen Anne coins) – minted at Edinburgh.

Edin – Edinburgh.

EEC – European Economic Community.

EF (over price column) – Extremely Fine condition.

E.I.C. – East India Co (supplier of metal).

Elephant and castle

eleph, eleph & castle – elephant or elephant and castle provenance mark (below the bust) taken from the badge of the African ('Guinea') Company, which imported the metal for the coins.

Eng – English shilling. In 1937, English and Scottish versions of the shilling were introduced. English versions: lion standing on crown (1937-1951); three leopards on a shield (1953-66).

exergue – segment below main design, usually containing the date.

On this penny the exergue is the area containing the date

ext – extremely.

F – face value only.

F (over price column) – Fine condition.

(F) – forgeries exist of these pieces. In some cases the forgeries are complete fakes, in others where the date is rare the date of a common coin has been altered. Collectors are advised to be very cautious when buying any of these coins.

Fair – rather worn condition.

Fantasies – non-currency items, often just produced for the benefit of collectors.

far colon – colon father from DEF than in close colon variety.

FDC – Fleur de coin. A term used to describe coins in perfect mint condition, with no flaws, scratches or other marks.

fig(s) – figure(s).

fillet – hair band.

flan – blank for a coin or medal.

GEOE – lettering error.

Florin of Victoria with the design in the Gothic style

Gothic – Victorian coins featuring Gothic-style portrait and lettering.

guinea-head – die used for obverse of guinea.

H – mintmark of The Mint, Birmingham, Ltd.

hd – head.

hp, harp (early, ord etc.) – varieties of the Irish harp on reverse.

hearts – motif in top RH corner of Hanoverian shield on reverse.

illust – illustration, or illustrated.

im – initial mark.

inc, incuse – incised, sunk in.

inv – inverted.

JH – Jubilee Head.

The Jubilee Head was introduced on the coinage in 1887 to mark Victoria's Golden Jubilee

KN – mintmark of the Kings Norton Metal Co Ltd.

L.C.W. – Initials of Leonard Charles Wyon, engraver.

lge – large.

LIMA – coins bearing this word were struck from bullion captured by British ships from foreign vessels carrying South American treasure, some of which may have come from Peru (capital Lima).

1902 pennies showing the low horizon variety (A) and the normal horizon (B)

low horizon – on normal coins the horizon meets the point where Britannia's left leg crosses behind the right. On this variety the horizon is lower.
LVIII etc – regnal year in Roman numerals on the edge.
matt – type of proof without mirror-like finish.
M (on gold coins) – minted at Melbourne (Australia).
'military' – popular name for the 1813 guinea struck for the payment of troops fighting in the Napoleonic Wars.
mm – mintmark.
Mod eff – modified effigy of George V.
mule – coin struck from wrongly paired dies.
N (on William III coins) – minted at Norwich.

William III shilling with N (for Norwich mint) below the bust

no. – number.
obv – obverse, usually the 'head' side of a coin.
OH – Old Head.
ord – ordinary.
OT – ornamental trident.
P (on gold coins) – minted at Perth (Australia).
pattern – trial piece not issued for currency.

piedfort – a coin which has been specially struck on a thicker than normal blank. In France, whence the term originates, the Kings seem to have issued them as presentation pieces from the 12th century onwards. In Britain medieval and Tudor examples are known, and their issue has now been reintroduced by the Royal Mint, starting with the 20 pence piedfort of 1982.
plain (on silver coins) – no provenance marks in angles between shields on reverse.
plain 4 – with upper serif only to horizontal bar of 4 (see crosslet 4).
pln edge prf – plain edge proof.
plume(s) – symbol denoting Welsh mines as source of metal.
proof, prf – coin specially struck from highly polished dies. Usually has a mirror-like surface.
prov, provenance – a provenance mark on a coin (e.g. rose, plume, elephant) indicates the supplier of the bullion from which the coin was struck.
PT – plain trident.
raised – in relief, not incuse.
RB – round beads in border.
rev – reverse, 'tail' side of coin.
r – right.
r & p – roses and plumes.

Roses and plumes provenance marks

rose – symbol denoting west of England mines as source of metal.
RRITANNIAR – lettering error.
rsd – raised.
S (on gold coins) – minted at Sydney (Australia).
SA (on gold coins) – minted at Pretoria (South Africa).

Scottish shilling 1953-66

Scot – Scottish shilling. Lion seated on crown, holding sword and sceptre (1937-51); lion rampant, on shield (1953-66).
SS C – South Sea Company (source of metal).

1723 shilling bearing the South Sea Company's initials

SEC – SECUNDO, regnal year (on edge).
sh – shield(s).
sm – small.
'spade' – refers to spadelike shape of shield on George III gold coins.

'Spade' guinea, reverse

TB – toothed beads in border.
TER – TERTIO, regnal year (on edge).
trnctn, truncation – base of head or bust where the neck or shoulders terminate.
Unc – Uncirculated condition.
var – variety.
VF – Very Fine condition.
VIGO – struck from bullion captured in Vigo Bay.
VIP – 'very important person'. The so-called VIP crowns were the true proofs for the years of issue. Probably most of the limited number struck would have been presented to high ranking officials.
W.C.C. – Welsh Copper Co (supplier of metal).
wire type – figure of value in thin wire-like script.
W.W. – initials of William Wyon, engraver.
xxri – lettering error.
y, Y (on William III coins) – minted at York.
YH – Young Head.

Victoria Young Head Maundy fourpence

Treasure

ON September 24, 1997 the Treasure Act 1996 came into being, replacing the old medieval law of treasure trove. This widened the definition of finds that are treasure, and under the new procedures which are set out in the Code of Practice on the Act, the new Treasure Valuation Committee assists the Secretary of State for Culture to submit an annual report.

In the past, before an object could be declared treasure and therefore be the property of the Crown, it had to pass three tests: it had to be made substantially of gold or silver; it had to have been deliberately hidden with the intention of recovery; and its owner or the heirs had to be unknown. If then a museum wanted to keep the coins (or artefacts) the lawful finder normally received the full market value; if not the coins were returned to the finder.

The new Act removes the need to establish that objects were hidden with intention of being recovered; it also sets out the precious metal content required for a find to qualify as treasure; and it extends the definition of treasure.

'All coins that contain at least 10 per cent of gold or silver by weight of metal and that come from the same find, provided a find consists of at least two coins with gold or silver content of at least 10 per cent. The coins must be at least 300 years old at the time of discovery. In the case of finds consisting of coins that contain less than 10 per cent gold or silver there must be at least ten such coins ... Single coins will not be treasure, unless they are found in association with objects that are treasure, or unless there is exceptionally strong evidence that they were buried with the intention of recovery (for example, a single coin found in plough soil without any sign of a container would not provide such evidence).'

As far as more modern coins are concerned, such as finds of guineas or sovereigns, the Act reads as follows: 'Only objects that are less than 300 years old, that are made substantially of gold or silver, that have been deliberately hidden with the intention of recovery and whose owners or heirs are unknown will come into this category. In practice such finds are rare and the only such discoveries that have been made within recent years have been hoards of gold and silver coins of the 18th, 19th or 20th centuries. Single coins found on their own will not qualify under this provi-

Cover of the latest report from the Treasure Trove Reviewing Committee

Front cover of the current 'The Treasure Act'.

sion unless there is exceptionally strong evidence to show that they were buried with the intention of recovery: for example, a single coin found in plough soil without any sign of a container would provide such. Therefore gold and silver objects that are clearly less than 300 years old need not be reported unless the finder has reason to believe that they may have been deliberately hidden with the intention of recovery.'

All this simplifies the task of coroners in determining whether or not a find is treasure, and it includes a new offence of non-declaration of treasure. Finally it states that lawful occupiers and landowners will have the right to be informed of finds of treasure from their land and they will be eligible for reward.

The Committee

The Treasure Trove Reviewing Committee was established in 1977 as an independent body to advise Ministers on the valuation of treasure trove finds. Under the new Act that body has been replaced by the Treasure Valuation Committee.

Under the new arrangements the national museums will no longer submit valuations to the Treasure Valuation Committee but instead the committee itself will commission valuation reports from expert advisers. All the interested parties (the finder, the landowner and the museum that intends to acquire the find) will be given the chance to comment on these valuations or indeed commission independent valuations of their own.

These reports are now delivered very quickly and there is no doubt that the new procedures are as transparently fair as it is possible to be. There is an annual report of the committee's findings published and available from the Department of National Heritage at £2.95. (A very interesting publication which is also available from the Book Department of Spink and Son Ltd.) The latest published report for the period 1996-1997 deals with 35 finds and is attractively illustrated throughout in colour.

At present the committee is chaired by Lord Stewartby, who is well known to coin collectors as the author of the standard work on Scottish coins and many learned articles on a wide area of early coins.

The current committee consists of:
Rt Hon Lord Stewartby (Chairman)
Mr John Casey, university lecturer and expert on Roman coins
Mr Patrick Finn, coin dealer
Mr Dennis Jordan, President of the National Council for Metal Detecting
Dr Jack Ogden, National Association of Goldsmiths
Professor Norman Palmer, a leading authority on the law of treasure trove

Information for finders and metal detectorists:
Copies of The Treasure Act 1966, Code of Practice (England Wales) 1997, can be obtained from the Department of National Heritage. This gives much useful information including a current list of coroners in the UK, and a list of coins commonly found that contain less than 10 per cent of gold or silver. It also gives advice on the care of finds, identification and storage, etc.

There is also a very useful leaflet entitled 'The Treasure Act, information for finds of treasure' which deals with everything in a question and answer way, for example:
What should I do if I find something that may be treasure?;
How do I report a find of treasure?;
What if I do not report a find of treasure?;
How do I know that I will receive a fair price for my find?
Note: both these publications can presently be obtained free of charge from:
Department of National Heritage,
2-4 Cockspur Street,
London SW1Y 5DH.
Tel: 020 7211 6200

Forgeries

MOST collectors know that there have been forgeries since the earliest days of coin production, so it is only to be expected that some new forgeries appear on the scene every year. It seems that there is always someone willing to deceive the collector and the dealer. However, nowadays very few forgers end up making much money. As a result of the actions of the British Numismatic Trade Association, the trade is much more tightly knit than ever before, and anxious to stamp out new forgeries before they have a chance to become a serious menace.

They were last a matter of serious concern in the late 1960s and early 1970s, when an enormous number of 1887 £5 pieces and United States $20 manufactured in Beruit came on to the market. Also in the early 1970s the group of Dennington forgeries could have made a serious impact on the English hammered gold market, but for lucky early detection. (Unfortunately we have noticed a number of these are still in circulation, and so we will deal with them later in this article.)

In the late 1970s a crop of forgeries of Ancient British coins came to light causing a panic in academic and trade circles. This caused a lack of confidence in the trade and it has taken a number of years for everyone to feel happy that there was no further problem. The BNTA firmly pursues any mention of forgeries and one hopes that a new spate of copies of Anglo-Saxon coins from the West Country are not allowed to develop. They are being sold as replicas, but they are still deceptive in the wrong hands. Bob Forrest compiled a list of these and it was published by the IAPN Bulletin of Forgeries in 1995/6 Vol.20 No.2. He has now done an update of this which will be available at the end of the year.

The worrying forgeries

We mentioned earlier the 'Dennington' forgeries. It is now many years since the trial of Anthony Dennington at the Central Criminal Court, where he was found guilty of six charges of 'causing persons to pay money by falsely pretending that they were buying genuine antique coins' *The Times*, July 10, 1969). There are a small number of these pieces still circulating in the trade, and since they have deceived some collectors and dealers, we thought we should record them more fully here. The following is a list of the pieces which appeared in the IBSCC Bulletin in August 1976.

1 Henry III gold penny
2 Edward III Treaty period noble
3 Another, with saltire before King's name
4 Henry IV heavy coinage noble
5 Henry V noble, Class C (mullet at King's sword arm)
6 Henry V/VI mule noble
7 Henry VI noble, annulet issue, London
8 Edward IV ryal, Norwich
9 Another, York
10 Elizabeth I Angel

Dennington forgeries: Edward III noble (top) and Mary Fine Sovereign

11   Mary Fine Sovereign 1553
12   James I unite, mintmark mullet
13   James I rose ryal, 3rd coinage, mint mark lis
14   James I 3rd coinage laurel
15   Commonwealth unite 1651
16   Commonwealth half unite 1651
17   Charles II touch piece

One can only reiterate that these copies are generally very good and you must beware of them. The following points may be useful.

1   The coins are usually slightly 'shiny' in appearance, and the edges are not good, since they have been filed down and polished.

2   They are usually very 'hard' to touch, whereas there is a certain amount of 'spring' in the genuine articles.

3   They usually feel slightly thick, but not always, not quite like an electrotype but certainly thicker than normal.

4   Although the Mary Fine sovereign reproduction is heavy, at 16.1986 gr, these pieces are usually lighter in weight than the originals.

As far as forgeries of modern coins are concerned, the most worrying aspects has been the enormous increase in well produced forgeries in the last 25 years.

They are so well produced that it is often impossible for the naked eye to detect the difference, and it has therefore become the job of the scientist and metallurgist. Many of these pieces have deceived dealers and collectors, although they do not seem to have caused too great a crisis of confidence. This increase in the number of modern counterfeits has been due to the enormous rise in coin values since the 1960s.

It is well known that the vast majority of these modern forgeries has emanated from the Middle East, as we have suggested earlier, where it is *not* illegal to produce counterfeits of other countries' coins. It has proved to be very good business for a lot of these small forgers in Beruit, and one can only rely on the alertness of the coin trade so that reports are circulated quickly whenever a new forgery is spotted.

Unfortunately, the main problem is still that the forger has every encouragement to continue production of copies, when one thinks of the profit involved. At the time of writing, it only takes about £290 worth of gold to make an 1887-dated five pound piece of correct composition, valued at around £650. We cannot, therefore, be complacent.

There is not enough space here to tell you in detail what to look for, and anyway detecting forgeries requires specialist knowledge, so a list of faults would not help. If you turn to the catalogue section of COINS MARKET VALUES you will find that as far as British coins are concerned we have placed **(F)** beside a number of coins which we know have been counterfeited, and which frequently turn up. However, you should watch out for sovereigns, in particular, of which there are forgeries of every date from 1900 to 1932 and even recent dates such as 1957 and 1976.

A list follows of the pieces you should be particularly careful about, especially if you notice that they are being offered below the normal catalogue value. Most modern forgeries of, say, Gothic crowns, seem to be offered at prices which are 10 per cent or 20 per cent below the current market price. The moral is, do not automatically think you have a bargain if the price is low – it could be a forgery!

Modern cast copies of Anglo-Saxon pennies: Ceolwulf 1st above, and Ceonwulf below

1738, 1739 two guineas
1793, 1798 guineas (there could also
  be other dates)
1820 pattern two pounds
1839 five pounds (in particular the
  plain edge variety)
1887 five pounds
1887 (two pounds (there seem to be
  many forgeries of these)
1893 five pounds, two pounds
1902 five pounds, two pounds
1911 five pounds, two pounds
  1817, 1819, 1822, 1825, 1827,
  1887, 1889, 1892, 1892M,
  1908C, 1913C sovereigns;
  also every date from 1900 to
  1932 inclusive, plus 1957,
  1959, 1963, 1966, 1967,
  1974, 1976
1847 Gothic crowns
1905 halfcrowns

A 'Behra' counterfeit of the 1950s. The last of a series bearing the dates 1902 to 1920, where the original pattern piece was a genuine South African sovereign of unknown date but post 1924. An attempt was made to remove the SA mint mark on the tool used to prepare the dies but traces still remained and were transferred to all the dies.

Other safeguards against forgery

(a) The best method of protection against purchasing forgeries is to buy your coins from a reputable dealer who is a member of the British Numismatic Trade Association or the International Association of Professional Numismatists, or one who will unconditionally guarantee that all his coins are genuine.

(b) Legal tender coins, which include five and two pound pieces, sovereigns, half sovereigns and crowns, are protected by the Forgery and Counterfeiting Act, and it is the responsibility of the police to prosecute in cases where this Act has been contravened.

(c) If your dealer is unhelpful over a non legal tender item which you have purchased and which you think has been falsely described, you can take legal action under the Trades Description Act 1968. However, we should warn you that it can be a tedious and long-winded business, but if you want to proceed in this you should contact your local Trading Standards Office or Consumer Protection department.

The different types of forgery

There are many different forgeries, but essentially they can be divided into two main groups. First of all there are contemporary forgeries intended to be used as face-value money (as in the cases, some years ago, of the counterfeit 50p pieces, which even worked in slot machines), and secondly forgeries intended to deceive collectors.

Contemporary forgeries, those pieces struck in imitation of currency coins, are obviously not a serious problem to numismatists. The recent ones cause more trouble to bank clerks, anyway, and are not of sufficiently good standard to deceive numismatic experts. In general, those produced in the Middle Ages were base (which was how the forger made a profit), consisting wholly of base metal or occasionally having a thin coating of the proper metal on the outside. Sometimes they were struck, but more often they were cast. Whatever the problems they caused at the time of issue, they are now often as interesting as the regular coins of the period.

However, one can be less light-hearted about copies which are made to deceive collectors. The following five methods of reproduction have been used.

Electrotyping. These copies would normally deceive an expert.

Casting. Old casts are easily recognisable, having marks made by air bubbles on the surface, and showing a generally 'fuzzy' effect. Much more of a problem are the modern cast copies, produced by sophisticated 'pressure-casting', which can be extremely difficult for all but most expert to distinguish from the originals (more of this later).

The fabrication of false dies. With hammered coins counterfeits are not difficult for an expert to detect. However, the sophisticated die production techniques used in Beirut have resulted in the worrying features of modern gold and silver coins described later.

The use of genuine dies put to some illegal use such as restriking (a mintmaster in West Germany was convicted in 1975 of that very issue).

Alteration of a genuine coin. (Ask your dealer how many George V pennies he has seen with the date altered to 1933 – it does happen!)

Counterfeit Coin Club
There is now a Counterfeit Coin Club which produces a small journal four times a year. If you are interested in joining, write to its President: Ken Peters, 2 Kings Road, Biggin Hill, Kent TN16 3XU.

Literature on forgery
The back numbers of Spink's *Numismatic Circulars* and Seaby's *Coin and Medal Bulletins* are useful sources of information on the forgeries that have been recorded over the years. The ISBCC (set up by an IAPN in 1975 by the late Vincent Newman) also produced a series of important forgery bulletins, mainly on modern coins, and are very useful if you can find them on the second-hand shelves. The IAPN themselves still produce very good reports on forgeries for their own members.

As far as hammered coins are concerned, still the most useful work is that by L.A. Lawrence in the *British Numismatic Journal* as long ago as 1905! ('Forgery in relation to Numismatics'. BNJ 1905-1907, a series of articles; occasionally it can be found bound as one volume).

COINS FOR SALE

HAMMERED GOLD
James I 1/4 Laurel NVF/VF £250.00
James I 1/4 Laurel EF Excellent portrait .
£450.00

£5 && £2 PIECES
1911 Pr. £2 GEM FDC Rare £575.00
1937 Pr. £5 UNC £625.00

GUINEAS
1678 2 Gns. Charles II EL.
Below Nice EF/A/UNC Extr. rare ......
£1,750.00
1685 James II Gn. Nice NEF .. £850.00
1686 James II Gn. Nice UNC .£2,250.00
1688 James II Gn. Nice UNC .£2,250.00
1700 Wm. III Gn. Nice UNC ..£2,250.00
1714 Anne Gn. Nice UNC ...£1,950.00
1745 Geo. II Gn. EF A/UNC ...£995.00
1790 Gn. Nice BU Scarce £350.00
1792 Gn. Nice BU Rare £350.00
1813 Military. Nice BU £995.00

1/2 GUINEAS
1786 Nice BU Rare £325.00
1813 1/2 Gn. Superb BU £295.00

SOVEREIGNS
George III 1760 - 1820
1820 BU GEM £575.00

George IV 1821 - 1830
1825 Plain edge, Nice BU,
     Very few minted £2,500.00
1826 Pr. BU GEM £2,000.00
1826 VF £150.00

William IV 1831 - 1837
1832 Superb BU £695.00

Victoria 1838 - 1887
Young Head Shield Rev.
1852 GVF £85.00
1855 Sydney NVF Extr. rare ...£595.00
1857 GVF + ... £90.00
1864 EF £90.00
1864 GVF £75.00
1866 NEF £72.00
1866 Syd. VF £100.00
1866 EF DN 4 .... £80.00
1869 EF DN 60 .... £80.00
1877 S BU £140.00
1877 S Nice VF £75.00
1878 S Nice BU Rare £250.00
1884 M Nice BU Scarce £195.00
1884 S ABU £100.00
1885 A ABU/BU £100.00

Veiled Hd. 1893 - 1901
1893 L Nice BU £90.00
1894 M EF £68.00
1894 S EF £70.00

1896 M BU £85.00
1899 M NEF/EF £62.00
1899 L EF £68.00
1899 L BU £90.00
1899 L EF £68.00
1901 M NEF/EF £65.00
1901 L NEF £62.00
2000 BU GEM £55.00

HALF SOVEREIGNS
1817 F £60.00
1817 Nice BU £225.00
1817 Superb BU/FDC £260.00
1820 Superb BU/FDC Scarce ..£275.00
1825 Geo. IV Laur. Hd. Nice BU £500.00
1828 Geo. IV Superb BU/FDC
     Proof-like Exceptional ...£595.00
1835 Wm. IV Nice BU Very rare .£550.00
1837 Wm. IV Nice BU Very rare .£650.00
1839 Pr. Nice UNC Extr. rare ...£850.00
1853 BU GEM Extr. rare in this grade ..
£350.00
1873 M Nice VF Rare £65.00
1880 GF £48.00
1887 Pr. Nice BU Extr. rare ...£250.00
1887 BU £70.00
1902 MP UNC £70.00
1982 ABU/BU £30.00
1982 BU GEM £33.00
2000 BU GEM £34.00
2000 Pr. GEM/FDC orig. R.M. Box ....
£70.00
1 oz Kruger BU GEM £210.00

CROWNS
1662 Rose Below NVF £110.00
1662 Rose Below GF £80.00
1664 GF £85.00
1667 GF £80.00
1679 Vir. EF £475.00
1688 GF Rare £145.00
1696 NVF/VF £75.00
1696 VF £95.00
1794 CM Doll. Nice ABU £375.00
1795 Doll. Oval C/M GEM UNC £575.00
1818 LIX Nice UNC £250.00
1818 UNC £225.00
1819 LIX Nice UNC £225.00
1821 NEF/EF £125.00
1821 UNC Toned £375.00
1845 EF £195.00
1847 Gothic UNC Nice £700.00
1887 Nice BU £65.00
1902 EF £70.00
1902 Superb UNC £120.00
1930 Nice BU Rare £195.00
1933 NVF/VF £68.00
1935 BU GEM £14.00
1935 EF £9.00
1937 BU GEM £16.00
1953 BU £5.00
1960 BU £5.00

HALF CROWNS
James I 3rd C. VF £325.00
1676 EF Nice tone £295.00
1685 GF/NVF £125.00
1686 James II GF Rare £100.00
1687 James II F £65.00
1687 NVF Rare £100.00
1689 Wm. & Mary EF Nice ...£250.00
1689 NVF/VF £75.00
1696 B GF £48.00
1700 Duo Nice BU Rare £450.00
1708 ABU £350.00
1709 NVF/VF £65.00
1715 F/GF £125.00
1723 SSC Nice GVF + Rare ...£295.00
1735 VF Rare £150.00
1736 Vir. UNC Very rare, Nice ..£450.00
1746 Pr. GEM UNC Toned Extr. rare ...
£850.00
1817 LH Nice UNC £125.00
1820 SH GEM UNC Very rare ..£250.00
1826 Pr. UNC Nice tone Extr. rare .....
£495.00
1831 Pr. UNC Nice tone Extr. rare .....
£595.00
1874 EF £50.00
1879 BU GEM Very rare £225.00
1887 Jub. Hd. BU £20.00
1887 EF £12.00
1893 BU £55.00
1902 Superb UNC £65.00
1920 EF Rare £14.00
1928 BU £15.00
1947 BU £4.00

FLORINS
1849 Nice UNC £120.00
1870 BU GEM Very rare £250.00
1881 Nice BU £175.00
1885 Nice BU Rare £140.00
1887 BU £20.00
1900 Nice BU £50.00
1902 BU £50.00
1920 EF Rare £12.00
1905 BU Very rare £350.00
1925 BU GEM Very rare £195.00

SHILLINGS
Charles I S.2785 VF £85.00
James I GF £45.00
1715 BU Rare £250.00
1718 BU Rare £250.00
1758 BU £50.00
1763 North Fine Very rare ...£150.00
1763 North Nice UNC £450.00
1787 BU £40.00
1839 Pr. Superb Pl. Edge ...£225.00
1887 Nice UNC £12.00
1902 BU £25.00

British Coin Prices

CELTIC COINAGE

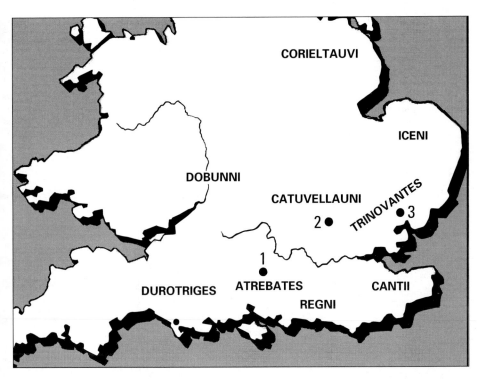

The distribution of the tribes in Britain based on the map in 'The coinage of Ancient Britain', by R.P. Mack, published by Spink and Son Ltd and B.A. Seaby Ltd.

Key to towns:
1. Calleva Atrebatum (Silchester)
2. Verulamium (St Albans)
3. Camulodunum (Colchester)

It is always difficult to produce a priced catalogue of coins, but none is more difficult than the early British series. The market has developed considerably since the publication of R.D. Van Arsdell's *Celtic Coinage of Britain,* which is an essential book for collectors (584 pages, 54 plates and many other illustrations, maps and diagrams).

A word of caution, though; quite a number of forgeries exist, some of relatively recent production, and unfortunately also numerous items from undeclared hoards are on the market, which makes it essential to buy from a reputable dealer.

We are very grateful for the help of Robert Van Arsdell since he produced the synopsis of the material which we have used. We have kept this very basic, and simply linked it up for easy reference with *The Coinage of Ancient Britain* by R. P. Mack, third edition, London 1975 (now out of print), and with the *British Museum Catalogue of British Iron Age Coins* by R. Hobbs, where it is possible. In the following lists Mack types are indicated by 'M' and BMC types by 'B'. The V numbers relate to the Van Arsdell catalogue. The existence of forgeries is indicated by **(F).**

Gold staters without legends

AMBIANI	F	VF
Large flan type M1, 3, V10, 12	£450	£1500

Ambiani large flan type

Defaced die type M5, 7, V30, 33 ...	£225	£700
Abstract type M26, 30, V44, 46	£175	£375
Gallic War type M27, a, V50, 52 (F) ...	£110	£225

Gallic War gold stater

SUESSIONES		
Abstract type M34a, V85	£200	£375

VE MONOGRAM		
M82, a, b, V87 (F)	£235	£525

WESTERHAM		
M28, 29, V200, 202 , B1-24	£175	£350

Chute Gold Starter, V1205

CHUTE		
M32, V1205, B35-76 (F)	£110	£220

CLACTON		
Type I M47, V1458, B137-144	£235	£525
Type II M46, a, V30, 1455, B145-179	£225	£500

CORIELTAUVI		
Scyphate type M—, V—, B3187-93	£250	£600

CORIELTAUVI (N.E. COAST TYPE)		
Type I M50-51a, V800, B182-191 ...	£175	£375
Type II M52-57, S27, V804	£160	£350

Norfolk Wolf stater VA610-3

NORFOLK	F	V
Wolf type M49, a, b, V610, B212-278	£125	£35

CORIELTAUVI		
South Ferriby Kite & Domino type,		
M449-450a, V.811, B3146-3186	£180	£40

Coritani (South Ferriby)

WHADDON CHASE		
M133-138, V1470-1478, B279-350 (F)	£165	£37
Middle , Late Whaddon Chase		
V1485-1509	£185	£42

Whaddon Chase stater

WONERSH		
M147, 148, V1522, B351-56	£250	£65

WEALD		
M84, 229, V144, 150, B2466-68	£275	£75

ICENI		
Freckenham Type I M397-399, 403b,		
V620, B3384-95	£200	£45
Freckenham Type II M401, 2, 3a, 3c,		
V626, B3396-3419	£200	£45
Snettisham Type M—, V—, B3353-83	£235	£52

Iceni gold stater

ATREBATIC		
M58-61, V210-216, B445-76	£150	£37

Atrebatic stater

SAVERNAKE FOREST
M62, V1526, B359-64 .... £175 £425

DOBUNNIC
M374, V1005, B2937-40 .... £275 £600

Gold quarter staters without legends

	F	VF
AMBIANI		
Large flan type M2, 4, V15, 20 (F)	£185	£550
Defaced die type M6, 8, V35, 37	£160	£425
GEOMETRIC		
M37, 39, 41, 41A, 42, V65, 146, 69,		
67	£60	£125
SUSSEX		
M40, 43-45, V143, 1225-1229	£65	£140
VE MONOGRAM		
M83, V87 (F)	£130	£300

Atrebatic quarter stater, Bognor Cog Wheel

ATREBATIC
M63-67, 69-75, V220-256, B478-546 £90 £225

Caesar's trophy, quarter stater VA145

KENTISH
Caesar's Trophy type V145 .... £85 £185

Gold staters with legends

	F	VF
COMMIUS		
M92, V350, B724-730	£375	£1100
TINCOMARUS		
M93, 93, V362, 363, B761-74	£450	£1250
VERICA		
Equestrian type M121, V500,		
B1143-58	£225	£500
Vine leaf type M125, V520, B1159-76	£275	£600

Verica gold stater

	F	VF
EPATICCUS		
M262, V575, B2021-23	£800	£2000
DUBNOVELLAUNUS		
In Kent M283, V176, B2492-98	£325	£700
In Essex M275, V1650, B2425-40 ...	£200	£475
EPPILLUS		
In Kent M300-1, V430, B1125-28 ...	£800	£2250
ADDEDOMAROS (THREE TYPES)		
M266, 7, V1605, B2390-94 (F)	£165	£400
TASCIOVANUS		
Bucranium M149, V1680,		
B1591-1607 (F)	£240	£550

VOLISIOS DUMNOCOVEROS

Equestrian M154-7, V1730-1736,		
B1608-13	£240	£500
TASCIO/RICON M184, V1780,		
B1625-36	£475	£1250
SEGO		
M194, V1845, B1625-27	£700	£2000
ANDOCO		
M197, V1860, B2011-14	£475	£1250

Tasciovanus Celtic Warrior

Cunobeline Gold Stater, V1910

CELTIC COINAGE

CUNOBELINE	F	VF
Two horses M201, V1910, B1769-71	**£600**	**£1450**
Corn ear M203 etc. V2010,		
B1772-1835 **(F)**	**£200**	**£425**

ANDOCO Stater

ANTED of the Dobunni		
M385-6, V1062-1066, B3023-27 **(F)**	**£350**	**£750**
EISU		
M388, V1105, B3039-42 **(F)**	**£450**	**£1100**
INAM		
M390, V1140, B3056 **(F)**	extremely rare	
CATTI		
M391, V1130, B3057-60 **(F)**	**£250**	**£525**
COMUX		
M392, V1092, B3061-63 **(F)**	**£650**	**£1500**
CORIO		
M393, V1035, B3064-3133 ... ... ·	**£325**	**£675**
BODVOC		
M395, V1052, B3135-42 **(F)**	**£600**	**£1350**

Bodvoc

VEP CORF		
M459-460, V940, 930, B3296-3300 **(F)**	**£350**	**£850**
DUMNOC TIGIR SENO		
M461, V972, B3325-27 **(F)**	**£600**	**£1350**
VOLISIOS DUMNOCOVEROS		
M463, V978, B3330-36	**£375**	**£800**

Cunobeline quarter stater V.1913-1

Gold quarter staters with legends

TINCOMARUS

Abstract type M95, V365	**£160**	**£425**
Medusa head type M97, V387,		
B811-24	**£225**	**£550**
Tablet type M101-4, V387-390,		
B825-79	**£125**	**£300**

Tincommius Medusa head gold quarter stater

EPPILLUS	F	V
CALLEVA M107, V407, B986-1015 ...	**£135**	**£3.**

Eppillus CALLEVA type

VERICA		
Horse type M111-114, V465-468,		
B1143-46	**£100**	**£2**
TASCIOVANUS		
Horse type M152-3, V1690,1692,		
B1641-1650	**£120**	**£2**
CUNOBELINE		
Various types, B1836-55 from	**£125**	**£2**

Silver coins without legends

DUROTRIGES		
Silver stater M317, V1235,		
B2525-2731 **(F)**	**£40**	**£1**
Geometric type M319, V1242,		
B2734-79	**£40**	**£1**
Starfish type M320, V1270,		
B2780-81	**£50**	**£1**

Starfish Unit

DOBUNNIC		
Face M374a, b, 5, 6, 8, V1020,		
B2950-3000	**£25**	**£**
Abstract M378a-384d, V1042,		
B3012-22	**£20**	**£**

Corieltauvi, showing boar and horse

CORIELTAUVI		
Boar type M405a, V855, B3194-3250	**£60**	**£1**
South Ferriby M410 etc, V875	**£50**	**£1**

Iceni Unit, V730

CENI	F	VF
Boar type M407-9, V655-659, B3440-3511	£25	£65
Wreath type M414, 5, 440, V679, 675, B3763-74	£20	£50
Face type M412-413e, V665, B3536-55	£60	£145
QUEEN BOUDICA		
Face type M413, 413D, V790, 792, B3556-3759	£40	£110

Silver coins of Boudica (left) and Commius (right)

COMMIUS		
Head left M446b, V355, 357, B731-58	£30	£100

Silver coins with legends

EPPILLUS	F	VF
CALLEVA type M108, V415, B1016-1115	£40	£110
EPATICCUS		
Eagle type M263, V580, B2024-2289	£25	£65
Victory type M263a, V581, B2294-2328	£30	£85

Verica, Lion type unit V505

VERICA		
Lim type M123, V505, B1332-59 ...	£40	£120

Silver unit, Epaticcus

CARATACUS		
Eagle Type M265, V593, B2376-2384 (**F**)	£110	£275
TASCIOVANUS		
Equestrian M158, V1745, B1667-68	£70	£225
VER type M161, V1699, B1670-73 ...	£70	£225
CUNOBELINE		
Equestrian M216-8, 6, V1951, 1953, 2047, B1862	£70	£225
Bust right M236, VA2055, B1871-73	£65	£210
ANTED of the Dobunni		
M387, V1082, B3032-38	£70	£175
EISU		
M389, V1110, B3043-55	£60	£150

CELTIC COINAGE

BODVOC
M396, V1057, B3143-45 (F) £110 £275

ANTED of the Iceni
M419-421, V710, 711, 715,
B3791-4009 ... ... £25 £60

ECEN
M424, V730, B4033-4215 ... ... £20 £45

EDNAM
M423, 425b, V740, 734, B4219-4281 £30 £65

ECE
M425a, 426, 7, 8, V761, 764,
762, 766, B4348-4538 ... ... £25 £50

AESU
M432, V775, B4558-72 ... ... £50 £125

PRASUTAGUS
King of the Iceni (husband of Boudica),
B4577-4580 ... ... £500 £1100

ESUP ASU
M4566, VA924, B3272 ... ... £75 £175

VEP CORF
M460b, 464, V394, 950, B3277-3382,
B3305-3314 ... ... £45 £110

DUMNOC TIGIR SENO
M462, V974 B3328-3329 ... ... £160 £400

VOLISIOS DUMNOCOVEROS
M463a, V978, 980, B3339 ... ... £130 £350

ALE SCA
M469, V996 ... ... £175 £400

Bronze, base metal coins without legends

	F	VF
POTIN		
Experimental type M22a, V104	£40	£85

Potin coin class II

Class I M9-22, V122-131	£25	£70
Class II M23-25, V136-139	£35	£85
Thurrock Types V1402-1442	£30	75

ARMORICAN

	F	V
ARMORICAN		
Billon stater	£30	£7
Billon quarter stater	£50	£11
DUROTRIGES		
Bronze stater M318, V1290	£20	£4
Cast type M332-370, V1322-1370 ...	£35	£9
NORTH THAMES		
M273, 274, 281, V1646 1615, 1669	£35	£1C
NORTH KENT		
M295, 296, V154	£70	£2C

Bronze coins with legends

DUBNOVELLAUNUS in Essex		
M277, 8, V1665, 1667	£45	£14
TASCIOVANUS		
Head, beard M168, 9, V1707	£45	£17
VERLAMIO M172, V1808	£40	£16
Head, VER M177, V1816	£55	£20
Boar, VER M179, V1713	£55	£20
Equestrian M190, V1892	£85	£30
Centaur M192, V1882	£95	£30
ANDOCO		
M200, V1871	£60	£17
CUNOBELINE		
Victory, TASC M221, V1971	£35	£12
Victory, CUN M22, a, V1973	£35	£13
Winged animal, M225, V2081	£35	£14

Cunobeline bronze with Centaur reverse

Head, beard, M226, 9, V2131, 2085	£35	£14
Panel, sphinx, M230, V1977	£35	£15
Winged beast, M231, V1979	£35	£14
Centaur, M242, V2089	£35	£14
Sow, M243, V2091	£35	£14
Warrior, M244, V2093	£30	£11
Boar, TASC, M245, V1983	£45	£18
Bull, TASC M246, V2095	£30	£12
Metal worker, M248, V2097	£30	£12
Pegasus, M249, V2099	£30	£9
Horse, CAMV, M250, V2101	£35	£14
Jupiter, horse, M251, V2103	£40	£16
Janus head, M252, V2105	£40	£17
Jupiter, lion, M253, V1207	£35	£14
Sphinx, fig, M260, a, V2109	£35	£15

ENGLISH HAMMERED
Gold from 1344 and Silver from *circa* 600

Prices in this section are approximately what collectors can expect to pay for the commonest types of the coins listed; for most other types prices will range upwards from these amounts. Precise valuations cannot be given since they vary from dealer to dealer and, in any case, have to be determined by consideration of a number of factors eg, the coin's condition (which is of prime importance in deciding its value).

For more detailed information refer to *English Hammered Coins*, Volumes 1 and 2, by J.J. North and published by Spink and Son Ltd. Any serious collectors should also obtain a copy of the important new volume, *The Herbert Schneider Collection, Volume One, English Gold Coins 1257-1603*, published by Spink and Son, 1996.

GOLD COINS
The Plantagenet Kings

Henry III gold penny

HENRY III 1216-1272   F   VF
Gold Penny
This specimen sold for £159,500 (including buyers premium) at a Spink auction on 9 July 1996.

Edward III quarter noble

EDWARD III 1327-77
Third coinage

	F	VF
Florins or Double leopard	ext. rare	
Half florins or leopard...	ext. rare	
Quarter florins or helms	ext. rare	
Nobles ... ... from	£950	£2000
Half nobles ... ... from	£1350	£3500
Quarter nobles	£300	£700

Fourth coinage
Pre-treaty with France (i.e. before 1315) with French title

	F	VF
Nobles	£325	£650
Half nobles	£250	£525
Quarter nobles	£140	£325

Transitional treaty period, 1361. Aquitaine title added

	F	VF
Nobles	£390	£750
Half nobles	£220	£475
Quarter nobles	£150	£300

Edward III 1327-1377, Half noble, Transitional Treaty

Treaty period 1361-9 omit FRANC

	F	VF
Nobles, London	£325	£650
Nobles, Calais		
(C in centre of rev.)	£370	£775
Half nobles, London	£225	£425
Half nobles, Calais	£350	£800
Quarter nobles, London	£140	£285
Quarter nobles, Calais	£160	£350

Post-treaty period 1369-77 French title resumed

	F	VF
Nobles, London	£400	£800
Nobles, Calais		
(flag at stern or C in centre)	£400	£800
Half nobles, London	ext. rare	
Half nobles, Calais	£550	£1200

There are many other issues and varieties in this reign. These prices relate to the commoner pieces.

Richard II London half noble

RICHARD II 1377-99

	F	VF
Nobles, London	£525	£1100
Nobles, Calais		
(flag at stern)	£550	£1200
Half nobles, London	£600	£1350

HAMMERED GOLD

	F	VF
Half nobles, Calais		
(flag at stern)	£900	£2200
Quarter nobles, London	£300	£600

There are many different varieties and different styles of lettering.

HENRY IV 1399-1413
Heavy coinage

	F	VF
Nobles (120grs) London	£3500	£8500
Nobles, Calais (flag at stern)	£4250	*
Half nobles, London	£2750	*
Half nobles, Calais	£3250	*
Quarter nobles, London	£850	£1900
Quarter nobles, Calais	£950	£2500

Light coinage

	F	VF
Nobles (108grs)	£900	£1850
Half nobles	£2250	*
Quarter nobles	£400	£850

Henry V noble

HENRY V 1413-22

	F	VF
Nobles, many varieties, from	£375	£700
Half nobles	£400	£800
Quarter nobles	£200	£425

This reign sees an increase in the use of privy marks to differentiate issues.

Henry VI noble, Annulet issue

HENRY VI 1422-61
Annulet issue (1422-27)

	F	VF
Nobles, London	£350	£675
Nobles, Calais (flag at stern)	£450	£900
Nobles, York	£475	£950
Half nobles, London	£250	£500
Half nobles, Calais	£475	£1000
Half nobles, York	£500	£1050
Quarter nobles, London	£160	£300
Quarter nobles, Calais	£190	£450
Quarter nobles, York	£240	£500

Henry VI, Quarter-Noble, Annulet issue

Rosette-mascle issue 1427-30 ... ...

	F	VF
Nobles, London	£650	£1400
Nobles, Calais	£800	£1650
Half nobles, London	£850	£1850
Half nobles, Calais	£1000	£2400
Quarter nobles, London	£400	£800
Quarter nobles, Calais	£450	£950

Pinecone-mascle issue 1430-4

	F	VF
Nobles, London	£650	£1400
Half nobles, London	£1250	£3250
Quarter noble	£650	£1500

Henry VI quarter noble, leaf-mascle

Leaf-mascle issue 1434-5

	F	VF
Nobles	£1400	£3500
Half nobles	£1650	£4000
Quarter nobles	£950	£2000

Leaf-trefoil issue 1435-8

	F	VF
Nobles	£1800	£4500
Quarter noble	£1250	£2500

Trefoil issue 1438-43

	F	VF
Nobles	£1600	£4000

Henry VI Gold Noble, Pinecone-mascle, London

Leaf-pellet issue 1445-54

	F	VF
Nobles	£1650	£4000

Cross-pellet issue 1454-60

	F	VF
Nobles	£2000	*

EDWARD IV 1st reign 1461-70
Heavy coinage 1461-64/5

	F	VF
Nobles (108grs)	£2500	£6000
Quarter noble	ext. rare	

COIN MARKET VALUES

Edward IV noble, heavy coinage

Light coinage 1464-70		F	VF
Ryals or rose nobles (120grs),			
London		£350	£675
Flemish copy		£275	£525

Edward IV Light Coinage 1464-70, Ryal, York

		F	VF
Ryals, Bristol (B in waves)		£425	£850
Ryals, Coventry (C in waves))		£725	£1700
Ryals, Norwich (N in waves)		£850	£2000
Ryals, York (E in waves)		£450	£900
Half ryals, London		£300	£600
Half ryals, Bristol (B in waves) ...		£450	£950
Half ryals, Coventry (C in waves) ...		£1750	£5000
Half ryals Norwich (N in waves) ...		£1500	£4250
Half ryals, York (E in waves)		£350	£700
Quarter ryals		£200	£450
Angels		£3250	*

Edward IV angel, first reign

HAMMERED GOLD

	F	VF
HENRY VI (restored) 1470-71		
Angels, London	£650	£1400
Angels, Bristol (B in waves)	£1000	£2400
Half angels, London	£1500	£3500
Half angels, Bristol (B in waves) ...	£2000	*
EDWARD IV 2nd reign 1471-83		
Angels, London	£275	£550
Angels, Bristol (B in waves)	£1200	£2750
Half angels, some varieties	£275	£550
EDWARD IV or V		
mm halved sun and rose		
Angels	£1000	£2500
EDWARD V 1483		
mm boar's head on obverse, halved		
sun and rose on reverse.		
Angels	£3500	*
Half angel	ext. rare	
RICHARD III 1483-5		
Angel, reading EDWARD, with R		
over E by mast	ext. rare	
Angels, as before, but *mm* boar's		
head	ext. rare	
Angels, reading RICARD or RICAD	£900	£1850
Half angels	£3000	*

Gold Angel, mm boar's head on obverse, and halved sun and rose on reverse

The Tudor Monarchs

Henry VII sovereign

HENRY VII 1485-1509	F	VF
Sovereigns of 20 shillings (all ext.		
rare) from	£6500	£14000
Ryals ... ... from	£7000	£17500
Angels, varieties, different *mm* from	£280	£550
Half angels	£200	£450

HAMMERED GOLD

Henry VII 1485-1509, Angel with Mint Mark pheon

HENRY VIII 1509-47

First coinage 1509-26

	F	VF
Sovereigns of 20 shillings *mm*		
crowned portcullis only	£3500	*
Angels (6s 8d) ... ... from	£275	£550
Half angels	£225	£500

Second coinage 1526-44

	F	VF
Sovereigns of 22s 6d, various *mm* ...	£2750	£6250
Angels (7s 6d)	£425	£850
Half angels *mm* lis	£550	£1200
George-nobles *mm* rose	£3000	£7000
Half-George noble	ext. rare	
Crowns of the rose *mm* rose	ext. rare	
Crowns of the double-rose		
HK (Henry and Katherine of Aragon)	£275	£550
HA (Henry and Anne Boleyn) ...	£525	£1000
HI (Henry and Jane Seymour) ...	£325	£700
HR (HENRICUS REX)	£275	£550
Halfcrowns of the double-rose		
HK	£275	£650
HI	£325	£700
HR	£425	£850

Third coinage 1544-47

	F	VF
Sovereigns of 20s, London ... from	£1800	£4750
Sovereigns of 20s, Southwark	£1600	£3850
Sovereigns of 20s, Bristol	£2500	£6000
Half sovereigns, London	£300	£650
Half sovereigns, Southwark	£325	£700
Half sovereigns, Bristol	£500	£1200

Henry VIII Angel, 3rd coinage with mint mark lis
(shown slightly enlarged)

	F	VF
Angels	£250	£550
Half angels	£275	£550
Quarter angels	£250	£525
Crowns, HENRIC 8, London	£250	£550
Crowns, Southwark	£325	£675
Crowns, Bristol	£300	£600

	F	VF
Halfcrowns, London	£235	£500
Halfcrowns, Southwark	£285	£600
Halfcrowns, Bristol	£300	£650

EDWARD VI 1547-53
Posthumous coinage in name of Henry VIII (1547-51)

	F	VF
Sovereigns, London	£2100	£5000
Sovereigns, Bristol	£2500	£6000
Half sovereigns, London	£300	£650
Half sovereigns, Southwark	£300	£650
Crowns, London	£325	£700
Crowns, Southwark	£425	£900
Halfcrowns, London	£300	£700
Halfcrowns, Southwark	£300	£700

Coinage in Edward's own name
First period 1547-49

	F	VF
Half sovereigns, Tower, read EDWARD 6	£625	£1350

Edward VI sovereign, posthumous coinage
(not actual size)

	F	VF
Half sovereigns, Southwark	£550	£1200
Crown	£2000	*
Halfcrowns	£1600	*

Second period 1549-50

	F	VF
Sovereigns	£1900	£4500
Half sovereigns, uncrowned bust		
London	£2000	*
Half sovereigns, SCUTUM on obv. ...	£550	£1350
Half sovereigns, Durham House		
MDXL VII	£3000	*
Half sovereigns, crowned bust,		
London	£525	£1250
Half sovereigns, half-length bust,		
Durham House	£3000	£8000
Crowns, uncrowned bust	£800	£1650
Crowns, crowned bust	£675	£1450
Halfcrowns, uncrowned bust	£750	£1500
Halfcrowns, crowned bust	£650	£1350

Edward VI fine sovereign of 30s third period with mint mark ostrich head

Edward VI Sovereign of 20 Shillings. Third Period

Third period 1550-53

	F	VF
Fine' sovereigns of 30s, king enthroned	£8000	£20000
Sovereigns of 20s, half-length figure ...	£100	£2650
Half sovereigns, similar to last	£675	£1500
Crowns, similar but SCUTUM on rev ...	£750	£1750
Halfcrowns, similar	£800	£1900
Angels	£3500	£9000
Half angel		ext. rare

MARY 1553-4

	F	VF
Sovereigns, different dates, some undated, some *mms*	£2100	£4750
Ryals, dated MDUI (1553)	£7500	£16500
Angels, *mm* pomegranate	£650	£1400
Half angels	£2000	£6000

Mary Gold Sovereign of 1553

	F	VF
PHILIP AND MARY 1554-8	£1750	£4250
Angels, *mm* lis	£4250	*
Half angels		

Philip and Mary angel

Elizabeth I 1558-1603
Hammered issues

	F	VF
'Fine' sovereigns of 30s, different issues from	£1700	£4000
Ryals	£3500	£9000
Angels, different issues	£325	£700
Half angels	£300	£650
Quarter angels	£275	£600

Elizabeth I quarter angel

	F	VF
Pounds of 20 shillings, different mint marks from	£750	£1700
Half pounds, different issues	£450	£950
Crowns —	£425	£900
Halfcrowns —	£425	£900

Elizabeth I hammered halfcrown

Milled issues

	F	VF
Half pounds, one issue but different marks	£900	£2500
Crowns —	£900	£2500
Halfcrowns —	£1200	£3250

The Stuart Kings

James I Thistle crown

James I gold Spur-ryal

3rd coinage 1619-25

	F	VF
Rose-ryals, varieties	£1000	£3000
Spur-ryals	£1900	£4500
Angels	£725	£1650
Laurels, different busts	£240	£475
Half Laurels	£185	£400
Quarter laurels	£135	£250

James I laurel

JAMES I 1603-25
1st coinage 1603-4

	F	VF
Sovereigns of 20 shillings two bust	£750	£1800
Half sovereigns	£1650	£4000
Crowns	£900	£2500
Halfcrowns	£400	£950

2nd coinage 1604-19

	F	VF
Rose-ryals of 30 shillings	£825	£2100
Spur-ryals of 15 shillings	£1900	£4500
Angels	£550	£1350
Half angels	£1450	£4000
Unites, different busts	£275	£550
Double crowns —	£210	£450
Britain crowns —	£150	£300

CHARLES I 1625-49
Tower Mint 1625-42
Initial marks: lis, cross calvary,
negro's head, castle, anchor,
heart, plume, rose, harp, port-
cullis, bell, crown, tun, triangle,
star, triangle in circle

Charles I Unite, Tower Mint, 1625-43

	F	VF
Angels, varieties	£850	£2650
Angels, pierced as touchpieces	£450	£900
Unites –	£250	£550
Double Crowns –	£225	£450
Crowns –	£140	£300

*James I
Rose-ryal of
30 shillings*

	F	VF
Halfcrowns —	£140	£275
Thistle crowns, varieties	£150	£325

Charles I Double Crown, Tower Mint with mint mark heart

Tower Mint under Parliament 1642-9
Initial marks: (P), (R), eye, sun, sceptre

	F	VF
Unites, varieties	£450	£900
Double crowns –	£425	£900
Crowns –	£225	£450

Briot's milled issues 1631-2
Initial marks: anemone and **B**, daisy and **B, B**

Angels	£3000	*
Unites	£1000	£2500
Double crowns	£850	£1850
Crowns	£1250	*

Coins of provincial mints
Bristol 1645

Unites	£6000	*
Half unites		ext. rare

Chester 1644

Unites	£8500	*

Exeter 1643-44

Unites	£8500	*

Oxford 1642-46

Triple unites, from	£2500	£5500
Unites from	£700	£1500
Half unites from	£700	£1500

Truro 1642-43

Half unites		ext. rare

Shrewsbury 1644

Triple unites and unites		ext. rare

Worcester 1643-44

Unites		ext. rare

HAMMERED GOLD

Siege pieces 1645-49
Pontefract besieged 1648-49

	F	VF
Unites **(F)**		ext. rare

Commonwealth 1650 gold unite

COMMONWEALTH 1649-60

	F	VF
Unites *im* sun	£450	£950
– *im* anchor	£1250	£3000
Double crowns *im* sun	£350	£750
– *im* anchor	£1100	£2650
Crowns *im* sun	£325	£650
– *im* anchor	£1250	*

Commonwealth crown

CHARLES II 1660-85
Hammered Coinage 1660-62

Charles II gold unite

	F	VF
Unites, two issues from	£600	£1400
Double crowns –	£500	£1200
Crowns –	£475	£1000

Charles I Oxford triple unite, 1643

SILVER COINS

In this section column headings are mainly F (Fine) and VF (Very Fine), but for pennies of the early Plantagenets – a series in which higher-grade coins are seldom available – prices are shown under the headings Fair and F. Again it should be noted that throughout the section prices are approximate, for the commonest types only, and are the amounts collectors can expect to pay – not dealers' buying prices. Descriptions of some early Anglo-Saxon coins are, of necessity, brief because of pressure on space. Descriptions such as 'cross/moneyer's name' indicate that a cross appears on the obverse and the moneyer's name on the reverse. For more details see Standard Catalogue of British Coins – Volume 1 published by Spink & Son Ltd, and English Hammered Coins, Volumes 1 and 2, by J. J. North, published by Spink and Son Ltd. (A new edition of Volume 2 was published in 1991 and a new edition of Volume 1 was published in 1994).

Anglo-Saxon Sceats and Stycas

Examples of Sceats

EARLY PERIOD c 600-750	F	VF
Silver sceats ... ...from	£55	£130

A fascinating series with great variation of styles of early art. Large numbers of types and varieties.

NORTHUMBRIAN KINGS c 737-867

Silver sceats c 737-796 ...from	£120	£275
Copper stycas c 810-867 ...from	£15	£35

Struck for many kings. Numerous moneyers and different varieties. The copper styca is the commonest coin in the Anglo-Saxon series.

ARCHBISHOPS OF YORK c 732-900

Silver sceats ... ...from	£75	£165
Copper stycas ... ...from	£25	£60

From here onwards until the reign of Edward I all coins are silver pennies unless otherwise stated

Kings of Kent

HEABERHT c 764	F	VF
Monogram/cross		ext. rare

One moneyer (EOBA).

ECGBERHT c 765-780		
Monogram/cross	£900	£2000

Two moneyers (BABBA and UDD)

EADBERHT PRAEN 797-798		
EADBERHT REX/moneyer	£950	£2000

Three moneyers

Penny of Eadberht Praen

CUTHRED 789-807	F	VF
Non-portrait, various designs from	£400	£850
Bust right	£500	£1250

Different moneyers, varieties etc.

BALDRED c 825		
Bust right	£800	£2000
Cross/cross	£600	£1500

different types and moneyers

Baldred penny, bust right

ANONYMOUS c 823		
Bust right	£550	£1400

Different varieties and moneyers.

Archbishops of Canterbury

JAENBERHT 766-792	F	VF
Various types (non-portrait) from	£850	£2100

AETHELHEARD 793-805		
Various types (non-portrait) from	£700	£1600

WULFRED 805-832		
Various groups (portrait types) from	£475	£1000

CEOLNOTH 833-870		
Various groups (portrait types) from	£375	£800

Ceolnoth penny

ETHERED 870-889
arious types (portrait, non-portrait)

	F	VF
	£1100	*

ÆLEGMUND 890-914
arious types (all non-portrait) from

	F	VF
	£350	£800

Kings of Mercia

Offa portrait penny

OFFA 757-796

	F	VF
Non-portrait from	£375	£800
Portrait from	£650	£1400

Many types and varieties

Cynethryth (wife of Offa) portrait penny

CYNETHRYTH (wife of Offa)

Portraits	£1450	£4000
Non-portrait	£1000	£2250

COENWULF 796-821
Various types (portrait, non-portrait) from

	£275	£550

Coenwulf portrait penny

CEOLWULF 1821-823
Various types (portrait) ... ...

	£600	£1400

BEORNWULF 823-825
Various types (portrait) ... ...

	£750	£1750

Beornwulf penny

LUDICA 825-827
Two types (portrait) (F) ... ...

	£2250	*

WIGLAF 827-829, 830-840
Two groups (portrait, non-portrait)

	£1500	£3750

BERHTWULF 840-852
Two groups (portrait, non-portrait) ... ...

	£700	£1500

HAMMERED SILVER

Berhtwulf penny

BURGRED 852-874
One type (portrait), five variants

	F	VF
	£95	£185

CEOLWULF II 874-c 877
Two types (portrait)) ... ...

	F	VF
	£1750	£4500

Kings of East Anglia

BEONNA c 758
Silver sceat ... ...

	F	VF
	£375	£800

AETHELBERHT LUL (died 794)
Portrait type (F) ... ...   ext. rare

Eadwald penny

EADWALD c 796
Non-portrait types ... ...

	F	VF
	£800	£2250

AETHELSTAN I c 850
Various types (portrait, non-portrait) ...

	£275	£600

AETHELWEARD c 850
Non-portrait types ... ...

	£425	£950

EADMUND 855-870
Non-portrait types ... ...

	£175	£400

Viking Invaders 878-954

ALFRED
Imitations of Alfred pennies and halfpennies from
(Many different types, portrait and non portrait)

	F	VF
	£300	£625

ANGLIA
AETHELSTAN II 878-890
Cross/moneyer ... ...

	£900	*

OSWALD (Unknown in history except from coins)
A/cross ... ...

	£1250	*

ST EADMUND
Memorial coinage, various legends etc. ... ...
Many moneyers.

	£80	£160

Halfpenny, similar ... ...

	£350	£850

HAMMERED SILVER

St Eadmund memorial penny

	F	VF
ST MARTIN OF LINCOLN c 925		
Sword/cross	£1500	*
AETHELRED c 870		
Temple/cross	£1200	*
YORK		
SIEVERT-SIEFRED-CNUT c 897		
Crosslet/small cross	£100	£180
Many different groups and varieties		
Halfpenny, similar	£375	£800
EARL SIHTRIC (unknown)		
Non-portrait	£1450	*
REGNALD c 919-921		
Various types, some blundered	£1000	*
SIHTRIC I 921-927		
Sword/cross	£1250	*
ANLAF GUTHFRITHSSON 939-941		
Raven/cross	£1200	£2750
Cross/cross	£1400	*
Flower/cross	£1500	*
ANLAF SIHTRICSSON 941-944, 948-952		
Various types	£1350	*
SIHTRIC II c 942-943		
Shield/standard	£1400	*
REGNALD II c 941-943		
Cross/cross	£1500	*
Shield/standard	£1650	*
ERIC BLOODAXE 948, 952-954		
Cross/moneyer	£1650	*
Sword/cross	£1850	*

St Peter of York halfpenny

	F	VF
ST PETER OF YORK c 905-927		
Various types ... ...from	£185	£400
Halfpenny, similar	£600	£1300

Kings of Wessex

	F	VF
BEORHTRIC 786-802		
Two types (non-portrait)		ext. rare
ECGBERHT 802-839		
FOUR GROUPS (portrait, non-portrait)	£700	£1750
Mints of Canterbury, London, Rochester, Winchester		

Aethelwulf Portrait Penny, Canterbury

	F	VF
AETHELWULF 839-858		
Four phases (portrait, non-portrait)	£225	£500
from Mints of Canterbury, Rochester (?)		
AETHELBERHT 858-866		
Two types (portrait) ... ...from	£225	£475
Many moneyers.		
AETHELRED I 865-871		
Portrait types ... ...from	£260	£650
Many moneyers.		
ALFRED THE GREAT 871-899		
Portrait in style of Aethelred I ...	£275	£650
Four other portrait types commonest being those		
with the London monogram reverse	£625	£1400
Halfpennies	£375	£900

Alfred the Great Penny, London monogram on reverse

	F	VF
Non-portrait types ... ...from	£250	£450
Many different styles of lettering etc.		
Halfpennies	£325	£700
EDWARD THE ELDER 899-924		
Non-portrait types:		
Cross/moneyer's name in two lines	£140	£325
Halfpennies as previous	£650	£1400

Rare penny of Edward the Elder with building on reverse

	F	VF
Portrait types:		
Bust/moneyer's name ·	£400	£950
Many types, varieties and moneyers.		
Types featuring buildings, floral		
designs, etc	£900	£2500
Many types, varieties and moneyers.		

Kings of all England

AETHELSTAN 924-39 ... ...   F   VF

Aethelstan 924-939, Penny, building type reverse

Non-portrait types:

	F	VF
Cross/moneyer's name in two lines	£165	£400
Cross/cross	£200	£500

Portrait types:

	F	VF
bust/moneyer's name in two lines	£550	£1500
Bust/small cross	£375	£900

Many other issues, some featuring buildings as illustrated above. There are also different mints and moneyer's names.

Aethelstan portrait penny with small cross on reverse

EADMUND 939-46

Non-portrait types:

	F	VF
Cross or rosette/moneyer's name in two lines	£170	£425
Silver halfpenny, similar	£650	£1500

Eadmund penny, two-line type

Portrait types:

	F	VF
Crowned bust/small cross	£400	£950
Helmeted bust/cross crosslet ...	£675	£1500

Many other issues and varieties; also different mint names and moneyers.

EADRED 946-55

Non-portrait types:

	F	VF
Cross/moneyer's name in two lines	£130	£300
Silver halfpenny similar	£525	£1000
Rosette/moneyer's name	£200	£450

HAMMERED SILVER

Eadred penny, portrait type

Portrait types:

	F	VF
Crowned bust/small cross	£300	£700

Again many variations and mint names and moneyers.

HOWEL DDA (King of Wales), died c948
Small cross/moneyer's name in two lines (GILLYS) ... ...   ext. rare

EADWIG 955-59
Non-portrait types:

		F	VF
Cross/moneyer's name ... from		£175	£375
Many variations, some rare.			
Silver halfpennies, similar		£900	£1600

Portrait types:

		F	VF
Bust/cross ... ... from		£1650	*

EADGAR 959-75
Non-portrait types:

		F	VF
Cross/moneyer's name ... from		£100	£210
Cross/cross ... ... from		£100	£200
Rosette/rosette ... ... from		£135	£300
Halfpennies ... ... from		£950	£2000

Eadgar, 959-957, Non Portrait Penny, Winchester

Portrait types

	F	VF
Pre-Reform	£500	£1200
Halfpenny, diademed bust/London monogram	£600	£1200
Reform (c.972)	£550	£1100

Many other varieties.

EDWARD THE MARTYR 975-78
Portrait types:

	F	VF
Bust left/small cross	£650	£1400

Many different mints and moneyers.

AETHELRED II 978-1016

Aethelred II 978-1016, Penny, Last small cross type

	F	VF
First small cross ... ... from	£375	£900
First hand ... ... from	£85	£165
Second hand ... ... from	£90	£160
Benediction hand ... ... from	£600	£1500

HAMMERED SILVER

	F	VF
CRUX ... ... from	£70	£140

Aethelred II CRUX type penny

Aethelred II , Long Cross penny

	F	VF
Long Cross	£70	£135
Helmet	£80	£160
Agnus Dei	£3000	*

Other issues and varieties, many mint names and moneyers.

Aethelred II long cross penny

CNUT 1016-35
	F	VF
Quatrefoil ... ... from	£65	£125

Cnut quatrefoil type penny

	F	VF
Pointed helmet ... ... from	£55	£110

Cnut pointed helmet type penny

	F	VF
Small cross ... ... from	£50	£95
Jewel cross ... ... from	£375	£800

Other types, and many different mint names and moneyers.

HAROLD I 1035-40
	F	VF
Jewel cross ... ... from	£165	£370

	F	VF
Long cross with trefoils ... from	£170	£375
Long cross with fleurs-de-lis from	£160	£350

Many different mint names and moneyers.

HARTHACNUT 1035-42
	F	VF
Jewel cross, bust left	£800	£1900
– bust right	£700	£1600
Arm and sceptre types	£600	£1400

Different mint names and moneyers.

	F	VF
Scandinavian types struck at Lund	£175	£400

EDWARD THE CONFESSOR 1042-66
	F	VF
PACX type ... ... from	£140	£300
Radiate crown/small cross from	£75	£140
Trefoil quadrilateral	£75	£150
Small flan ... ... from	£65	£130
Expanding cross types ... from	£75	£150

Edward the Confessor Penny, Expanding Cross Type

	F	VF
Helmet types	£80	£150
Sovereign/eagles	£95	£200
Hammer cross	£75	£140

Edward the Confessor Hammer Cross Penny

	F	VF
Bust facing	£70	£135
Cross and piles	£85	£150
Large bust, facing, with sceptre	£900	£2250

Other issues, including a unique gold penny; many different mint names and moneyers.

HAROLD II 1066
	F	VF
Crowned head left with sceptre	£375	£800

Harold II Penny, bust left with sceptre

	F	VF
Similar but no sceptre	£425	£900

Harold II, bust left, without sceptre

	F	VF
Crowned head right with sceptre	£700	£1500

The Norman Kings

WILLIAM I 1066-87

		F	VF
Profile/cross fleury	...from	£165	£400
Bonnet	...from	£120	£250
Canopy	...from	£210	£500
Two sceptres	...from	£170	£425
Two stars	...from	£120	£250
Sword	...from	£190	£450

William I profile/cross fleury penny

		F	VF
Profile/cross and trefoils	...from	£275	£625
PAXS	...from	£100	£170

WILLIAM II 1087-1100

William II, cross voided type penny

		F	VF
Profile	...from	£300	£700
Cross in quatrefoil	...from	£275	£600
Cross voided	...from	£275	£600
Cross pattee over fleury	...from	£350	£700
Cross fleury and piles	...from	£375	£850

Henry I penny; small bust/cross and annulets

HENRY I 1100-1135

		F	VF
Annulets	...from	£275	£650
Profile/cross fleury	...from	£210	£450
PAX	...from	£225	£475
Annulets and piles	...from	£250	£600
Voided cross and fleurs	...from	£450	£950
Pointing bust and stars	...from	£575	£1250
Quatrefoil and piles	...from	£225	£475
Profile/cross and annulets	from	£700	£1650
Cross in quatrefoil	...from	£435	£900

Henry I, full face/cross fleury penny

HAMMERED SILVER

	F	VF
Full face/cross fleury	£140	£325
Double inscription	£325	£750
Small bust/cross and annulets	£250	£600
Star in lozenge fleury	£250	£550
Pellets in quatrefoil	£130	£300
Quadrilateral on cross fleury	£110	£250
Halfpennies	£1000	£2500

STEPHEN 1135-54

		F	VF
Cross moline (Watford)	...from	£100	£235

Stephen 'Watford' Penny

	F	VF
Cross moline PERERIC	£330	£700
Voided cross and mullets	£150	£375

Stephen Penny, voided cross pattée with mullets

	F	VF
Profile/cross fleury	£285	£700
Voided cross pommée (Awbridge)	£165	£400

There are also a number of irregular issues produced during the Civil War, all of which are very rare. These include several extremely rare and attractive pieces bearing the names of Empress Matilda and barons, such as Eustace Fitzjohn and Robert de Stuteville.

The Plantagenet Kings

HENRY II 1154-89

	Fair	F

Henry II Cross and Crosslets (Tealby) Penny

	Fair	F
Cross and crosslets ('Tealby' coinage)	£25	£50

The issue is classified by bust variants into six groups, struck at 32 mints.

Henry II Short Cross Penny 1b

HAMMERED SILVER

	F	VF
Short cross pennies	£30	£80

The 'short cross' coinage was introduced in 1180 and continued through successive reigns until Henry III brought about a change in 1247. HENRICVS REX appears on all these coins but they can be classified into reigns by the styles of the busts and lettering. We recommend a copy of C.R. Wren's illustrated guide The Short Cross Coinage 1180-1247, as the best guide to identification.

Richard I, 1189-1199, Short Cross Penny

RICHARD I 1189-99

Short cross pennies	£40	£95

JOHN 1199-1216

Short cross pennies	£35	£70

John Short Cross Penny

HENRY III 1216-72

Short cross pennies	£20	£35
Long cross pennies no sceptre	£15	£35
Long cross pennies with sceptre	£15	£35

Henry III, Long Cross Penny, no sceptre

Henry III, Long Cross Penny with sceptre

The 'long cross' pennies, first introduced in 1247, are divided into two groups: those with sceptre and those without. They also fall into five basic classes, with many varieties. We recommend C.R. Wren's, The Voided Long Cross Coinage, 1247-79 as the best guide to identification.

Edward I, 1st coinage, Long Cross penny

EDWARD I 1272-1307
1st coinage 1272-78

	F	VF
Long cross pennies ... ...from	£20	£6(

similar in style to those of Henry III but with more realistic beard.

Edward I Penny, London

New coinage 1278-1307

Groats	: £950	£300(
Pennies, various classes, mints from	£12	£3(
Halfpennies – ... ...from	£20	£5(
Farthings – ... ...from	£25	£7(

Edward I Farthing, London

Any new collector wishing to become serious about this area should obtain a copy of Edwardian English Silver Coins 1279-1351. Sylloge of coins of the British Isles 39 (The JJ North collection)

EDWARD II 1307-27

Pennies, various classes, mints from	£15	£5(
Halfpennies ... ...from	£50	£12!
Farthings ... ...from	£35	£7!

EDWARD III 1327-77
1st and 2nd coinages 1327-43

Pennies (only 1st coinage) various types and mints	£225	£45(
Halfpennies, different types and mints	£15	£4(
Farthings	£30	£7!

3rd coinage 1344-51 (Florin Coinage)

Pennies, various types and mints	£15	£5!
Halfpennies –	£15	£4(
Farthings	£30	£6!

Edward III 1327-77, Groat Treaty Period

4th coinage 1351-77

	F	VF
Groats, many types and mints from	£35	£95

Edward III halfgroat Post-Treaty

		F	VF
Halfgroats –	... ...	£20	£50
Pennies –	... ...	£18	£45
Halfpennies, different types	...	£35	£90
Farthings, a few types	... ...	£90	£225

Henry IV halfpenny

RICHARD II 1377-99

	F	VF
Groats, four types from	£230	£550

Henry VI Annulet issue halfgroat

	F	VF
Halfgroats	£180	£450
Pennies, various types, London	£250	£600
Pennies, various types, York ...	£45	£130
Pennies, Durham	£150	£450
Halfpennies, three main types ...	£30	£75
Farthings, some varieties	£100	£250

HENRY IV 1399-1413

	F	VF
Groats, varieties ... ...from	£1450	£4000
Halfgroats –	£475	£1200
Pennies –	£200	£600
Halfpennies	£150	£350
Farthings –	£500	*

Henry V Groat

HAMMERED SILVER

HENRY V 1413-22

	F	VF
Groats, varieties ... ...from	£80	£200
Halfgroats	£70	£190
Pennies	£30	£75
Halfpennies	£20	£60
Farthings	£130	£350

HENRY VI 1422-61
Annulet issue 1422-1427

	F	VF
Groats	£30	£70
Halfgroats	£25	£60
Pennies	£20	£50
Halfpennies	£15	£40
Farthings	£100	£275

Rosette-Mascle issue 1427-1430

	F	VF
Groats	£35	£90
Halfgroats	£30	£70
Pennies	£30	£70
Halfpennies	£20	£50
Farthings	£125	£300

Pinecone-Mascle 1430-1434

	F	VF
Groats	£35	£80
Halfgroats	£30	£70
Pennies	£30	£70
Halfpennies	£20	£45
Farthings	£125	£300

Leaf-Mascle issue 1434-1435

	F	VF
Groats	£70	£170
Halfgroats	£70	£160
Pennies	£50	£125
Halfpennies	£30	£70

Leaf-Trefoil 1435-1438

	F	VF
Groats	£50	£120
Halfgroats	£40	£110
Pennies	£45	£110
Halfpennies	£25	£55
Farthings	£135	£325

Trefoil 1438-1443

	F	VF
Groats	£60	£150
Halfgroats	£150	£350
Halfpennies	£30	£70

Trefoil-Pellet 1443-1445

	F	VF
Groats	£75	£200

Henry VI Groat, Leaf-Pellet issue

Leaf-Pellet 1445-1454

	F	VF
Groats	£45	£120
Halfgroats	£40	£110
Pennies	£35	£90
Halfpennies	£25	£50
Farthings	£135	£300

HAMMERED SILVER

Unmarked 1445-1454	F	VF
Groats	£300	£750
Halfgroats	£200	£500

Cross-Pellet 1454-1460		
Groats	£80	£200
Halfgroats	£200	£500
Pennies	£45	£100
Halfpennies	£40	£90
Farthings	£150	£400

Lis-Pellet 1454-1460		
Groats	£175	£475

These are many different varieties, mintmarks and mints in this reign. These prices are for commonest prices in each issue.

EDWARD IV 1st Reign 1461-1470
Heavy coinage 1461-4

	F	VF
Groats, many classes, all London	£90	£220
Halfgroats, many classes, all London	£250	£525
Pennies, different classes. London, York and Durham	£145	£275
Halfpennies, different classes, all London	£45	£100
Farthings. London	£300	£600

Edward IV Groat. Light Coinage

Light coinage 1464-70

	F	VF
Groats, many different issues, varieties, *mms* and mints from	£35	£90
Halfgroats, ditto	£30	£70
Pennies, ditto	£30	£65
Halfpennies, ditto	£25	£60
Farthings Two issues	£275	£600

Henry VI (restored), Groat, London

HENRY VI (restored) 1470-71

	F	VF
Groats, different mints, *mms* from	£125	£300
Halfgroats – from	£210	£450
Pennies – from	£275	£575
Halfpennies – from	£95	£225

EDWARD IV 2nd reign 1471-83	F	VF
Groats, different varieties, mints etc	£35	£95
Halfgroats	£30	£70
Pennies	£30	£70
Halfpennies	£20	£60

EDWARD V 1483
(The coins read EDWARD but are now considered to be attributable to Richard III)
(Mintmark boar's head)

Groats	£1750	£4000
Halfgroats		ext. rar
Penny		ext. rar

Richard III Groat, London Mint

RICHARD III 1483-85

Groats, London and York mints, various combinations of *mms*	£270	£575
Halfgroats	£575	£1200
Pennies, York and Durham (London mint unique)	£125	£325
Halfpennies	£110	£260
Farthing		ext. rare

PERKIN WARBECK, PRETENDER'
Groat, 1494 [cf. BNJ XXVI, p. 125] £700 £2000

The Tudor Monarchs

HENRY VII 1485-1509
Facing bust issues:

Henry VII Groat London open crown type

Groats, all London

Open crown without arches ...	£75	£250
Crown with two arches unjewelled	£60	£150
Crown with two jewelled arches	£55	£120
Similar but only one arch jewelled	£40	£110
Similar but tall thin lettering ...	£45	£120
Similar but single arch, tall thin lettering	£40	£110
Halfgroats, London		
Open crown without arches, tressure unbroken	£275	£650
Double arched crown	£45	£100

	F	VF
Unarched crown	£30	£70
Some varieties and different *mms.*		
Halfgroats, Canterbury		
Open crown, without arches ...	£30	£80
Double arched crown	£30	£70
Some varieties and different *mms.*		
Halfgroats, York		
Double arched crown	£35	£85
Unarched crown with tressure		
broken	£30	£70
Double arched crown with keys		
at side of bust	£25	£70
Many varieties and different mms.		
Pennies, facing bust type		
London	£185	£400
Canterbury, open crown	£200	£450
– arched crown	£45	£120
Durham, Bishop Sherwood		
(S on breast)	£55	£140
York	£40	£90
Many varieties and mms.		
Pennies, 'sovereign enthroned' type		
London, many varieties	£35	£80
Durham –	£40	£90
York –	£30	£75
Halfpennies, London		
Open crown	£45	£120
Arched crown	£30	£80
Crown with lower arch	£25	£65
Some varieties and mms.		
Halfpennies, Canterbury		
Open crown	£90	£200
Arched crown	£75	£150
Halfpennies, York		
Arched crown and key below bus	£80	£180
Farthings, all London	£125	£300
Profile issues:		
Testoons im lis, three different		
legends	£4500	£8500

Henry VII profile issue testoon

	F	VF
Groats, all London		
Tentative issue (double band to		
crown)	£140	£400

Henry VII Groat, Tentative issue

	F	VF
Regular issue (triple band to		
crown)	£60	£160
Some varieties, and *mms*		
Halfgroats		
London	£65	£175
– no numeral after king's name	£400	£900
Canterbury	£35	£90
York, two keys below shield ...	£45	£100
– XB by shield	£325	£750

HENRY VIII 1509-47
With portrait of Henry VII
1st coinage 1509-26

	F	VF
Groats, London	£75	£200
Groats, Tournai	£325	£925
Groats, Tournai, without portrait	£1750	*
Halfgroats, London	£65	£180
Halfgroats, Canterbury, varieties	£40	£120
Halfgroats, York, varieties	£35	£120
Halfgroats, Tournai	£1250	*
Pennies, 'sovereign enthroned'		
type, London	£35	£90
Pennies, Canterbury, varieties ...	£65	£140
Pennies, Durham, varieties ...	£30	£70
Halfpennies, facing bust type,		
London	£30	£70
Canterbury	£65	£140
Farthings, portcullis type, London	£275	£650

Henry VIII second coinage groat,
with Irish title HIB REX

With young portrait of Henry VIII
2nd coinage 1526-44

	F	VF
Groats, London, varieties, *mms*	£45	£125
Groats, Irish title, HIB REX	£300	£750
Groats, York *mms*	£80	£200
Halfgroats, London *mms*	£35	£100
Halfgroats, Canterbury *mms* ...	£30	£90
Halfgroats, York *mms*	£30	£90
Pennies 'sovereign enthroned' type		
London, varieties, *mms*	£30	£90
Canterbury, varieties, *mms* ...	£70	£170
Durham –	£30	£90
York	£90	£250

Henry VIII, Halfpenny, 2nd Coingage, London

	F	VF
Halfpennies, facing bust type		
London, varieties, *mms*	£25	£70
Canterbury	£40	£90
York	£65	£140
Farthings, portcullis type	£325	£700

HAMMERED SILVER

With old bearded portrait   F   VF
3rd coinage 1544-47
Posthumous issues 1547-51

	F	VF
Testoons (or shillings)		
London (Tower mint), varieties,		
mms	£500	£1500
Southwark, varieties, mms ...	£525	£1600
Bristol, varieties, mms	£650	£1800
Groats, six different busts,		
varieties, mms		
London (Tower mint)	£55	£180
Southwark	£55	£180
Bristol	£60	£190
Canterbury	£60	£190
London (Durham House)	£160	£500

Henry VIII third coinage groat

	F	VF
Halfgroats, only one style of		
bust (except York which has		
two), varieties, mms		
London (Tower mint)	£50	£160
Southwark	£55	£175
Bristol	£50	£160
Canterbury	£35	£125
York	£50	£150
London (Durham House)	£300	£600

Henry VIII Penny, 3rd Coinage Tower

Henry VIII Penny, 3rd Coinage, Bristol

	F	VF
Pennies (facing bust) varieties, mms		
London (Tower mint)	£35	£110
Southwark	£65	£170
London (Durham House)	£325	£750
Bristol	£45	£140
Canterbury	£35	£120
York	£35	£120
Halfpennies (facing bust) varieties, mms		
London (Tower mint)	£35	£100
Bristol	£70	£175
Canterbury	£45	£110
York	£35	£110

EDWARD VI 1547-53
1st period 1547-49

	F	VF
Shillings, London (Durham House),		
mm bow, patterns (?)		ext. rare
Groats, London (Tower),		
mm arrow	£450	£1300
Groats, London (Southwark),		
mm E, none	£475	£1400
Halfgroats, London (Tower),		
mm arrow	£425	£1000
Halfgroats, London (Southwark),		
mm arrow, E	£400	£950
Halfgroats, Canterbury, mm none	£225	£550
Pennies, London (Tower),		
mm	£275	£650
Pennies, London (Southwark),		
mm E	£350	£850
Pennies, Bristol,		
mm none	£200	£575
Halfpennies, London (Tower),		
mm uncertain	£350	£900
Halfpennies, Bristol, mm none	£300	£800

Edward VI 2nd period shilling. Tower mint with mintmark Y.

Edward VI, Shilling, 2nd period Canterbury with mintmark t.

2nd period 1549-50

	F	VF
Shillings, London (Tower) various		
mms	£95	£300
Shillings, Bristol, mm TC	£650	£1750
Shillings, Canterbury, mm T or t	£135	£450
Shillings, London (Durham House),		
mm bow, varieties	£200	£600

3rd period £550-53

	F	VF
Base silver (similar to issues of 2nd period)		
Shillings, London (Tower),		
mm lis, lion, rose	£125	£400
Pennies, London (Tower),		
mm escallop	£65	£175
Pennies, York, mm mullet	£50	£150
Halfpennies, London (Tower) ...	£185	£500

     COINS MARKET VALUES

	F	VF

'ine Silver
Crown 1551 mm Y, 1551-53
mm tun ... ... | £300 | £700 |

Mary Groat

Mary Portrait Penny

Edward VI Halfcrown 1551, walking horse

Halfcrown, walking horse, 1551,
mm Y ... ... | £225 | £550 |
Halfcrowns, galloping horse,
1551-52, mm tun ... ... | £300 | £800 |

*Edward VI
1552 halfcrown
galloping
horse*

Halfcrowns, walking horse, 1553,
mm tun ... ... | £650 | £1500 |
Shillings, mm Y, tun ... ... | £60 | £190 |
Sixpences, London (Tower),
mm y, tun ... ... | £70 | £225 |
Sixpences, York, mm mullet ... | £120 | £400 |
Threepences, London (Tower),
mm tun ... ... | £130 | £450 |
Threepences, York mm mullet ... | £270 | £650 |
Pennies, sovereign type ... ... | £700 | £1650 |
Farthings, portcullis type ... ... | £700 | * |

MARY 1553-54

	F	VF
Groats, mm pomegranate	£65	£220
Halfgroats, similar	£550	*
Pennies, rev VERITAS TEMP FILIA ...	£375	*
Pennies, rev CIVITAS LONDON	£375	*

PHILIP AND MARY 1554-58

	F	VF
Shillings, full titles, without date	£170	£600
– also without XII	£175	£600
– dated 1554	£200	£650
– dated 1554, English titles ...	£225	£700
– dated 1555, English titles only	£200	£650
– dated 1554, English titles only also without XII	£350	*
– 1555, as last	£475	*
– 1554 but date below bust ...	£650	*
– 1555 but date below bust ...	£650	*
– 1555 similar to previous but without ANG	£750	*
Sixpences, full titles, 1554	£160	£600
– full titles, undated	ext rare	
– English titles, 1555	£200	£650
– similar but date below bust, 1554	£525	*
– English titles, 1557	£220	£700
– similar, but date below bust, 1557	£750	*
Groats, mm lis	£80	£260
Halfgroats, mm lis	£350	£1000

Philip and Mary Shilling, 1554 and full titles

	F	VF
Pennies, mm lis	£300	£700
Base pennies, without portrait	£50	£160

HAMMERED SILVER

ELIZABETH I 1558-1603   F   VF
Hammered coinage, 1st issue 1558-61
Shillings ELIZABETH

	F	VF
Wire-line circles	£250	£750
Beaded inner circles	£100	£325
ET for Z	£60	£185

Edward VI shilling greyhound countermark (reign of Elizabeth), and Elizabeth I hammered groat

Groats

	F	VF
Wire-line inner circles	£120	£400
Beaded inner circles	£45	£160
ET for Z	£35	£150

Halfgroats

	F	VF
Wire-line inner circles	£130	£375
Beaded inner circles	£30	£85

Elizabeth I Penny, wire-line inner circle

Pennies

	F	VF
Wire-line inner circles	£175	£475
Beaded inner circles	£20	£70
Countermarked shillings of Edward VI, 1560-61		
With portcullis mark (Current for 4½d) **(F)**	£1350	*
With greyhound mark (current for 2½d) **(F)**	1500	*

Hammered coinage, 2nd issue 1561-82

	F	VF
Sixpences, dated 1561-82	£30	£110
Threepences, 1561-82	£25	£75
Halfgroats, undated	£40	£100
Threehalfpences, 1561-62, 1564-70, 1572-79, 1581-82	£25	£90
Pennies, undated	£20	£70
Threefarthings, 1561-62, 1568, 1572-78, 1581-82	£55	£140

Elizabeth I Halfcrown, 1601

Hammered coinage, 3rd issue 1583-1603

	F	VF
Crowns, im **1**	£525	£1100
Crowns, im **2**	£675	£1650
Halfcrowns, im **1**	£325	£750
Halfcrowns, im **2 (F)**	£900	£2500
Shillings ELIZAB	£55	£175
Sixpences, 1582-1602	£35	£120
Halfgroats, E D G ROSA etc	£15	£65
Pennies	£20	£65
Halfpennies, portcullis type ...	£20	£60

There are many different mintmarks, such as lis, bell, lion etc., featured on the hammered coins of Elizabeth I, and these marks enable one to date those coins which are not themselves dated. For more details see J.J. North's English Hammered Coinage, *Volume 2.*

Elizabeth I Miled Coinage, Sixpence, 1562

Milled Coinage
Shillings

	F	VF
large size	£245	£750
Intermediate	£120	£400
Small	£100	£350
Sixpences		
1561	£40	£150
1562	£35	£120
1563-64, 1566	£50	£200
1567-68	£50	£180
1570-71	£110	£375
Groats, undated	£110	£375
Threepences, 1561, 1562-64 ...	£70	£250
Halfgroats	£90	£300
Threefarthings	ext rare	

The Stuart Kings

JAMES I 1603-25
1st coinage 1603-04

	F	VF
Crowns, rev EXURGAT etc	£475	£1100
Halfcrowns –	£475	£1500
Shillings, varieties	£50	£200
Sixpences, dated 1603-04, varieties	£35	£150
Halfgroats, undated	£25	£70
Pennies –	£25	£65

James I Sixpence, 1603

2nd coinage 1604-19

	F	VF
Crowns rev QVAE DEVS etc ...	£450	£950
Halfcrowns –	£650	£2000

James I 2nd coinage shilling

	F	VF
Shillings, varieties	£40	£150
Sixpences, dated 1604-15, varieties etc.	£30	£110
Halfgroats, varieties	£15	£55
Pennies	£15	£40
Halfpennies	£15	£40

James I Shilling, 3rd Coinage

3rd coinage 1619-25

	F	VF
Crowns	£250	£600
– Plume over reverse shield ...	£300	£700
Halfcrowns	£110	£300
– Plume over reverse shield ...	£185	£500

	F	VF

James I halfcrown with plume over shield on reverse

	F	VF
Shillings	£45	£165
– Plume over reverse shield ...	£100	£300
Sixpences dated 1621-24	£35	£130
Halfgroats	£15	£35
Pennies	£15	£30
Halfpennies	£15	£35

James I sixpence of 1622

CHARLES I 1625-1649
Tower Mint 1625-1643

Crowns
(Obv. King on horseback. Rev. shield)

	F	VF
1st horseman/square shield im lis, cross calvary	£275	£700
As last/plume above shield im lis, cross calvary, castle ...	£600	£1400
2nd horseman/oval shield im plume, rose harp. Some varieties, from	£250	£600
3rd horseman/round shield im bell, crown, tun, anchor, triangle, star, portcullis, triangle in circle. Some varieties, from	£265	£650

Halfcrowns
(Obv. King on horseback. Rev. shield)

Charles I Tower halfcrown: first horseman

77

HAMMERED SILVER

	F	VF
1st horseman/square shield		
im lis, cross calvary, negro's head, castle, anchor.		
Many varieties, from	£100	£300
2nd horseman/oval shield		
im plume, rose, harp, portcullis.		
Many varieties, from	£80	£200
3rd horseman/round shield		
im bell, crown, tun, portcullis, anchor, triangle, star		
Many varieties, from	£55	£150
4th horseman/round shield		
im star, triangle in circle	£35	£120

Charles I Tower Halfcrown, mintmark triangle

Shillings

	F	VF
1st bust/square shield		
***im* lis, cross calvary**		
Some varieties	£50	£175
2nd bust/square shield		
im cross calvary, negro's head, castle, anchor, heart, plume		
Many varieties, from	£50	£170
3rd bust/oval shield		
im plume, rose	£40	£140
4th bust/oval or round shield		
im harp, portcullis, bell, crown, tun		
Many varieties, from	£40	£150
5th bust/square shield		
im tun, anchor, triangle		
Many varieties, from	£35	£130
6th bust/square shield		
im anchor, triangle, star, triangle in circle		
Some varieties, from	£35	£130

Sixpences
(early ones are dated)

	F	VF
1st bust/square shield, date above		
1625 *im* lis, cross calvary		
1626 *im* cross calvary	£50	£170
2nd bust/square shield, date above		
1625, 1626 *im* cross calvary		
1626, 1627 *im* negro's head		
1626, 1628 *im* castle		
1628, 1629 *im* anchor		
1629 *im* heart		
1630 *im* heart, plume	£90	£250

	F	VF
3rd bust/oval shield		
im plume, rose	£45	£170
4th bust/oval or round shield		
im harp, portcullis, bell, crown, tun	£35	£130

Charles I Tower sixpence mm bell

	F	VF
5th bust/square shield		
im tun, anchor, triangle		
Many varieties, from	£35	£130
6th bust/square shield		
im triangle, star	£30	£135
Halfgroats		
Crowned rose both sides		
im lis, cross calvary, blackamoor's head	£18	£50
2nd bust/oval shield		
im plume, rose	£20	£60
3rd bust/oval shield		
im rose, plume	£20	£60
4th bust/oval or round shield,		
im harp, crown, portcullis, bell, tun, anchor, triangle, star		
Many varieties from	£15	£55
5th bust/round shield		
im anchor	£25	£85
Pennies		
Uncrowned rose both sides		
im one or two pellets, lis, negro's head	£15	£40
2nd bust/oval shield		
im plume	£20	£60
3rd bust/oval shield		
im plume, rose	£15	£55
4th bust/oval shield		
im harp, one or two pellets, portcullis, bell, triangle	£15	£50
5th bust/oval shield		
im one or two pellets, none	£15	£40
Halfpennies		
Uncrowned rose both sides		
im none	£15	£40

Tower Mint, under Parliament 1643-48

	F	VF
Crowns		
(Obv. King on horseback, Rev. shield)		
4th horseman/round shield		
im (**P**), (**R**), eye sun	£300	£750
5th horseman/round shield		
im sun, sceptre	£400	£850
Halfcrowns		
(Obv. King on horseback, Rev. shield)		
3rd horseman/round shield		
im (**P**), (**R**), eye sun	£55	£200
im (**P**), foreshortened horse	£150	£400
5th horseman (tall)/round shield		
im sun, sceptre	£65	£225

Charles I Parliament shilling, mm eye

Sixpence of Broit's 2nd milled issue

Briot's hammered issues 1638-39

	F	VF
im: anchor, triangle over anchor		
Halfcrowns	£550	£1250
Shillings	£325	£850

	F	VF
Shillings (revs. all square shield)		
6th bust (crude)		
im **(P)**, **(R)**, eye, sun	£40	£150
7th bust (tall, slim)		
im sun, sceptre	£40	£165
8th bust (shorter, older)		
im sceptre	£45	£200
Sixpences (revs. all square shield)		
6th bust		
im **(P)**, **(R)**, eye sun	£70	£200
7th bust		
im **(R)**, eye, sun, sceptre ...	£65	£180
8th bust, (crude style)		
im eye, sun	£90	£300
Halfgroats		
4th bust/round shield		
im **(P)**, **(R)**, eye sceptre ...	£30	£70
7th bust (old/round shield)		
im eye, sun, sceptre	£25	£60
Pennies		
7th bust/oval shield		
im one or two pellets	£20	£55

Charles I Crown of Exeter

PROVINCIAL MINTS

York 1642-44		
im: lion		
Halfcrowns, varieties from	£110	£300
Shillings –	£90	£250
Sixpences –	£150	£400
Threepences –	£40	£100

Aberystwyth 1638-42		
im: open book		
Halfcrowns, varieties from	£400	£1000
Shillings –	£180	£500
Sixpences –	£170	£500
Groats –	£35	£80

Charles I Briot's crown

Briot's 1st milled issued 1631-32

im: flower and **B**		
Crowns	£350	£900
Halfcrowns	£190	£500
Shillings	£140	£425
Sixpences	£70	£225
Halfgroats	£35	£70
Pennies	£35	£75

Briot's 2nd milled issue 1638-39

im: anchor, anchor and B, anchor and mullet		
Halfcrowns	£160	£400
Shillings	£80	£220
Sixpences	£40	£100

Aberystwyth groat

Threepences –	£30	£65
Halfgroats –	£40	£95
Pennies –	£60	£165
Halfpennies	£150	£375

Aberystwyth – Furnace 1647-48		
im: crown		
Halfcrowns from	£1200	£3000
Shillings		ext. rare

HAMMERED SILVER

	F	VF
Sixpences		ext. rare
Groats	£185	£450
Threepences	£200	£475
Halfgroats	£225	£550
Pennies	£600	£1350

Shrewsbury 1642
mm: plume without band

	F	VF
Pounds, varieties from	£1000	£3000
Halfpounds –	£475	£1000
Crowns –	£425	£950
Halfcrowns –	£300	£700
Shillings –	£675	£1500

Oxford 1642-46
mm: plume with band

	F	VF
Pounds, varieties from	£1000	£3000
Halfpounds –	£400	£825
Crowns –	£375	£800
Halfcrowns –	£100	£275
Shillings –	£110	£325
Sixpences –	£140	£325
Groats –	£65	£175
Threepences –	£50	£150
Halfgroats –	£80	£200
Pennies –	£100	£250

Bristol 1643-45
im: Bristol monogram, acorn, plumelet

	F	VF
Halfcrowns, varieties from	£140	£375

Charles I halfcrown of York with mm lion

	F	VF
Shillings –	£150	£350
Sixpences –	£150	£400
Groats –	£125	£300
Threepences –	£140	£400
Halfgroats –	£200	£475
Pennies –	£300	£700

Charles I sixpence, Bristol 1644

A, B, and plumes issues
Associated with Thomas Bushell; previously assigned to Lundy

	F	VF
Halfcrowns, varieties from	£525	£1500

	F	VF
Shillings –	£250	£65•
Sixpences –	£150	£40•
Groats –	£100	£22!
Threepences –	£100	£22!
Halfgroats –	£350	£80•

Truro 1642-43
im: rose, bugle

	F	VF
Crowns, varieties	£225	£50•
Halfcrowns –	£550	£120•
Shillings –		ext. rare

Bristol shilling 1644

Exeter 1643-46
im Ex, rose, castle

	F	VF
Halfpounds		ext. rare
Crowns, varieties	£200	£450•
Halfcrowns	£135	£350•
Shillings	£180	£450•
Sixpences	£180	£450•
Groats	£70	£160•
Threepences	£80	£180•
Halfgroats –	£125	£350•
Pennies	£250	£525•

Worcester 1643-4
im: castle, helmet, leopard's head, lion, two lions, lis, rose, star

	F	VF
Halfcrowns, many varieties ...	£450	£1100

Salopia (Shrewsbury) 1644
im: helmet, lis, rose (in legend)

	F	VF
Halfcrowns, many varieties ...	£550	£1650

Worcester or Salopia (Shrewsbury)
im: bird, boar's head, lis, castle, cross, and annulets, helmet, lion, lis, pear, rose, scroll

	F	VF
Shillings, varieties	£700	£1800
Sixpences	£750	£1750
Groats	£400	£1200
Threepences	£300	£700
Halfgroats	£400	£950

'HC' mint (probably Hartlebury Castle, Worcester 1646)
im: pear, three pears

	F	VF
Halfcrowns	£1000	£2650

Chester 1644
im: cinquefoil, plume, prostrate gerb, three gerbs

	F	VF
Halfcrowns, varieties	£550	£1250
Shillings		ext. rare
Threepences	£750	£1750

Welsh Marches mint? 1644	F	VF
Halfcrowns...	£500	£1100

Welsh Marches mint, halfcrown

SIEGE PIECES
Carlisle besieged 1644-45

	F	VF
Three shillings	£2650	£6000
Shillings (F)	£1850	£4000

Newark besieged many times
(surrendered May 6, 1646)

	F	VF
Halfcrowns, 1645-46 (F)	£375	£750

Newark Besieged, Shilling, dated 1645

	F	VF
Shillings, 1645-46, varieties (F)	£300	£600
Ninepences, 1645-46	£275	£550
Sixpences	£250	£600

Pontefract besieged 1648-49

	F	VF
Two shillings, 1648		ext. rare
Shillings, 1648, varieties	£700	£1500

Ponefract Besieged 1648, Siege Shilling

Scarborough besieged 1644-45
Many odd values issued here, all of which are extremely rare. The coin's value was decided by the intrinsic value of the piece of metal from which it was made.

HAMMERED SILVER

	F	VF

Examples: 5s 8d, 2s 4d, 1s 9d, 1s 3d, 7d etc. (F). Collectors could expect to pay at least **£2250** or more in F and **£4500** in VF for any of these.

COMMONWEALTH 1649-60

	F	VF
Crowns, *im* sun 1649,51-54, 56 ...	£350	£700
Halfcrowns, *im* sun 1649, 1651-6	£130	£350
—*im* anchor 1658-60	£475	£1000

Commonwealth Shilling, 1651

	F	VF
Shillings, *im* sun 1649, 1661-87	£85	£200
—*im* anchor 1658-60	£325	£650

A superb 1651 sixpence

	F	VF
Sixpences, *im* sun 1649, 1651-7	£80	£180
—*im* anchor 1658-6	£300	£625
Halfgroats undated	£25	£70
Pennies undated	£25	£60
Halfpennies undated	£25	£60

CHARLES II 1660-85
Hammered coinage 1660-62

	F	VF
Halfcrowns, three issues ... from	£175	£475
Shillings— ... ... from	£80	£325

Charles II hammered issue shilling

	F	VF
Sixpences—	£65	£200
Fourpences, third issue only ...	£25	£70
Threepences— ... ... from	£25	£65
Twopences, three issues ... from	£20	£50
Pennies— ... ... from	£25	£60

'ROYAL' AND 'ROSE' BASE METAL FARTHINGS

Until 1613 English coins were struck only in gold or silver — the monarchy considered that base metal issues would be discreditable to the royal prerogative of coining. However, silver coins had become far too small, farthings so tiny that they had to be discontinued. So to meet demands for small change James I authorised Lord Harington to issue copper farthing tokens. Subsequently this authority passed in turn to the Duke of Lennox, the Duchess of Richmond and Lord Maltravers. It ceased by order of Parliament in 1644.

	Fair	F	VF	EF
JAMES I **Royal farthing tokens**				
Type 1 Harington (circa 1613). Small copper flan with tin-washed surface, mint-mark between sceptres below crown	£10	£30	£75	£12!
Type 2 Harington (circa 1613). Larger flan, no tin wash	£15	£15	£40	£8
Type 3 Lennox (1614-25). IACO starts at 1 o'clock position	£3	£10	£25	£6(
Type 4 Lennox (1622-25). Oval flan, IACO starts at 7 o'clock	£8	£25	£65	£12
CHARLES I **Royal farthing tokens**				
Type 1 Richmond (1625-34). Single arched crown	£2	£8	£25	£5
Type 2 Transitional (circa 1634). Double arched crown	£6	£20	£50	£10(
Type 3 Maltravers (1634-36). Inner circles	£3	£10	£30	£6(
Type 4 Richmond (1625-34). As Type 1 but oval	£8	£25	£60	£12(
Type 5 Maltravers (1634-36). Double arched crown	£10	£30	£70	*
Rose farthing tokens (rose on reverse)				
Type 1 Small thick flan	£3	£10	£30	*
Type 2 Same, but single arched crown	£2	£7	£25	*
Type 3 Same, but sceptres below crown	£10	£25	£50	*

James I Harington farthings, types 1, 2 and 3 (left to right)

Charles I Richmond, Maltravers and Rose farthings (left to right)

MILLED COINAGE from 1656

Again it must be stressed that the prices shown in this guide are the approximate amounts collectors can expect to pay for coins — they are not dealers' buying prices. Information for this guide is drawn from auction results and dealers' lists, with the aim of determining firm valuations. Prices still vary enormously from sale to sale and from one dealer's list to another. Allowance must also be made for the variance in the standards of grading. The prices given here aim at a reasonable assessment of the market at the time of compilation, but they are not the product of computers, which would, in any case, provide only average (not necessarily accurate) prices. It is not possible to forecast such values because of the erratic fluctuations that can occur, not only in boom conditions but also during times of economic uncertainty, and an annual catalogue of this type cannot be up to date on the bullion prices of common sovereigns, for example. If you are buying or selling bullion gold coins, refer to current quotations from bullion dealers.

With some denominations in the silver and copper series, column headings indicating condition change at the beginning of the lists of George III coins. The condition (grade) of a coin is of great importance in determining its market value. Notes on grading and on abbreviations etc. used in these price guides appear elsewhere in this publication.

Cromwell gold patterns

These were struck by order of Cromwell, with the consent of the Council. The dies were made by Thomas Simon, and the coins were struck on Peter Blondeau's machine. The fifty shillings and the broad were struck from the same dies, but the fifty shillings has the edge inscription PROTECTOR LITERIS LITERAE NUMMIS CORONA ER SALUS, while the broad is not so thick and has a grained edge. No original strikings of the half broad are known, but some were struck from dies made by John Tanner in 1738. All three denominations are dated 1656.

Oliver Cromwell gold half broad 1656

	F	VF	EF	Unc
Fifty shillings	£3500	£8500	£15000	*
Broad	£2000	£3500	£6000	£7500
Half broad	£2500	£4000	£6500	£8500

Five guineas

	F	VF	EF	Unc
CHARLES II				
1668-78 pointed end to trnctn of bust ...	£1200	£2500	£6500	*
1668, 69, 75—eleph below bust	£1200	£2500	£6500	*
1675-8—eleph & castle below bust	£1200	£2500	£6500	*
1678-84 rounded end to trnctn	£1100	£2000	£5800	*
1680-4—eleph & castle	£1500	£2750	£7000	*
JAMES II				
1686 sceptres in wrong order on rev ...	£1200	£2250	£6000	£10000
1687-8 sceptres correct	£1200	£2250	£6000	£10000
1687-8 eleph & castle	£1250	£2500	£6500	£10000
WILLIAM AND MARY				
1691-4 no prov mark	£1200	£2000	£5250	£9500
1691-4 eleph & castle	£1350	£2500	£6000	£10000
WILLIAM III				
1699-1700 no prov mark	£1200	£2000	£4750	£8500
1699 eleph & castle	£1400	£2500	£5500	£9500
1701 new bust 'fine work'	£1350	£2250	£5250	£8500

Charles II 1676 five guineas, elephant and castle

George II 1729 five guineas

Charles II 1664 two guineas elephant below bust

James II 1687 two guineas

ANNE
Pre-Union with Scotland

	F	VF	EF	Unc
1703 VIGO below bust	*	*	£35000	*
1705-6 plain below	£1350	£2750	£6000	£9500

Post-Union with Scotland

	F	VF	EF	Unc
1706	£1250	£2500	£5500	£9000
1709 Larger lettering, wider shield and crowns	£1250	£2500	£5250	£8500
1711, 1713-4 broader bust	£1250	£2500	£5250	£8500

Pre-Union reverses have separate shields (top and right) for England and Scotland. Post-Union reverses have the English and Scottish arms side by side on the top and bottom shields.

GEORGE I

	F	VF	EF	Unc
1716, 17, 20, 26	£1750	£2750	£7000	£10000

GEORGE II

	F	VF	EF	Unc
1729, 31, 35, 38, 41 YH	£1350	£2250	£4000	£7000
1729 E,I,C, below head	£1350	£2500	£4500	£7500
1746 OH, lima below	£1350	£2750	£4750	£8000
1748, 53 plain below	£1350	£2750	£4750	£8000

GEORGE III

	F	VF	EF	Unc
1770, 73, 77 patterns only	*	*	£25000	£40000

Two guineas

CHARLES II

	F	VF	EF	Unc
1664, 5, 9, 71 pointed end to trnctn	£650	£1650	£3500	£6500
1664 elephant below	£650	£1650	£3500	£6500
1675-84 rounded end to trnctn	£550	£1500	£3000	£6000
1676, 78, 82-84 eleph & castle below bust	£700	£1750	£4500	£7500
1678 elephant below				ext. rare

JAMES II

	F	VF	EF	Unc
1687	£800	£1950	£4500	£7500
1688/9	£850	£2000	£5000	£8000

WILLIAM AND MARY

	F	VF	EF	Unc
1691, 3, 4 eleph & castle	£800	£1650	£3750	£6000
1693, 4 no prov mark	£750	£1400	£3250	£5500

WILLIAM III

	F	VF	EF	Unc
1701	£1000	£2250	£3500	£6500

ANNE
(none struck before Union)

	F	VF	EF	Unc
1709, 11, 13, 14	£650	£1200	£2500	£5000

GEORGE I

	F	VF	EF	Unc
1717,20,26	£650	£1250	£2500	£4000

GEORGE II

	F	VF	EF	Unc
1734, 5, 8, 9,YH (**F**)	£400	£650	£1500	£2250
1739, 40 intermediate head (**F**)	£450	£700	£1750	£2750
1748, 53 OH	£475	£750	£2000	£3000

GEORGE III

	F	VF	EF	Unc
1768, 73, 77 patterns only	*	*	£12500	£22500

Guineas

CHARLES II

	F	VF	EF	Unc
1663 pointed trnctn	£550	£1250	£3000	£5500
1663—eleph	£550	£1250	£3500	*
1664 trnctn indented	£550	£1250	£3000	*
1664—eleph	*	*	£6000	*

GUINEAS

	F	VF	EF	Unc
1664-73 sloping pointed trnctn	£400	£950	£2750	£5500
1664, 5, 8 — eleph	£500	£1250	£3250	*
1672-84 rounded trnctn	£350	£750	£2500	*
1674-84 — eleph & castle	£500	£1000	£4000	*
1677, 8 — eleph	*	£1750	*	*

JAMES II
	F	VF	EF	Unc
1685, 6 1st bust	£300	£750	£2000	£3000
1685 — eleph & castle	£350	£850	£2250	*
1686-8 2nd bust	£350	£800	£2000	£3000
1686-8 — eleph & castle	£350	£850	£2100	*

WILLIAM AND MARY
	F	VF	EF	Unc
1689-94 no prov mark	£300	£750	£1750	£3500
1689-94 eleph & castle	£325	£850	£2000	*
1692 eleph	£550	£1200	*	*

Charles II 1663 guinea elephant below bust

WILLIAM III
	F	VF	EF	Unc
1695, 6 1st bust	£250	£500	£1500	£2500
1695, 7 — eleph & castle	*	*	*	*
1697-1701 2nd bust	£250	£500	£1500	*
1698-1701 — eleph & castle	£450	£1100	*	*
1701 3rd bust 'fine work'	£350	£750	£2500	*

ANNE
Pre-Union[1]
	F	VF	EF	Unc
1702, 1705-7 plain below bust	£300	£600	£1500	£2750
1703 VIGO below	£1250	£5000	£12500	*

Post Union[1]
	F	VF	EF	Unc
1707, 8 1st bust	£250	£500	£1000	£2000
1707 — eleph & castle	£400	£850	£2750	*
1707-9 2nd bust	£250	£500	£1000	£2000
1708-9 — eleph & castle	£450	£1100	£3500	*
1710-1714 3rd bust	£250	£500	£1000	£1750

[1]See note in prices of five guinea pieces for Anne.

Anne 1713 guinea

GEORGE I
	F	VF	EF	Unc
1714 1st head PR. EL. (Prince Elector) in rev legend	£600	£1200	£2200	£3500
1715 2nd head, tie with two ends	£275	£650	£1250	£2500
1715 3rd head, hair not curling round trnctn	£225	£550	£1150	£2250
1716-23 4th head, tie with loop	£200	£500	£950	£2000
1721, 2 — eleph & castle	£500	*	*	*
1723-7 5th head, smaller, older bust	£225	£550	£1150	£2250
1726 — eleph & castle	£500	£1350	*	*

GEORGE II
	F	VF	EF	Unc
1727 1st YH, small lettering	£450	£850	£2250	£3750
1727, 8 — larger lettering	£300	£500	£1800	*
1729-32 2nd YH (narrower)	£250	£500	£1500	*
1729, 31, 2 — E.I.C. below	£350	£800	£1900	£3000
1732-8 — larger lettering	£200	£500	£1350	£2000
1732 — — E.I.C. below	£350	£600	£1750	*
1739, 40, 43 intermediate head	£200	£450	£1000	£1900
1739 — E.I.C. below	£350	£750	£2000	*
1745, 6 — larger lettering	£200	£600	£1350	*
1745 — LIMA below	£500	£1000	£2750	*
1747-53, 5, 6, 8, 9, 60, OH	£200	£300	£850	£1750

GEORGE III
	F	VF	EF	Unc
1761, 1st head	£500	£1000	£2500	£3500
1763, 4, 2nd head	£300	£850	£2500	*
1765-73, 3rd head	£140	£275	£650	£1200
1774-9, 81-6, 4th head	£125	£225	£400	£700
1789-99, 5th head, 'spade' rev (F)	£110	£200	£325	£425
1813, 6th head, rev shield in Garter ('Military guinea')	£250	£500	£850	£1200

George III 1768 guinea

William and Mary 1691 half guinea

William III 1695 half guinea

George I 1719 half guinea

George I half guinea, 1725

George II 1756 half guinea

George III 1788 half guinea with 'spade' type shield on reverse

George I 1718 quarter guinea

Half Guineas

	F	VF	EF	Unc
CHARLES II				
1669-72 bust with pointed trnctn	£300	£650	£1750	*
1672-84 rounded trnctn...	£300	£650	£1750	*
1676-8, 80, 82-4 — eleph & castle	£350	£850	£2500	*
JAMES II				
1686-8 no prov mark	£300	£650	£1750	£2750
1686 eleph & castle	£650	*	*	*
WILLIAM AND MARY				
1689 1st busts	£350	£750	£1750	£2750
1690-4 2nd busts	£350	£750	£1750	*
1691-2 — eleph & castle	£400	£850	£2000	*
1692 — eleph				ext. rare
WILLIAM III				
1695 no prov mark	£200	£450	£1250	£2250
1695, 6 eleph & castle	£350	£750	£2000	*
1697-1701 larger harp on rev	£250	£500	£1500	*
1698 — eleph & castle	£300	£650	£2000	*
ANNE				
Pre-Union[1]				
1702, 5 plain below bust	£400	£850	£2000	*
1703 VIGO below	£2500	£7500	£12000	*
Post-Union[1]				
1707-14 plain	£200	£400	£800	£1750

[1]See note in prices of five guineas for Anne.

	F	VF	EF	Unc
GEORGE I				
1715, 17-23, 1st head	£150	£300	£600	£1200
1721 eleph & castle	£300	£800	*	*
1724-7, smaller older head	£150	£300	£600	£1200
GEORGE II				
1728-39 YH	£150	£300	£850	£1750
1729-32, 9 — E.I.C. below	£175	£350	£1200	*
1740, 3, 5, 6, intermediate head	£150	£300	£750	*
1745 — LIMA below	£650	£1250	£2750	*
1747-53, 5, 6, 58-60 OH	£150	£300	£600	£1500
GEORGE III				
1762, 3, 1st head	£250	£500	£1250	*
1764-6, 8, 9, 72-5, 2nd head	£125	£300	£600	£1000
1774, 5, 3rd head	£500	£1000	£2000	*
1775-9, 81, 83-6, 4th head	£75	£100	£250	£450
1787-91, 93-8, 1800, 5th head	£60	£80	£175	£350
1801-3, 6th head	£60	£75	£165	£300
1804, 6, 8-11, 13, 7th head	£60	£75	£165	£300

Third guineas

	F	VF	EF	Unc
GEORGE III				
1797-1800 1st head	£40	£60	£100	£250
1801-3 — date close to crown on reverse	£40	£60	£100	£250
1804, 6, 8-11, 2nd head	£40	£70	£125	£250

Quarter guineas

	F	VF	EF	Unc
GEORGE I				
1718	£40	£75	£110	£200
GEORGE III	F	VF	EF	Unc
1762	£45	£75	£150	£250

Britannias
(See under Decimal Coinage)

Five pounds

	F	VF	EF	Unc
GEORGE III				
1820 pattern **(F)**	*	*	*	£35000
GEORGE IV				
1826 proof	*	*	£5500	£7500
VICTORIA				
1839 proof with 'Una and				
the Lion' rev **(F)**	*	£7500	£14500	£19000
1887 JH **(F)**	£350	£475	£600	£800
1887 proof	*	*	£1200	£2000
1887 proof no 8P	*	*	£1500	£2500
1893 OH **(F)**	£400	£750	£1000	£1400
1893 proof	*	*	£1250	£2250
EDWARD VII				
1902 **(F)**	£350	£450	£550	£700
1902 proof	*	*	£600	£750
GEORGE V				
1911 proof **(F)** ...	*	*	£950	£1250
GEORGE VI				
1937 proof	*	*	*	£600

ELIZABETH II

In 1984 the Royal Mint issued the first of an annual issue of Brilliant Uncirculated £5 coins. These bear the symbol 'U' in a circle to the left of the date on the reverse to indicate the standard of striking.

1981 proof	£400
1984	£400
1985	£425
1986	£425
1987 new effigy	£425
1988	£425
1989 500th anniversary of the sovereign, BU ...	£450
1990 Queen Mother's 90th birthday, proof	£575
1990	£435
1991	£450
1992	£450
1993 Coronation, proof	£700
1993	£475
1994	£500
1995	£535
1996 Queen's 70th Birthday, proof	£645
... ... BU	£575
1997 Golden Wedding, proof	£650
1997	£535
1998 Prince Charles 50th Birthday, proof	£600
1998 New Portrait	£535
1999 Diana Memorial, proof	£600
1999 Millennium, proof	£600
1999	£450
2000 Millennium, proof	£495
2000 Queen Mother Centenary, proof	£495
2000	£450

Two pounds

	F	VF	EF	Unc
GEORGE III				
1820 pattern **(F)**	*	*	£9500	£12500

George III 1820 pattern two pounds

	F	VF	EF	Unc
GEORGE IV ...	F	VF	EF	Unc
1823 St George				
on reverse **(F)**	£250	£400	£650	£1200
1826 proof, shield				
reverse	*	*	£2000	£3000

William IV 1831 proof two pounds

	F	VF	EF	Unc
WILLIAM IV				
1831 proof	*	*	£3000	£4500
VICTORIA				
1887 JH **(F)** ...	£185	£220	£265	£300
1887 proof	*	*	£500	£800
1893 OH **(F)** ...	£220	£300	£400	£550
1893 proof	*	*	£500	£900
EDWARD VII				
1902 **(F)**	175	£210	£265	£300
1902 proof	*	*	£275	£325
GEORGE V				
1911 proof **(F)**	*	*	*	£450

1937 proof two pounds

	F	VF	EF	Unc
GEORGE VI				
1937 proof ...	*	*	*	£375

TWO POUNDS

ELIZABETH II	F	VF	EF	Unc
1983 proof				£225
1986 Commonwealth Games, proof				£225
1987 proof				£250
1988 proof				£250
1989 500th anniversary of the sovereign, proof				£275
1990 proof				£250
1991 proof				£250
1993 proof				£250
1994 gold proof				£425
1994 gold proof 'mule'				£750
1995 VE day gold proof				£375
1995 50th Anniversary of UN, proof				£300
1996 European Football Championship				£350
1997 Bimetal gold proof				£350
1998 New portrait, proof				£300
1999 Rugby World Cup...				£300
2000 proof				£275

Sovereigns

GEORGE III	F	VF	EF	Unc
1817 (F)	£110	£225	£450	£700
1818	£110	£250	£550	£800
1819 ... ...£12500	£25000	£55000	*
1820	£110	£250	£500	£750

GEORGE IV				
Type Laureate head/St George				
1821	£110	£225	£500	£700
1822 (F)	£110	£225	£500	£700
1823	£150	£300	£750	£950
1824	£110	£225	£500	£700
1825	£250	£500	£1250	*

George IV 1826 proof sovereign

Type bare head/shield				
1825 (F)	£100	£200	£425	£700
1826	£100	£200	£450	£750
1826 proof	*	*	£950	£2000
1827 (F)	£100	£200	£450	£750
1828 (F)	£650	£2000	£4000	*
1829	£100	£200	£425	£700
1830	£100	£200	£425	£700

WILLIAM IV				
1831	£125	£275	£550	£850
1831 proof	*	*	£1500	£2850

William IV 1831 proof sovereign

1832 (F)	£110	£200	£500	£700
1833	£110	£225	£550	£750
1835	£110	£200	£500	£700
1836	£110	£200	£500	£700
1837	£120	£225	£550	£750

VICTORIA				
Type 1, YH obv, shield rev				
1838	£85	£125	£275	£650

Victoria 1839 proof sovereign

	F	VF	EF	Unc
1839	£95	£175	£750	£1200
1839 proof	*	*	£1200	£2500
1841	£500	£900	£3000	*
1842	*	*	£100	£250
1843	*	*	£100	£200
1843 narrow shield	£750	£1500	£2750	*
1844	*	*	£100	£200
1845	*	*	£100	£200
1846	*	*	£100	£200
1847	*	*	£100	£200
1848	*	*	£100	£200
1849	*	*	£100	£200
1850	*	*	£100	£200
1851	*	*	£100	£200
1852	*	*	£100	£200
1853	*	*	£90	£200

Victoria 1853 sovereign, shield on reverse

1853 proof	*	*	£4000	£6500
1854	*	*	£100	£200
1855	*	*	£100	£200
1856	*	*	£100	£200
1857	*	*	£100	£200
1858	*	*	£125	£250
1859	*	*	£80	£175
1859 'Ansell' ...	£120	£400	£1250	*
1860	*	*	£100	£200
1861	*	*	£80	£175
1862	*	*	£80	£175
1863	*	*	£70	£150
1863 die number below				
wreath on rev	*	*	£70	£150
1863 '827' on				
truncation ...	£1500	£2250	£3750	*
1864 die no. ...	*	*	£70	£150
1865 die no. ...	*	*	£70	£150
1866 die no. ...	*	*	£70	£150
1868 die no. ...	*	*	£70	£150
1869 die no. ...	*	*	£70	£150
1870 die no. ...	*	*	£70	£150
1871 die no. ...	*	*	£70	£110
1871 S (Sydney mint)				
below wreath	*	*	£125	£250
1872	*	*	£70	£125
1872 die no. ...	*	*	£60	£100
1872 M (Melbourne mint)				
below wreath	*	*	£100	£250
1872 S	*	*	£100	£250
1873 die no. ...	*	*	£70	£150
1873 S	*	*	£100	£250
1874 die no. ...	£300	£850	£2500	*
1874 M	*	*	£100	£250
1875 S	*	*	£100	£250
1877 S	*	*	£80	£200

88

COINS MARKET VALUES

	F	VF	EF	Unc
1878 S	*	*	£100	£200
1879 S	*	*	£80	£200
1880 M	£200	£750	£1500	£2750
1880 S	*	*	£100	£250
1881 M	*	£80	£125	£250
1881 S	*	*	£100	£250
1882 M	*	*	£100	£250
1882 S	*	*	£75	£175
1883 M	*	£125	£300	£600
1883 S	*	*	£75	£150
1884 M	*	*	£100	£250
1884 S	*	*	£75	£175
1885 M	*	*	£100	£200
1885 S	*	*	£75	£175
1886 M	£250	£1000	£2000	£3000
1886 S	*	*	£80	£175
1887 M	£200	£500	£1250	£2000
1887 S	*	*	£80	£175

Type II. YH obv, St George and Dragon rev

	F	VF	EF	Unc
1871	*	*	£75	£120
1871 S below head	*	£75	£120	£200
1872	*	*	£90	£150
1872 M below head	*	£85	£150	£300
1872 S	*	*	£150	£250
1873	*	*	£75	£125
1873 M	*	£75	£150	£300
1873 S	*	*	£150	£250
1874	*	*	£75	£125
1874 M	*	*	£150	£300
1874 S	*	*	£100	£200
1875 M	*	*	£150	£300
1875 S	*	*	£100	£200
1876	*	*	£75	£175
1876 M	*	*	£150	£300
1876 S	*	*	£125	£250
1877 M	*	*	£125	£300
1878	*	*	£75	£125
1878 M	*	*	£125	£300
1879	*	£95	£450	£750
1879 M	*	*	£125	£250
1879 S	*	*	£250	£650
1880	*	*	£70	£125
1880 M	*	*	£125	£300
1880 S	*	*	£150	£300
1881 M	*	*	£150	£300
1881 S	*	*	£125	£300
1882 M	*	*	£80	£175
1882 S	*	*	£75	£125
1883 M	*	*	£75	£150
1883 S	*	*	£70	£100
1884	*	*	£70	£120
1884 M	*	*	£80	£120
1884 S	*	*	£70	£100
1885	*	*	£80	£120
1885 M	*	*	£80	£125
1885 S	*	*	£70	£110
1886 M	*	*	£80	£125
1886 S	*	*	£70	£100
1887 M	*	*	£80	£120
1887 S	*	*	£70	£110

Jubilee head coinage

	F	VF	EF	Unc
1887 **(F)**	*	*	£60	£85
1887 proof	*	*	£300	£450
1887 M on ground below dragon	*	*	£100	£250
1887 S on ground below dragon	*	*	£250	£500
1888	*	*	*	£70
1888 M	*	*	*	£90
1888 S	*	*	*	£90
1889	*	*	*	£70
1889 M	*	*	*	£90

SOVEREIGNS

	F	VF	EF	Unc
1889 S	*	*	*	£80
1890	*	*	*	£70
1890	*	*	*	£80
1890 S	*	*	*	£80
1891	*	*	*	£70
1891 M	*	*	*	£80
1891 S	*	*	*	£80
1892	*	*	*	£70
1892 M	*	*	*	£80
1892 S	*	*	*	£80
1893 M	*	*	*	£80
1893 S	*	*	*	£80

Old head coinage

	F	VF	EF	Unc
1893	*	*	*	£65
1893 proof	*	*	£350	£500
1893 M	*	*	*	£65
1893 S	*	*	*	£65
1894	*	*	*	£65
1894 M	*	*	*	£65
1894 S	*	*	*	£65
1895	*	*	*	£65
1895 M	*	*	*	£65
1895 S	*	*	*	£65
1896	*	*	*	£65
1896 M	*	*	*	£65
1896 S	*	*	*	£65
1897 M	*	*	*	£65
1897 S	*	*	*	£65
1898	*	*	*	£65
1898 M	*	*	*	£65
1898 S	*	*	*	£65
1899	*	*	*	£65

1898 Victoria Old Head sovereign

	F	VF	EF	Unc
1899 M	*	*	*	£65
1899 P (Perth mint) on ground below dragon	*	*	*	£200
1899 S	*	*	*	£150
1900	*	*	*	£65
1900 M	*	*	*	£65
1900 P	*	*	*	£110
1900 S	*	*	*	£100
1901	*	*	*	£65
1901 M	*	*	*	£65
1901 P	*	*	*	£110
1901 S	*	*	*	£85

EDWARD VII

	F	VF	EF	Unc
1902	*	*	*	£65
1902 proof	*	*	£80	£125
1902 M	*	*	*	£65
1902 P	*	*	*	£65
1902 S	*	*	*	£65
1903	*	*	*	£65
1903 M	*	*	*	£65
1903 P	*	*	*	£65
1903 S	*	*	*	£65
1904	*	*	*	£65
1904 M	*	*	*	£65
1904 P	*	*	*	£65
1904 S	*	*	*	£65
1905	*	*	*	£65
1905 M	*	*	*	£65
1905 P	*	*	*	£65

SOVEREIGNS

	F	VF	EF	Unc
1905 S	*	*	*	£65
1906	*	*	*	£68
1906 M	*	*	*	£68
1906 P	*	*	*	£68
1906 S	*	*	*	£65
1907	*	*	*	£65
1907 M	*	*	*	£65
1907 P	*	*	*	£65
1907 S	*	*	*	£65
1908	*	*	*	£65
1908 C (Canada, Ottawa mint) on ground below dragon (F)	*	*	£750	£1750
1908 M	*	*	*	£65
1908 P	*	*	*	£65
1908 S	*	*	*	£65
1909	*	*	*	£65
1909 C	*	*	£75	£150
1909 M	*	*	*	£65
1909 P	*	*	*	£65
1909 S	*	*	*	£65
1910	*	*	*	£65
1910 C	*	*	£75	£150
1910 M	*	*	*	£65
1910 P	*	*	*	£65
1910 S	*	*	*	£65

GEORGE V

	F	VF	EF	Unc
1911	*	*	*	£60
1911 proof	*	*	£150	£250
1911 C	*	*	*	£70
1911 M	*	*	*	£60
1911 P	*	*	*	£60
1911 S	*	*	*	£60
1912	*	*	*	£60
1912 M	*	*	*	£60
1912 P	*	*	*	£60
1912S	*	*	*	£60
1913	*	*	*	£60
1913 C (F)	*	£75	£125	£225
1913 M	*	*	*	£60
1913 P	*	*	*	£60
1913 S	*	*	*	£60
1914	*	*	*	£60
1914 C	*	*	£85	£125
1914 M	*	*	*	£60
1914P	*	*	*	£60
1914 S	*	*	*	£60
1915	*	*	*	£60
1915 M	*	*	*	£60
1915 P	*	*	*	£60
1915 S	*	*	*	£60
1916	*	*	*	£60
1916 C	*	£2000	£5000	*
1916 M	*	*	*	£60
1916 P	*	*	*	£60
1916 S	*	*	*	£60
1917 (F)	*	£2000	£3250	*
1917 C	*	*	£60	£90
1917 M	*	*	*	£60
1917 P	*	*	*	£60
1917 S	*	*	*	£60
1918 C	*	*	£60	£90
1918 I (Indian mint, Bombay), on ground below dragon	*	*	*	£70
1918 M	*	*	*	£60
1918 P	*	*	*	£ 60
1918 S	*	*	*	£60
1919 C	*	*	£65	£100
1919 M	*	*	*	£60
1919 P	*	*	*	£60
1919 S	*	*	*	£60
1920 M	*	£850	£2500	*

	F	VF	EF	Unc
1920 P	*	*	*	£60
1920 S			highest	rarity
1921 M	*	£2000	£4000	£6000
1921 P	*	*	*	£70
1921 S	*	£500	£1200	£2500
1922 M	*	£1750	£3500	£6000
1922 P	*	*	*	£70
1922 S	*	£2750	£8500	£13500
1923 M	*	*	*	£70
1923 S	*	£2000	£4000	£6500
1923 SA (South Africa, Pretoria Mint) on ground below dragon	*	£1250	£1750	£2500
1924 M	*	*	£60	£90
1924 P	*	*	*	£75
1924 S	*	£500	£1000	£1500
1924 SA	*	*	£2000	£3000
1925	*	*	*	£70
1925 M	*	*	*	£70
1925 P	*	*	£120	£175
1925 S	*	*	*	£70
1925 SA	*	*	*	£60
1926 M	*	*	*	£70
1926 P	*	£100	£200	£450
1926 S	*	£4000	£10000	£17500
1926 SA	*	*	*	£60
1927 P	*	*	£125	£250
1927 SA	*	*	*	£60
1928 M	*	£800	£1750	£2500
1928 P	*	*	£85	£120
1928 SA	*	*	*	£60
1929 M	*	£400	£900	£1500
1929 P	*	*	*	£60
1929 SA	*	*	*	£60
1930 M	*	*	£150	£300
1930 P	*	*	*	£60
1930 SA	*	*	*	£60
1931 M	*	£125	£250	£500
1931 P	*	*	*	£60
1931 SA	*	*	*	£60
1932 SA	*	*	*	£60

GEORGE VI

	F	VF	EF	Unc
1937 proof only		*	*	£400

ELIZABETH II

	F	VF	EF	Unc
1957	*	*	*	£55
1958	*	*	*	£55
1959	*	*	*	£55
1962	*	*	*	£55
1963	*	*	*	£55
1964	*	*	*	£55
1965	*	*	*	£55
1966	*	*	*	£55
1967	*	*	*	£55
1968	*	*	*	£55
1974	*	*	*	£55
1976	*	*	*	£55
1978	*	*	*	£55
1979	*	*	*	£55
1979 proof	*	*	*	£85
1980	*	*	*	£55
1980 proof	*	*	*	£85
1981	*	*	*	£55
1981 proof	*	*	*	£85
1982	*	*	*	£55
1982 proof	*	*	*	£85
1983 proof	*	*	*	£100
1984 proof	*	*	*	£100
1985 proof	*	*	*	£125
1986 proof	*	*	*	£125
1987 proof	*	*	*	£125
1988 proof	*	*	*	£150
1989 500th anniversary of the sovereign, proof	*	*	*	£140

SOVEREIGNS

	F	VF	EF	Unc
1990 proof	*	*	*	£150
1991 proof	*	*	*	£160
1992 proof	*	*	*	£160
1993 proof	*	*	*	£160
1994 proof	*	*	*	£160
1995 proof	*	*	*	£160
1996 proof	*	*	*	£160
1997 proof	*	*	*	£160
1998 new portrait proof*	*	*	*	£160
1999 proof	*	*	*	£180
2000				£70
2000 proof				£135

Half sovereigns

GEORGE III	F	VF	EF	Unc
1817	£60	£90	£200	£400
1818	£50	£100	£175	£500
1820	£55	£100	£250	£500

GEORGE IV
Laureate head/ornate shield, date on rev

	F	VF	EF	Unc
1821	£250	£600	£1250	£2000
1823 plain shield	£70	£100	£350	£575
1824	£65	£100	£300	£550
1825	£65	£100	£300	£550

Bare head, date on obv/shield, full legend rev

	F	VF	EF	Unc
1826	£65	£90	£300	£550
1827	£65	£90	£300	£600
1828	£65	£90	£325	£650

WILLIAM IV

	F	VF	EF	Unc
1834 reduced size	£80	£125	£450	£750
1835 normal size	£80	£125	£400	£650
1836 sixpence obverse die				
... ...	£400	£1000	£1950	£2750
1836	£100	£200	£500	£750
1837	£80	£100	£400	£650

Victoria 1839 proof half sovereign

VICTORIA
Young head/shield rev

	F	VF	EF	Unc
1838	*	£100	£200	£400
1839 proof only	*	*	*	£1250
1841	*	£100	£200	£400
1842	*	£100	£200	£425
1843	*	£100	£200	£475
1844	*	£100	£200	£425
1845	*	£150	£300	*
1846	*	£100	£200	£475
1847	*	£100	£200	£425
1848	*	£125	£250	£500
1849	*	£100	£200	£450
1850	£100	£225	£750	£1000
1851	*	£100	£200	£450
1852	*	£100	£200	£400
1853	*	£100	£200	£425
1854	£125	£250	£600	*
1855	*	£100	£200	£400
1856	*	£100	£200	£400
1857	*	£75	£175	£350
1858	*	£75	£175	£350
1859	*	£75	£175	£350
1860	*	£75	£175	£350
1861	*	£100	£200	£425
1862	£300	£750	£1500	*
1863	*	£100	£200	£375
1863 die no.	*	£75	£150	£325

	F	VF	EF	Unc
1864 die no.	*	£75	£150	£300
1865 die no.	*	£75	£150	£325
1866 die no.	*	£75	£150	£325
1867 die no.	*	£75	£150	£325
1869 die no.	*	£75	£150	£325
1870 die no.	*	£75	£150	£325
1871 die no. ...	*	£75	£150	£325
1871 S below shield	*	£100	£350	£850
1872 die no. ...	*	£75	£150	£325
1872 S	*	£100	£350	£850
1873 die no. ...	*	£75	£150	£325
1873 M below shield	*	£100	£350	£850
1874 die no. ...	*	*	£100	£325
1875 die no. ...	*	*	£100	£325
1875 S	*	*	£350	£850
1876 die no. ...	*	*	£100	£300
1877 die no. ...	*	*	£90	£250
1877 M	£50	£100	£450	£950
1878 die no. ...	*	*	£90	£250
1879 die no. ...	*	*	£90	£250
1879 S	£50	£100	£350	£800
1880	*	*	£90	£220
1880 die no. ...	*	*	£90	£220
1880 S	£75	£125	£450	£1000
1881 S	£75	£125	£450	£1000
1881 M	£75	£150	£450	£1000
1882 S	£100	£300	£1500	£3500
1882 M	*	£175	£750	£1600
1883	*	*	£90	£200
1883 S	*	£90	£325	£750
1884	*	*	£90	£200
1884 M	*	£90	£375	£750
1885	*	*	£85	£200
1885 M	£75	£200	£750	£1800
1886 S	*	£75	£325	£750
1886 M	£50	£125	£500	£1500
1887 S	*	£75	£450	£1250
1887 M	£65	£250	£1000	£2500

Jubilee head/shield rev

	F	VF	EF	Unc
1887	*	*	£60	£80
1887 proof	*	*	£200	£375
1887 M	*	£150	£350	£750
1887 S	*	£150	£400	*
1889 S	*	£150	£350	*
1890	*	*	£50	£80
1891	*	*	£50	£80
1891 S	*	*	£400	£750
1892	*	*	£50	£85
1893	*	*	£50	£85
1893 M	*	*	£450	£1000

Old head/St George reverse

	F	VF	EF	Unc
1893	*	*	£45	£60
1893 proof	*	*	£225	£450
1893 M	£750	*	*	*
1893 S	£60	£120	£300	£800
1894	*	*	£45	£60
1895	*	*	£45	£60
1896	*	*	£45	£60
1896 M	£70	£125	£450	£1000
1897	*	*	£40	£65
1897 S	*	£90	£250	£450
1898	*	*	£40	£65
1899	*	*	£40	£65
1899 M	£70	£125	£450	£1500
1899 P Proof only	*	*	*	£10000
1900	*	*	£40	£60
1900 M	£70	£125	£450	£1500
1900 P	£300	£500	£1200	£2500
1900 S	*	£80	£350	£1000
1901	*	*	£40	£65
1901 P proof only	*	*	*	£6000

EDWARD VII

	F	VF	EF	Unc
1902	*	*	*	£55
1902 proof	*	*	£75	£100

1902
matt
proof
half
sovereign

	F	VF	EF	Unc
)02 S	*	*	£150	£450
)03	*	*	*	£60
)03 S	*	*	£90	£250
)04	*	*	*	£55
)04 P	£100	£200	£500	£1200
)05	*	*	*	£58
)06	*	*	*	£55
)06 M	*	*	£90	£350
)06 S	*	*	£85	£225
)07	*	*	*	£55
)07 M	*	*	£80	£200
)08	*	*	*	£55
)08 M	*	*	£80	£200
)08 P	*	£100	£600	*
)08 S	*	*	£80	£200
)09	*	*	*	£48
)09 M	*	*	£80	£275
)09 P	£70	£150	£400	£1500
)10	*	*	*	£48
)10 S	*	*	£80	£250

EORGE V

)11	*	*	*	£45
)11 proof	*	*	£100	£200
)11 P	*	*	£40	£80
)11 S	*	*	*	£50
)12	*	*	*	£45
)12 S	*	*	£40	£50
)13	*	*	*	£40
)14	*	*	*	£40
)14 S	*	*	*	£50
)15	*	*	*	£40
)15 M	*	*	£40	£50
)15 P	*	*	£40	£65
)15 S	*	*	*	£40
)16 S	*	*	*	£40
)18 P	*	£200	£500	£800
)23 SA proof...	*	*	*	£165
)25 SA	*	*	*	£40
)26 SA	*	*	*	£40

iEORGE VI

)37 proof	*	*	*	£150

LIZABETH II

)80 proof	*	*	*	£55
)82	*	*	*	£38
)82 proof	*	*	*	£60
)83 proof	*	*	*	£60
)84 proof	*	*	*	£60
)85 proof	*	*	*	£65
)86 proof	*	*	*	£65
)87 proof	*	*	*	£65
)88 proof	*	*	*	£65
)89 500th anniversary of the				
sovereign, proof	*	*	*	£85
)90 proof	*	*	*	£80
)91 proof	*	*	*	£80
)92 proof	*	*	*	£90
)93 proof	*	*	*	£85
)94 proof	*	*	*	£85
)95 proof	*	*	*	£85
)96 proof	*	*	*	£85
)97 proof	*	*	*	£85
)98 new portrait proof	*	*	*	£85
)99 proof	*	*	*	£90
)000	*	*	*	£35
)000 proof	*	*	*	£70

Crowns

CROMWELL

	F	VF	EF
1658	£700	£1450	£2500
1658 Dutch copy	£1000	£2000	£3500
1658 Tanner's copy	£1250	£2500	£4000

CHARLES II

	F	VF	EF
1662 1st bust...	£95	£400	£2500
1663 –	£100	£500	£2750
1664 2nd bust	£100	£450	£3500
1665 –	£400	£1000	*
1666 –	£95	£500	£3500
1666 – eleph	£175	£650	£4000
1667 –	£75	£400	£2500
1668 –	£70	£400	£2000
1668/7 –	£100	£450	£3000
1669 –	£200	£750	*
1669/8 –	£200	£750	£4000
1670 –	£80	£400	£2250
1670/69 –	£120	£450	*
1671 –	£75	£450	£2500
1671 3rd bust	£75	£400	£2250
1672 –	£75	£400	£2200
1673 –	£75	£400	£2250
1673/2 –	£80	£350	£2250
1674 –	£4000	*	*
1675 –	£300	£1000	*
1675/4 –	£300	£1000	*
1676 –	£60	£300	£1500
1677 –	£70	£300	£1500
1677/6 –	£70	£300	£1500
1678/7 –	£120	£500	*
1679 –	£65	£300	£1500
1679 4th bust –	£90	£300	£1500
1680 3rd bust –	£140	£500	£2000
1680/79 –	£70	£350	£1750
1680 4th bust –	£70	£300	£2000
1680/79 –	£125	£400	£2250
1681 – elephant & castle ...	£750	£2250	*
1681 –	£75	£400	£2250
1682 –	£100	£400	£2250
1682/1 –	£70	£400	£2250
1683 –	£175	£500	£2750
1684 –	£95	£450	£2250

JAMES II

	F	VF	EF
1686 1st bust...	£125	£550	£1750
1687 2nd bust	£100	£400	£850
1688 –	£125	£450	£900
1688/7 –	£100	£425	£875

WILLIAM AND MARY

	F	VF	EF
1691	£175	£600	£1750
1692	£195	£650	£1850
1692/2 inverted QVINTO... ...	£195	£650	£1850
1692/2 inverted QVARTO ...	£600	£1250	*

WILLIAM III

	F	VF	EF
1695 1st bust...	£85	£325	£750
1696 –	£85	£325	£750
1696 – GEI error...	£200	£650	*
1696/5 –	£125	£375	£900
1696 2nd bust		unique	
1696 3rd bust	£85	£325	£750
1697 –	£600	£2000	£10000
1700 3rd bust variety	£85	£325	£750

ANNE

	F	VF	EF
1703 1st bust VIGO	£200	£500	£2000
1705 –	£450	£850	£3000
1706 –	£125	£400	£800
1707 –	£100	£300	£700
1707 2nd bust	£85	£275	£600
1707 – E	£85	£275	£600
1708 –	£85	£300	£600

	F	VF	E
1708 – E...	£80	£300	
1708/7 –...	£90	£325	
1708 – plumes	£110	£300	£60
1713 3rd bust	£110	£300	£60

GEORGE I

	F	VF	
1716	£175	£400	£175
1718	£300	£600	£220
1718/6	£200	£450	£150
1720	£200	£450	£150
1720/18...	£175	£400	£160
1723 SS C	£175	£450	£150
1726 roses & plumes	£225	£550	£220

GEORGE II

	F	VF	
1732 YH	£140	£350	£75
1732 – proof	*	*	£300
1734	£140	£350	£75
1735	£140	£350	£65
1736	£140	£350	£65
1739	£140	£350	£62
1741	£140	£350	£60
1743 OH	£125	£350	£60

1691 William & Mary Crown

	F	VF	
1746 – LIMA	£125	£350	£60
1746 – proof	*	*	£225
1750	£150	£350	£70
1751	£200	£400	£85

GEORGE III

	F	VF	EF	Ur
Oval counter-stamp[1]	£75	£125	£250	£40
Octagonal Counterstamp[1]	£200	£350	£650	£95
1804 Bank of England dollar[1]	£50	£95	£225	£37
1818 LVIII...	£10	£45	£175	£40
1818 – error edge	£250	*	*	
1818 LIX	£10	£45	£150	£35

	F	VF	EF	Unc
819 –	£10	£45	£175	£400
819 – no edge
stops	£50	£100	£350	*
819/8 LIX	*	£100	£350	*
819 LIX	£10	£35	£175	£400
819 – no stop
fter TUTAMEN	£30	£50	£275	*
820 lx	*	*	£175	£400
820/19	£50	£150	£300	*

Beware of contemporary forgeries. The counterstamps are usually on Spanish-American dollars.

GEORGE IV

	F	VF	EF	Unc
821 1st hd SEC ...	£35	£150	£400	£1000
821 – prf	*	*	*	£1750
821 – TER error
edge	*	*	£1500	£2500
822 – SEC	£60	£200	£500	£1250
822 – – prf	*	*	*	*
822 – TER	£50	£175	£450	£1100
822 – – prf	*	*	*	£2500
823 – prf	*	*	*	£11000
826 2nd hd prf	*	*	£1250	£2250

WILLIAM IV

	F	VF	EF	Unc
831 w.w.	*	*	£3750	£5000
831 w.wyon	*	*	£4500	£6500
834 w.w.	*	*	*	£10000

VICTORIA

	F	VF	EF	Unc
839 proof	*	£750	£1500	£3000
844 star stops	£25	£100	£750	£1750
844 – prf	*	*	*	£5500
844 cinquefoil stops	£25	£100	£750	£1750
845	£25	£100	£750	£1750
845 proof	*	*	*	£5000
847	£25	£100	£850	£2000

Victoria 1847 Gothic crown

CROWNS

	F	VF	EF	Unc
1847 Gothic	£200	£400	£700	£1500
1847 – plain edge ...	*	£450	£800	£2000
1853 SEPTIMO	*	*	£2500	£4000
1853 plain	*	*	£3000	£5000
1887 JH	£12	£15	£25	£75
1887 – proof	*	*	£150	£350
1888 close date	£15	£25	£50	£85
1888 wide date	£45	£75	£120	£250
1889	£15	£25	£35	£75
1890	£15	£25	£35	£80
1891	£15	£25	£50	£100
1892	£15	£25	£50	£100
1893 LVI	£15	£25	£95	£200
1893 – proof	*	*	£150	£400
1893 LVII	£15	£65	£140	£275
1894 LVII	£15	£30	£95	£225
1894 LVIII...	£15	£30	£95	£240
1895 LVIII...	£15	£30	£95	£225
1895 LIX	£15	£30	£90	£200
1896 LIX	£15	£40	£175	£350
1896 LX	£15	£30	£90	£200
1897 LX	£15	£30	£90	£200
1897 LXI	£15	£30	£90	£220
1898 LXI	£15	£30	£125	£300
1898 LXII	£15	£30	£100	£225
1899 LXII	£15	£39	£85	£200
1899 LXIII...	£15	£30	£95	£225
1900 LXIII...	£15	£30	£95	£200
1900 LXIV...	£15	£30	£95	£225

EDWARD VII

	F	VF	EF	Unc
1902	£20	£35	£70	£100
1902 matt proof	*	*	£75	£100

GEORGE V

	F	VF	EF	Unc
1927 proof	£35	£60	£90	£140
1928	£60	£80	£120	£200
1929	£60	£80	£120	£200
1930	£60	£85	£125	£200
1931	£60	£85	£125	£200
1932	£85	£110	£200	£300
1933	£60	£85	£125	£200
1934	£300	£475	£750	£1200
1935	£5	£7	£10	£18
1935 rsd edge prf ...	*	*	£125	£225
1935 gold proof	*	*	*	£10000
1935 prf in good
silver (.925)	*	*	£650	£1250
1935 specimen	*	*	*	£40
1936	£65	£90	£175	£250

GEORGE VI

	F	VF	EF	Unc
1937	*	*	£8	£15
1937 proof	*	*	*	£30
1937 'VIP' proof	*	*	*	£350
1951	*	*	*	£5
1951 'VIP' proof	*	*	*	£200

ELIZABETH II

	F	VF	EF	Unc
1953	*	*	*	£7
1953 proof	*	*	*	£15
1953 'VIP' proof	*	*	*	£225
1960	*	*	*	£7
1960 'VIP' proof	*	*	*	£300
1960 polished dies ...	*	*	£4	£10
1965 Churchill	*	*	*	£1.50
1965 – 'satin' finish ...	*	*	*	£400

For issues 1972 onwards see under 25 pence in Decimal Coinage section.

George VI 1937
Crown (reverse)

Double florins

Victoria 1887 halfcrown

VICTORIA	F	VF	EF	Unc
1887 Roman 1	*	£10	£18	£35
1887 – proof	*	*	£125	£225
1887 Arabic 1	*	£12	£20	£45
1887 – proof	*	*	£90	£175
1888	*	£12	£28	£75
1888 inverted 1	£10	£20	£65	£150
1889	*	£10	£25	£60
1889 inverted 1	£10	£25	£65	£150
1890	*	£12	£25	£70

Three shilling bank tokens

Contemporary forgeries of these pieces, as well as of other George III coins, were produced in quite large numbers. Several varieties exist for the pieces dated 1811 and 1812. Prices given here are for the commonest types of these years.

GEORGE III	F	VF	EF	Unc
1811	*	£20	£50	£75
1812 draped bust ...	*	£20	£50	£75
1812 laureate head	*	£20	£50	£75
1813	*	£20	£50	£75
1814	*	£20	£50	£75
1815	*	£20	£50	£75
1816	£100	£250	£600	£1200

Halfcrowns

CROMWELL	F	VF	EF
1656	£800	£2000	£4000
1658	£450	£850	£1200

Cromwell 1658 halfcrown

	F	VF	E
CHARLES II	F	VF	E
1663 1st bust	£85	£400	£150
1664 2nd bust	£100	£350	£165
1666/3 3rd bust	£750	*	
1666/3 – elephant	£250	£750	£450
1667/4 –	£1450	*	
1668/4 –	£125	£275	
1669 –	£225	£600	
1669/4 –	£175	£450	
1670 –	£65	£275	£100
1671 3rd bust var	£65	£275	£100
1671/0 –	£75	£325	£110
1672 –	£80	£325	£110
1672 4th bust	£100	£350	£120
1673 –	£65	£275	£125
1673 – plume below	£1000	*	
1673 – plume both sides ...	£1750	*	
1674 –	£125	£350	
1674/3 –	£150	£500	
1675 –	£65	£275	£100
1676 –	£65	£275	£100
1677 –	£65	£275	£100
1678 –	£125	£450	
1679 –	£65	£275	£100
1680 –	£125	£350	
1681 –	£65	£275	£100
1681/0 –	£65	£275	£100
1681 – eleph & castle	£1250	*	
1682 –	£100	£350	
1682/1 –	£150	£500	
1682/79 –	£150	£500	
1683 –	£65	£275	£125
1683 – plume below	£3000	*	
1684/3 –	£150	£500	

James II 1687 halfcrown

JAMES II			
1685 1st bust	£75	£400	£95
1686 –	£75	£400	£95
1686/5 –	£125	£500	£125
1687 –	£75	£400	£95

	F	VF	EF
687/6 –	£85	£400	£1000
687 2nd bust	£100	£500	£1250
688 –	£75	£400	£1000

WILLIAM AND MARY

	F	VF	EF
689 1st busts 1st shield ...	£60	£200	£750
689 – 2nd shield	£60	£200	£750
690 – –	£75	£350	£800
691 2nd busts 3rd shield ...	£65	£225	£750
692 – –	£65	£225	£750
693 – –	£60	£200	£700
693 – – 3 inverted	£85	£300	£1000
693 3 over 3 inverted	£80	£250	£800

William and Mary 1693 Halfcrown

WILLIAM III

	F	VF	EF
696 large shield early harp	£25	£70	£300
696 – – B	£30	£125	£400
696 – – C	£35	£125	£400
696 – – E	£40	£150	£500
696 – – N	£35	£125	£450
696 – – Y	£30	£125	£400
696 – – y/E	£65	£250	£750
696 – ord harp	£75	£250	£750
696 – – C	£75	£250	£750
696 – – E	£85	£275	£600
696 – – N	£85	£275	£600
696 small shield	£20	£70	£300
696 – B	£30	£125	£450
696 – C	£55	£150	£500
696 – E	£85	£225	£600
696 – N	£30	£125	£450
696 – y	£40	£125	£450
696 2nd bust		unique	
697 1st bust large shield ...	£20	£75	£250
697 – – B	£30	£100	£350
697 – – C	£35	£100	£400
697 – – E	£35	£100	£400
697 – – E/C	£80	£200	£600
697 – – N	£30	£100	£500
697 – – y	£30	£100	£400

1697 Halfcrown of NORWICH: N below bust

	F	VF	EF
698 – –	£25	£80	£300
699 – –	£40	£125	£500

COINS MARKET VALUES

HALFCROWNS

	F	VF	EF
1700 – –	£25	£65	£300
1701 – –	£30	£70	£350
1701 – eleph & castle	£500	*	*
1701 – plumes	£120	£375	£1000

ANNE

	F	VF	EF
1703 plain	£300	£700	£1750
1703 VIGO	£50	£200	£500
1704 plumes	£125	£275	£850
1705 –	£75	£225	£650
1706 r & p	£35	£150	£400
1707 –	£30	£150	£400
1707 plain	£35	£100	£350
1707 E	£30	£100	£375
1708 plain	£20	£100	£350
1708 E	£30	£100	£450
1708 plumes	£40	£125	£475
1709 plain	£25	£100	£350
1709 E	£300	*	*
1710 r & p	£40	£125	£450
1712 –	£35	£100	£350
1713 plain	£50	£200	£600
1713 r & p	£30	£100	£400
1714 –	£30	£100	£450
1714/3	£150	*	*

GEORGE I

	F	VF	EF
1715 proof	*	*	£2500
1715 r & p	£90	£300	£600
1717 –	£100	£350	£700
1720 –	£150	£400	£800
1720/17 –	£85	£300	£650
1723 SS C	£75	£275	£600
1726 small r & p	£1250	£2500	£4000

Spanish Half Dollar with George III counterstamp (octagonal)

GEORGE II

	F	VF	EF
1731 YH proof	*	*	£2000
1731	£70	£250	£700
1732	£70	£250	£700
1734	£70	£250	£700
1735	£70	£250	£700
1736	£70	£250	£700
1739	£60	£200	£500
1741	£100	£275	£750
1741/39	£70	£200	£400
1743 OH	£60	£100	£400
1745	£60	£90	£325
1745 LIMA	£50	£100	£350
1746 -	£50	£100	£350
1746 plain, proof	*	*	£800
1750	£90	£250	£650
1751	£50	£275	£750

GEORGE III

	F	VF	EF	Unc
Oval counterstamp usually on Spanish half dollar	£125	£250	£400	*

97

HALFCROWNS

	F	VF	EF	Unc
1816 large head	*	£50	£100	£225
1817 –	*	£50	£100	£225
1817 small head ...	*	£50	£100	£200
1818	*	£50	£100	£225
1819	*	£50	£100	£225
1819/8	*	*	*	*
1820	*	£60	£125	£250

George IV halfcrown of 1821

GEORGE IV

	F	VF	EF	Unc
1820 1st hd 1st rev ...	*	£50	£125	£250
1821 –	*	£50	£125	£250
1821 proof	*	*	£450	£750
1823	£500	£1250	£3500	*
1823 – 2nd rev	*	£50	£125	£275
1824 – –	£25	£60	£175	£375
1824 2nd hd 3rd rev ...	£1250	*	*	*
1825 – –	*	£70	£90	£200
1826 – –	*	£25	£90	£200
1826 – – proof	*	*	£200	£450
1828 – –	*	£35	£175	£300
1829 – –	*	£35	£125	£250

William IV 1831 halfcrown

WILLIAM IV

	F	VF	EF	Unc
1831	*	*	*	*
1831 proof	*	*	£250	£475
1834 ww	£30	£75	£200	£500
1834 *ww* in script ...	£12	£40	£95	£250
1835	£25	£75	£175	£400
1836	£12	£40	£95	£250
1836/5	£30	£85	£250	*
1837	£35	£90	£250	£600

VICTORIA

From time to time halfcrowns bearing dates ranging from 1861 to 1871 are found, but except for rare proofs: 1853, 1862 and 1864, no halfcrowns were struck between 1850 and 1874, so pieces dated for this period are now considered to be contemporary or later forgeries.

	F	VF	EF	Unc
1839 plain and ornate fillets, ww	*	£650	£2000	
1839 – plain edge proof	*	*	£325	£65
1839 plain fillets, ww incuse	*	£900	£2000	£30(
1840	£15	£75	£185	£27
1841	£75	£225	£700	£100
1842	£15	£40	£185	£30
1843	£50	£125	£300	£50
1844	£15	£40	£160	£3(
1845	£15	£40	£225	£3(
1846	£20	£50	£175	£3(
1848	£75	£175	£450	£8(
1848/6	£75	£200	£550	£9(
1849 large date	£25	£75	£200	£4(
1849 small date	£50	£175	£375	£7(
1850	£25	£85	£275	£5(
1853 proof	*	£350	£600	£100
1862 proof	*	*	£1500	£225
1864 proof	*	*	£1500	£225
1874	*	£30	£95	£1(
1875	*	£25	£75	£1(
1876	*	£35	£120	£2(
1876/5	*	*	*	
1877	*	£25	£70	£1(
1878	*	£25	£70	£1(
1879	*	£35	£100	£2(
1880	*	£25	£70	£1(
1881	*	£25	£70	£1(
1882	*	£25	£90	£17
1883	*	£25	£80	£14
1884	*	£25	£80	£15
1885	*	£25	£80	£15
1886	*	£25	£70	£14
1887 YH	*	£25	£70	£15
1887 JH	*	£15	£25	£4
1887 – proof	*	*	£70	£13
1888	*	£20	£35	£6
1889	*	£20	£35	£6
1890	*	£25	£40	£7
1891	*	£25	£40	£7
1892	*	£25	£40	£7
1893 OH	*	£20	£25	£6
1893 – proof	*	*	£80	£15
1894	*	£20	£40	£7
1895	*	£20	£35	£6
1896	*	£20	£30	£6
1897	*	£15	£35	£6
1898	*	£20	£35	£6
1899	*	£20	£35	£6
1900	*	£20	£35	£6
1901	*	£20	£30	£6

EDWARD VII

	F	VF	EF	Unc
1902	*	£15	£30	£6
1902 matt proof	*	*	*	£6
1903	£50	£120	£400	£80
1904	£35	£90	£300	£65
1905 (F)	£150	£400	£850	£150
1906	*	£30	£100	£20
1907	*	£40	£100	£25
1908	*	£40	£200	£5(
1909	*	£25	£100	£20
1910	*	£20	£60	£15

GEORGE V

	F	VF	EF	Unc
1911	*	£110	£30	£6
1911 proof	*	*	*	£8
1912	*	£14	£35	£8
1913	*	£14	£40	£9
1914	*	*	£15	£3
1915	*	*	£15	£3
1916	*	*	£15	£3

	F	VF	EF	Unc
1917	*	*	£20	£35
1918	*	*	£15	£30
1919	*	*	£20	£40
1920	*	*	£20	£40
1921	*	*	£25	£50
1922	*	*	£20	£50
1923	*	*	£12	£20
1924			£25	£55
1925	£12	£25	£200	£350

George V 1926 halfcrown

	F	VF	EF	Unc
1926	*	*	£30	£65
1926 mod eff	*	*	£35	£60
1927	*	*	£20	£40
1927 new rev, proof only	*	*	*	£35
1928	*	*	£10	£25
1929	*	*	£10	£20
1930	£7	£35	£125	£200
1931	*	*	£10	£20
1932	*	*	£15	£35
1933	*	*	£9	£20
1934	*	*	£20	£40
1935	*	*	£6	£14
1936	*	*	£6	£12

GEORGE VI

	F	VF	EF	Unc
1937	*	*	*	£9
1937 proof	*	*	*	£12
1938	*	*	£4	£20
1939	*	*	*	£14
1940	*	*	*	£8
1941	*	*	*	£7
1942	*	*	*	£7
1943	*	*	*	£7
1944	*	*	*	£7
1945	*	*	*	£7
1946	*	*	*	£5
1947	*	*	*	£5
1948	*	*	*	£5
1949	*	*	*	£8
1950	*	*	*	£8
1950 proof	*	*	*	£10
1951	*	*	*	£8
1951 proof	*	*	*	£10

ELIZABETH II

	F	VF	EF	Unc
1953	*	*	*	£3
1953 proof	*	*	*	£9
1954	*	*	£3	£20
1955	*	*	*	£4
1956	*	*	*	£4
1957	*	*	*	£3
1958	*	*	£3	£15
1959	*	*	£4	£35
1960	*	*	*	£3
1961	*	*	*	£1
1962	*	*	*	£1
1963	*	*	*	£1
1964	*	*	*	*
1965	*	*	*	*
1966	*	*	*	*
1967	*	*	*	*

Florins

The first florins produced in the reign of Victoria bore the legend VICTORIA REGINA and the date, omitting DEI GRATIA (By the Grace of God). They are therefore known as 'Godless' florins.

The date of a Victorian Gothic florin is shown in Roman numerals, in Gothic lettering on the obverse for example: mdccclvii (1857). Gothic florins were issued during the period 1851-1887.

VICTORIA	F	VF	EF	Unc
1848 'Godless' proof with milled edge	*	*	*	£1750
1848 'Godless' proof with plain edge	*	*	*	£600

Victoria 1849 'Godless' florin

	F	VF	EF	Unc
1849 – ww obliterated by circle	£25	£50	£100	£225
1849 – ww inside circle	£15	£40	£85	£150
1851 proof only	*	*	*	£4000
1852	£15	£40	£95	£180
1853	£15	£40	£95	£170
1853 no stop after date	£20	£50	£100	£200
1853 proof	*	*	*	£1000
1854	£250	£500	*	*
1855	*	£35	£100	£200
1856	*	£50	£140	£300
1857	*	£40	£125	£250
1858	*	£40	£125	£250
1859	*	£40	£125	£250
1859 no stop after date	*	£50	£130	£250
1860	*	£50	£140	£300
1862	£25	£100	£200	*
1863	£50	£170	£300	*
1864	*	£40	£125	£250
1865	*	£40	£125	£250
1865 colon after date	*	£50	£140	£300
1866	*	£50	£135	£275
1866 colon after date	*	£55	£160	£300
1867	£15	£70	£170	£325
1868	*	£50	£130	£250
1869	*	£45	£125	£250
1870	*	£40	£120	£225
1871	*	£40	£120	£225

Victoria 1859 Gothic florin

FLORINS

	F	VF	EF	Unc
1872	*	£35	£125	£250
1873	*	£35	£125	£250
1874	*	£35	£125	£250
1874 xxiv/iii - (die 29) ...	£75	£175	£300	*
1875	*	£45	£125	£250
1876	*	£45	£125	£250
1877	*	£45	£125	£250
1877 no ww	*	*	*	*
1877 42 arcs	*	*	*	*
1878	*	£40	£125	£250
1879 ww 48 arcs ...	*	£40	£125	£250
1879 die no.	£12	£40	£125	£250
1879 ww. 42 arcs ...	£12	£40	£125	£250
1879 no ww, 38 arcs	*	£45	£125	£250
1880	*	£40	£125	£250
1881	*	£40	£125	£250
1881 xxri	*	£40	£110	£200
1883	*	£40	£110	£200
1884	*	£40	£110	£200
1885	*	£40	£110	£200
1886	*	£40	£110	£200
1887 33 arcs	*	*	*	*
1887 46 arcs	*	£40	£135	£250
1887 JH	*	£10	£15	£25
1887 – proof	*	*	*	£75
1888	*	£10	£30	£60
1889	*	£10	£30	£60
1890	£8	£15	£45	£80
1891	£20	£50	£140	£250
1892	£20	£50	£100	£200
1893 OH	*	£10	£25	£50
1893 proof	*	*	*	£110
1894	*	£10	£40	£ 75
1895	*	£10	£35	£60
1896	*	£10	£25	£50
1897	*	£10	£25	£ 50
1898	*	£10	£25	£50
1899	*	£10	£25	£50
1900	*	£10	£25	£50
1901	*	£10	£25	£50

Edward VII 1902 florin

EDWARD VII

	F	VF	EF	Unc
1902	*	£8	£25	£50
1902 matt proof	*	*	*	£45
1903	*	£25	£50	£90
1904	*	£32	£100	£195
1905	£35	£125	£400	£650
1906	*	£20	£50	£90
1907	*	£25	£60	£100
1908	*	£30	£80	£150
1909	*	£25	£75	£170
1910	*	£15	£40	£80

GEORGE V

	F	VF	EF	Unc
1911	*	*	£25	£45
1911 proof	*	*	*	£50
1912	*	*	£30	£65
1913	*	*	£35	£80
1914	*	*	£15	£30
1915	*	*	£12	£25
1916	*	*	£15	£30
1917	*	*	£18	£35
1918	*	*	£15	£30
1919	*	*	£18	£35
1920	*	*	£18	£35
1921	*	*	£18	£35
1922	*	*	£15	£30
1923	*	*	£15	£30
1924	*	*	£12	£35
1925	£15	£35	£125	£200
1926	*	*	£25	£60
1927 proof only	*	*	*	£40

George V 1928 florin

	F	VF	EF	Unc
1928	*	*	£7	£12
1929	*	*	£7	£12
1930	*	*	£10	£35
1931	*	*	£8	£20
1932	£15	£60	£150	£250
1933	*	*	£8	£15
1935	*	*	£8	£15
1936	*	*	£5	£10

GEORGE VI

	F	VF	EF	Unc
1937	*	*	*	£7
1937 proof	*	*	*	£12
1938	*	*	£4	£15
1939	*	*	*	£6
1940	*	*	*	£6
1941	*	*	*	£4
1942	*	*	*	£5
1943	*	*	*	£4
1944	*	*	*	£4
1945	*	*	*	£4
1946	*	*	*	£4
1947	*	*	*	£4
1948	*	*	*	£3
1949	*	*	*	£5
1950	*	*	*	£6
1950 proof	*	*	*	£8
1951	*	*	*	£5
1951 proof	*	*	*	£9

George VI 1949 florin

ELIZABETH II	F	VF	EF	Unc
1953	*	*	*	£2
1953 proof	*	*	*	£5
1954	*	*	*	£15
1955	*	*	*	£3
1956	*	*	*	£3
1957	*	*	*	£15
1958	*	*	*	£10
1959	*	*	*	£15
1960	*	*	*	£1
1961	*	*	*	£1
1962	*	*	*	*
1963	*	*	*	*
1964	*	*	*	*
1965	*	*	*	*
1966	*	*	*	*
1967	*	*	*	*

One and sixpence bank tokens

GEORGE III	F	VF	EF	Unc
1811	£5	£15	£30	£60
1812 laureate bust ...	£5	£15	£35	£75
1812 laureate head ...	£5	£15	£35	£75
1813	£5	£15	£35	£75
1814	£5	£15	£35	£75
1815	£5	£15	£35	£75
1816	£5	£15	£35	£75

Shillings

1658 shilling of Cromwell

CROMWELL	F	VF	EF
1658	£250	£550	£800
1658 Dutch copy	*	*	*

Charles II 1671 shilling, plumes below bust

CHARLES II	F	VF	EF
1663 1st bust	£65	£175	£400
1663 1st bust var	£65	£175	£400
1666 –	*	*	*
1666 – eleph	£250	£750	£2000
1666 guinea hd, eleph ...	£850	£1750	*

	F	VF	EF
1666 2nd bust	£500	£2000	£5000
1668 1st bust var	£350	£600	*
1668 2nd bust	£50	£175	£400
1668/7 –	£75	£200	£500
1669/6 1st bust var	£375	*	*
1669 2nd bust	*	*	*
1670 –	£85	£200	£600
1671 –	£95	£225	£650
1671 – plumes both sides	£200	£450	£1000
1672 –	£50	£150	£500
1673 –	£60	£175	£600
1673/2 –	£50	£150	£500
1673 – plumes both sides	£250	£600	£1250
1674 –	£50	£150	£500
1674/3 –	£50	£150	£500
1674 – plumes both sides	£200	£500	£1250
1674 – plumes rev only ...	£200	£500	£1250
1674 3rd bust	£300	£600	*
1675 –	£350	£700	*
1675/3 –	£350	£700	*
1675 2nd bust	£250	£550	*
1675/4 –	£250	£550	*
1675 – plumes both sides	£200	£500	£1250
1676	£40	£150	£500
1676/5 –	£50	£175	£500
1676 – plumes both sides	£200	£500	£1200
1677 –	£45	£150	£500
1677 – plume obv only ...	£350	£750	*
1678 –	£60	£175	£500
1678/7 –	£60	£175	£500
1679 –	£45	£125	£450
1679/7 –	£60	£150	£500
1679 plumes	£250	£650	£1250
1679 plumes obv only ...	£200	£600	£1250
1680 –	£600	£1250	*
1680 plumes	£200	£500	£1250
1680/79 –	*	*	*
1681 –	£100	£300	£600
1681/0 –	£100	£300	£600
1681/0 – eleph & castle ...	£850	*	*
1682/1 –	£200	£500	£1250
1683 –	£2000	*	*
1683 4th bust	£85	£250	£650
1684 –	£65	£200	£600

James II 1685 shilling

JAMES II	F	VF	EF
1685	£70	£250	£650
1685 no stops on rev	£125	£350	£750
1685 plume on rev	£3750	£6000	£10000
1686	£50	£200	£600
1686 V/S	£60	£225	£700
1687	£50	£200	£600
1687/6	£40	£175	£550
1688	£45	£200	£600
1688/7	£60	£225	£700
WILLIAM & MARY			
1692	£60	£300	£750
1693	£55	£250	£600

SHILLINGS

WILLIAM III

	F	VF	EF
1695	£15	£60	£175
1696	£15	£40	£125
1696 no stops on rev ...	£35	£100	£300
1669 in error	£500	£1250	*
1696 1st bust B	£20	£65	£200
1696 – C	£20	£65	£200
1696 – E	£20	£65	£200
1696 – N	£20	£65	£200
1696 – Y	£20	£65	£200
1696 – Y	£30	£80	£250
1696 2nd bust		unique	
1696 3rd bust C	£70	£200	£450
1696 – E	£150	*	*
1697 1st bust	£15	£35	£100
1697 – no stops on rev ...	£35	£100	£300
1697 – B	£30	£65	£200
1697 – C	£20	£65	£200

1697 Shilling of BRISTOL: B below bust

1697 – E	£20	£75	£250
1697 – N	£20	£75	£250
1697 – Y	£20	£75	£250
1697 – Y	£25	£75	£750
1697 3rd bust	£15	£35	£100
1697 – B	£25	£80	£275
1697 – C	£15	£65	£200
1697 – E	£25	£75	£250
1697 – N	£20	£75	£250
1697 – Y	£20	£75	£250
1697 3rd bust var	£15	£35	£100
1697 – B	£20	£65	£200
1697 – C	£85	£150	£350
1698	£25	£75	£200
1698 – plumes	£85	£150	£400
1698 4th bust	£85	£150	£400
1699 –	£90	£175	£425
1699 5th bust	£50	£100	£325
1699 – plumes	£60	£200	£450
1699 – roses	£95	£250	£500
1700 –	£15	£40	£120
1700 – no stops on rev ...	£40	£85	£200
1700 – plume	£650	*	*
1701 –	£40	£125	£250
1701 – plumes	£20	£150	£350

Anne 1702 shilling, VIGO below bust

ANNE

1702 – 1st bust	£40	£100	£225

1702 – plumes	£50	£125	£350
1702 – VIGO	£40	£85	£200
1703 2nd bust VIGO	£40	£95	£250
1704 –	£225	£600	£2000
1704 – plumes	£60	£175	£350
1705 –	£60	£175	£350
1705 – plumes	£40	£95	£250
1705 – r&p	£40	£85	£225
1707 – r&p	£40	£85	£225
1707 – E	£40	£75	£175
1707 – E★	£75	£150	£350
1707 3rd bust	£20	£35	£100
1707 – plumes	£45	£85	£225
1707 – E	£20	£60	£175
1707 Edin bust E★	*	*	*
1708 2nd bust E	£75	£200	£500
1708 – E★	£50	£90	£300
1708/7 – E★	£60	£150	£400
1708 – r&p	£60	£175	£450
1708 3rd bust	£20	£45	£120
1708 – plumes	£40	£85	£225
1708 – r&p	£40	£35	£225
1708 – E	£60	£120	£325
1708 – E	£75	£125	£450
1708 – Edin bust E★	£40	£95	£300
1709 –	£45	£100	£325
1709 – E	£90	£175	£400
1709 3rd bust	£15	£35	£100
1710 – r&p	£30	£65	£200
1710 4th bust prf	*	*	*
1710 – r&p	£35	£80	£225
1711 3rd bust	£65	£120	£350
1711 4th bust	£20	£40	£100
1712 – r&p	£25	£45	£175
1713/2 –	£30	£50	£200
1714 –	£25	£50	£175

George I 1723 SS C shilling

GEORGE I

1715 1st bust r&p	£25	£65	£200
1716 –	£85	£250	£500
1717 –	£25	£65	£225
1718 –	£30	£75	£200
1719 –	£70	£200	£350
1720 –	£25	£65	£200
1720 – plain	£20	£55	£175
1720 – large 0	£20	£55	£175
1721 –	£175	£500	£850
1721 r&p	£20	£55	£175
1721/0 –	£20	£55	£175
1721/19	£25	£65	£200
1721/18 –	£25	£65	£200
1722 –	£20	£65	£200
1723 –	£20	£65	£200
1723 – SS C	£20	£45	£110
1723 – SSC – C/SS	£30	£60	£150
1723 – SSC Fench			
arms at date...	£175	£500	£1250
1723 2nd bust SS C... ...	£50	£100	£200
1723 – r&p	£30	£85	£275
1723 – w.c.c...	£200	£400	£1000
1724 – r&p	£30	£85	£275
1724 – w.c.c	£200	£450	£1200

	F	VF	EF
1725 – r & p	£25	£85	£275
1725 – no obv stops	£50	£150	£350
1725 – w.c.c.	£300	£500	£1400
1726 – r & p	£400	*	*
1726 – w.c.c.	£350	£600	£1500
1727 – r & p	£400	*	*
1727 – – no stops on obv	£350	£900	*

GEORGE II

	F	VF	EF
1727 YH plumes	£65	£175	£350
1727 – r & p	£50	£100	£250
1728 –	£65	£200	£450
1728 – r & p	£50	£100	£250
1729 – –	£50	£100	£250
1731 – –	£25	£85	£225
1731 – plumes	£50	£150	£400
1732 – r & p	£40	£100	£225
1734 – –	£40	£90	£200
1735 – –	£40	£90	£200
1736 – –	£40	£90	£200
1736/5 – –	£45	£95	£225
1737 – –	£25	£85	£175
1739 – roses	£15	£45	£150
1741 – roses	£15	£50	£150

1763 'Northumberland' Shilling

	F	VF	EF
1743 OH roses	£15	£45	£150
1745 –	£15	£45	£150
1745 – LIMA	£20	£45	£150
1746 – – LIMA	£65	£150	£450
1746/5 – LIMA	£65	£175	£500
1746 – proof	*	£300	£550
1747 – roses	£15	£40	£125
1750 –	£15	£45	£150
1750/6 –	£20	£50	£175
1750 – 5 over 4	£20	£45	£150
1751 –	£25	£55	£200
1758 –	£12	£25	£40

1728 Young Head Shilling

GEORGE III

	F	VF	EF	Unc
1763 'Northumber-land'	£150	£225	£350	£500
1786 proof or pattern	*	*	*	£4000
1787 no hearts	£5	£10	£30	£50
1787 – no stop over head	£10	£25	£60	£85
1787 – no stops at date	£10	£30	£75	£100

SHILLINGS

	F	VF	EF	Unc
1787 – no stops on obv	£250	£500	£1750	*
1787 hearts	£5	£10	£30	£50
1798 'Dorrien and Magens'	*	£2250	£3500	£5000
1816	*	£3	£35	£75
1817	*	£3	£35	£75
1817 GEOE	£50	£125	£350	£750
1818	£4	£20	£45	£100
1819	*	£4	£40	£80
1819/8	*	*	£60	£125
1820	*	£4	£40	£100

GEORGE IV

	F	VF	EF	Unc
1820 1st hd 1st rev pattern or prf	*	*	*	£2000
1821 1st hd 1st rev	£10	£30	£100	£200
1821 – proof	*	*	£175	£350
1823 – 2nd rev	£20	£50	£175	*
1824 – –	£8	£25	£100	£200
1825 – –	£15	£35	£100	£200
1825 2nd hd	£10	£25	£90	£150
1826 –	*	£20	£85	£120

George IV 1824 shilling

	F	VF	EF	Unc
1826 – proof	*	*	£100	£170
1827	£10	£50	£150	£250
1829	*	£30	£120	£200

WILLIAM IV

	F	VF	EF	Unc
1831 proof	*	*	*	£300
1834	£10	£30	£85	£150
1835	£10	£35	£120	£200
1836	£15	£25	£85	£150
1837	£25	£75	£175	*

William IV 1837 shilling

VICTORIA

	F	VF	EF	Unc
1838	£8	£18	£65	£130
1839	£8	£20	£65	£130
1839 2nd YH	£8	£20	£65	£130
1839 – proof	*	*	*	£225
1840	£12	£35	£100	£160
1841	£12	£35	£100	£160
1842	£10	£20	£60	£95
1843	£12	£30	£90	£140
1844	£8	£20	£55	£95
1845	£8	£20	£60	£110
1846	£8	£20	£55	£95
1848/6	£30	£80	£350	*
1849	£12	£25	£70	£120

SHILLINGS

	F	VF	EF	Unc
1850	£150	£500	£950	*
1850/46	£150	£500	£950	*
1851	£25	£100	£300	*
1852	£8	£20	£65	£95
1853	£8	£20	£65	£90
1853 proof	*	*	*	£375
1854	£60	£250	£750	*
1855	£8	£20	£60	£90
1856	£8	£20	£60	£90
1857	£8	£20	£60	£90
1857 F:G:	£200	*	*	*
1858	£8	£20	£60	£90
1859	£8	£20	£60	£90
1860	£10	£25	£80	*
1861	£10	£25	£80	*
1862	£15	£35	£100	*

Victoria 1839 shilling

	F	VF	EF	Unc
1863	£15	£50	£200	*
1864	£8	£15	£60	£90
1865	£8	£15	£60	£90
1866	£8	£15	£60	£90
1866 BBITANNIAR ...	*	*	£350	*
1867	£8	£15	£70	£110
1867 3rd YH, die no.	£150	£250	*	*
1868	£8	£20	£70	£110
1869	£12	£30	£70	£130
1870	£10	£25	£70	£120
1871	£8	£20	£50	£80
1872	£8	£20	£50	£80
1873	£8	£20	£50	£80
1874	£8	£20	£50	£80
1875	£8	£20	£50	£80
1876	£10	£25	£60	£100
1877 die no.	£8	£20	£45	£75
1877 no die no	*	*	*	*
1878	£8	£20	£45	£75
1879 3rd YH	£45	£100	£200	*
1879 4th YH	£8	£20	£45	£75
1880	£6	£15	£35	£65
1880 longer line below SHILLING	*	*	*	*
1881	£6	£15	£35	£70
1881 longer line below SHILLING	£6	£15	£40	£70
1881 – Large rev lettering	£6	£15	£35	£70
1882	£10	£35	£75	£150
1883	£6	£15	£35	£65
1884	£6	£15	£35	£65
1885	£6	£15	£35	£65
1886	£6	£15	£35	£65
1887	£7	£20	£65	£110
1887 JH	*	*	£12	£25
1887 proof	*	*	*	£80
1888	*	£6	£25	£50
1889	£40	£100	£300	*
1889 large JH	*	*	£25	£50
1890	*	*	£25	£50
1891	*	*	£25	£50
1892	*	*	£25	£50

Victoria Jubilee Head and Old Head shillings

	F	VF	EF	Unc
1893 OH	*	*	£15	£30
1893 – proof	*	*	*	£100
1893 small obv letters	*	*	£18	£35
1894	*	*	£20	£45
1895	*	*	£18	£40
1896	*	*	£18	£40
1897	*	*	£18	£35
1898	*	*	£18	£35
1899	*	*	£18	£35
1900	*	*	£18	£35
1901	*	*	£15	£30

EDWARD VII

	F	VF	EF	Unc
1902	*	*	£20	£30
1902 matt prf	*	*	*	£30

Edward VII 1905 shilling

	F	VF	EF	Unc
1903	*	£15	£65	£140
1904	*	£12	£60	£120
1905	£40	£120	£375	*
1906	*	*	£25	£50
1907	*	*	£25	£60
1908	£8	£20	£55	£130
1909	£8	£20	£55	£130
1910	*	*	£20	£35

GEORGE V

	F	VF	EF	Unc
1911	*	*	£10	£18
1911 proof	*	*	*	£35
1912	*	*	£15	£45
1913	*	*	£25	£60
1914	*	*	£8	£15
1915	*	*	£8	£15
1916	*	*	£8	£15
1917	*	*	£10	£20
1918	*	*	£8	£18
1919	*	*	£12	£30
1920	*	*	£12	£30
1921	*	*	£20	£40

George V nickel trial shilling, 1924

	F	VF	EF	Unc
1922	*	*	£12	£35
1923	*	*	£10	£25
1923 nickel	*	*	£300	£550
1924	*	*	£10	£20
1924 nickel	*	*	£300	£550
1925	*	*	£12	£60
1926	*	*	£10	£35
1926 mod eff	*	*	£10	£25
1927 –	*	*	£10	£30
1927 new type	*	*	£6	£20
1927 – proof	*	*	*	£20
1928	*	*	*	£10
1929	*	*	£4	£12
1930	*	*	£8	£20
1931	*	*	£4	£12
1932	*	*	£4	£12
1933	*	*	£4	£12
1934	*	*	£5	£25
1935	*	*	*	£7
1936	*	*	*	£5

GEORGE VI

	F	VF	EF	Unc
1937 Eng	*	*	*	£5
1937 Eng prf	*	*	*	£7
1937 Scot	*	*	*	£3
1937 Scot prf	*	*	*	£6
1938 Eng	*	*	£2	£15
1938 Scot	*	*	£2	£12
1939 Eng	*	*	*	£5
1939 Scot	*	*	*	£5
1940 Eng	*	*	*	£5
1940 Scot	*	*	*	£5
1941 Eng	*	*	*	£4
1941 Scot	*	*	£2	£5
1942 Eng	*	*	*	£3
1942 Scot	*	*	*	£4
1943 Eng	*	*	*	£3
1943 Scot	*	*	*	£4
1944 Eng	*	*	*	£3
1944 Scot	*	*	*	£3
1945 Eng	*	*	*	£3
1945 Scot	*	*	*	£2
1946 Eng	*	*	*	£2
1946 Scot	*	*	*	£2
1947 Eng	*	*	*	£3
1947 Scot	*	*	*	£3

Reverses: English (left), Scottish (right)

	F	VF	EF	Unc
1948 Eng	*	*	*	£2
1948 Scot	*	*	*	£2
1949 Eng	*	*	*	£4
1949 Scot	*	*	*	£4
1950 Eng	*	*	*	£5
1950 Eng prf	*	*	*	£6
1950 Scot	*	*	*	£5
1950 Scot prf	*	*	*	£6
1951 Eng	*	*	*	£5
1951 Eng prf	*	*	*	£6
1951 Scot	*	*	*	£5
1951 Scot prf	*	*	*	£6

ELIZABETH II

	F	VF	EF	Unc
1953 Eng	*	*	*	£1
1953 Eng prf	*	*	*	£5
1953 Scot	*	*	*	£1

SHILLINGS

	F	VF	EF	Unc
1953 Scot prf	*	*	*	£5
1954 Eng	*	*	*	£1
1954 Eng	*	*	*	£1
1955 Eng	*	*	*	£1
1955 Scot	*	*	*	£1
1956 Eng	*	*	*	£2
1956 Scot	*	*	*	£6
1957 Eng	*	*	*	£2
1957 Scot	*	*	*	£5
1958 Eng	*	*	*	£6
1958 Scot	*	*	*	£1

Reverses: English (left), Scottish (right)

	F	VF	EF	Unc
1959 Eng	*	*	*	£1
1959 Scot	*	*	*	£20
1960 Eng	*	*	*	£1
1960 Scot	*	*	*	£2
1961 Eng	*	*	*	£1
1961 Scot	*	*	*	£5
1962 Eng	*	*	*	*
1962 Scot	*	*	*	*
1963 Eng	*	*	*	*
1963 Scot	*	*	*	*
1964 Eng	*	*	*	*
1964 Scot	*	*	*	*
1965 Eng	*	*	*	*
1965 Scot	*	*	*	*
1966 Eng	*	*	*	*
1966 Scot	*	*	*	*

Sixpences

CROMWELL	F	VF	EF
1658	of the highest rarity		
1658 Dutch copy	£650	£1250	£2500

CHARLES II			
1674	£25	£90	£300
1675	£120	£75	£300
1675/4	£30	£100	£325
1676	£30	£100	£325
1676/5	£30	£100	£325
1677	£20	£95	£300
1678/7	£30	£100	£325

Charles II 1678 sixpence

	F	VF	EF
1679	£30	£100	£325
1680	£40	£120	£350

SIXPENCES

	F	VF	EF
1681	£20	£70	£275
1682	£40	£120	£325
1682/1	£20	£75	£275
1683	£20	£75	£250
1684	£25	£90	£325

James II 1688 sixpence

JAMES II

	F	VF	EF
1686 early shields	£45	£150	£350
1687 –	£40	£150	£400
1687/6	£40	£150	£400
1687 later shield	£40	£150	£350
1687/6	£45	£175	£425
1688 –	£50	£200	£450

WILLIAM AND MARY

	F	VF	EF
1693	£45	£200	£400
1693 3 upside down	£55	£225	£450
1694	£70	£250	£500

William and Mary 1694 sixpence

WILLIAM III

	F	VF	EF
1695 1st bust early harp	£10	£35	£100
1696 – –	£5	£20	£75
1696 – – no obv stops	£10	£35	£100
1696/5	£15	£50	£150
1696 – – B	£10	£35	£120
1696 – – C	£10	£35	£120
1696 – – E	£15	£50	£125
1696 – – N	£10	£40	£120
1696 – – y	£10	£35	£100
1696 – – Y	£15	£50	£125
1696 – later harp	£15	£70	£175
1696 – – B	£25	£90	£225
1696 – – C	£30	£100	£250
1696 – – N	£25	£90	£225
1696 2nd bust	£100	£225	£500
1697 1st bust early harp	£5	£20	£75
1697 – – B	£10	£35	£120
1697 – – C	£15	£50	£120
1697 – – E	£15	£50	£120
1697 – – N	£10	£35	£120
1697 – – y	£15	£50	£120
1697 2nd bust	£30	£110	£275
1697 3rd bust later harp	£5	£20	£75
1697 – – B	£15	£40	£140
1697 – – C	£30	£60	£150
1697 – – E	£20	£50	£150
1697 – – Y	£20	£50	£125
1698 – –	£15	£40	£100
1698 – – plumes	£30	£80	£200
1699 – –	£45	£125	£300
1699 – – plumes	£35	£85	£250

William III 1699 sixpence, plumes

	F	VF	EF
1699 – – roses	£50	£125	£350
1700	£10	£25	£90
1701	£15	£30	£125

ANNE

	F	VF	EF
1703 VIGO	£20	£50	£120
1705	£25	£90	£200
1705 plumes	£20	£80	£175
1705 roses & plumes	£20	£60	£150
1707 –	£20	£55	£100
1707 plain	£15	£35	£85
1707 E	£15	£45	£150

Anne 1707 sixpence, E below bust

	F	VF	EF
1707 plumes	£20	£45	£150
1708 plain	£10	£30	£75
1708 E	£20	£60	£200
1708/7 E	£50	£120	£250
1708 E★	£20	£70	£225
1708/7 E★	£50	£120	£250
1708 Edin bust E★	£20	£75	£225
1708 plumes	£20	£55	£200
1710 roses & plumes	£20	£60	£225
1711	£10	£30	£75

George I 1717 sixpence

GEORGE I

	F	VF	EF
1717	£25	£95	£250
1720/17	£25	£95	£250
1723 SS C, Small letters on obv	£15	£30	£100
1723 SS C, large letters on both sides	£15	£30	£100
1726 roses & plumes	£30	£125	£300

GEORGE II

	F	VF	EF
1728 YH	£25	£85	£250
1728 – plumes	£20	£75	£150
1728 – r & p	£20	£65	£175
1731 – –	£20	£65	£175
1732 – –	£20	£65	£175
1734 – –	£25	£65	£200
1735 – –	£25	£70	£175
1736 – –	£20	£60	£175
1739 – roses	£15	£50	£125
1739 – – O/R	£35	£100	£250

	F	VF	EF
1741 – –	£15	£45	£125
1743 OH	£15	£45	£125
1745 – –	£15	£45	£125
1745/3 – –	£25	£55	£175
1745 – LIMA	£10	£30	£85
1746 – LIMA	£10	£30	£85
1746 – plain proof	*	*	£350

George II 1746 sixpence

	F	VF	EF
1750	£10	£30	£90
1751	£15	£40	£100
1757	£5	£10	£30
1757	£5	£10	£30
1758/7	£10	£25	£40

GEORGE III	F	VF	EF	Unc
1787 hearts	£8	£15	£20	£35
1787 no hearts	£8	£15	£20	£35
1816	£8	£15	£25	£55
1817	£8	£15	£25	£55
1818	£8	£18	£40	£95
1819	£8	£15	£25	£65
1819 small 8	£10	£20	£50	£125
1820	£8	£15	£30	£75
1820 1 inverted	£30	£100	£225	£450

GEORGE IV	F	VF	EF	Unc
1820 1st hd 1st rev (pattern or proof)	*	*	*	£1250
1821 1st hd 1st rev	£6	£18	£60	£100
1821 – – BBITANNIAR	£65	£125	£300	£550
1824 1st hd 2nd rev	£6	£18	£55	£100
1825 – –	£6	£18	£65	£100
1826 – –	£15	£60	£150	£275
1826 2nd hd 3rd rev	£5	£14	£60	£95

George IV 1825 sixpence

	F	VF	EF	Unc
1826 – – proof	*	*	*	£175
1827	1£15	£45	£130	£250
1828	£8	£20	£95	£175
1829	£6	£20	£85	£150

WILLIAM IV	F	VF	EF	Unc
1831	£6	£20	£80	£100
1831 proof	*	*	*	£175
1834	£6	£30	£50	£100
1835	£6	£20	£70	£125
1836	1£15	£35	£95	£150
1837	1£12	£30	£95	£150

VICTORIA	F	VF	EF	Unc
1838	£5	£10	£50	£85
1839	£5	£10	£50	£85
1839 proof	*	*	*	£150

	F	VF	EF	Unc
1840	£5	£10	£45	£80
1841	£5	£10	£45	£80
1842	£5	£10	£60	£110
1843	£5	£10	£50	£85
1844	£5	£10	£50	£85
1845	£5	£10	£50	£85
1846	£3	£8	£40	£80
1848	£15	£75	£300	£500
1848/6	£10	£50	£200	£400
1848/7	£10	£50	£200	£400
1850	£5	£15	£55	£110
1850 5 over 3	£15	£30	£150	£300
1851	£4	£12	£40	£85
1852	£4	£12	£40	£80
1853	£5	£15	£40	£75
1853 proof	*	*	*	£250
1854	£40	£100	£450	*
1855	£4	£12	£40	£70
1856	£4	£12	£40	£75
1857	£4	£12	£45	£75
1858	£4	£12	£45	£70
1859	£4	£12	£40	£70
1859/8	£4	£12	£45	£75
1860	£5	£15	£45	£75
1862	£20	£60	£250	£425
1863	£12	£40	£175	£350
1864	£5	£12	£40	£80
1865	£6	£14	£45	£85
1866	£5	£12	£40	£80
1866 no die no.	*	*	*	*
1867	£8	£20	£50	£95
1868	£8	£20	£50	£95
1869	£8	£25	£75	£130
1870	£8	£20	£60	£100
1871	£5	£12	£40	£75
1871 no die no.	£5	£12	£40	£75
1872	£5	£12	£40	£75
1873	£5	£12	£40	£70
1874	£5	£12	£40	£70
1875	£5	£12	£40	£75
1876	£6	£20	£55	£90
1877	£5	£12	£40	£70
1877 no die no.	£5	£12	£40	£70
1878	£5	£10	£35	£75
1878 DRITANNIAR	£35	£100	£250	*
1879 die no.	£8	£20	£55	£110
1879 no die no.	£5	£10	£35	£70
1880 2nd YH	£4	£10	£25	£60
1880 3rd YH	£3	£8	£20	£50
1881	£4	£10	£20	£50
1882	£8	£20	£50	£100
1883	£4	£10	£20	£50
1884	£4	£10	£20	£50
1885	£4	£10	£20	£50
1886	£4	£10	£20	£50
1887 YH	£4	£10	£20	£50
1887 JH shield rev	£2	£5	£10	£18

1887 Jubilee Head sixpence, withdrawn type

	F	VF	EF	Unc
1887 – proof	*	*	*	£75
1887 – new rev	£2	£5	£10	£15
1888	£3	£5	£10	£15
1889	£3	£7	£12	£30

SIXPENCES

	F	VF	EF	Unc
1890	*	£3	£12	£35
1891	*	£3	£12	£35
1892	*	£3	£12	£35
1893	£250	£650	£1250	*
1893 OH	*	£3	£15	£35
1893 proof	*	*	*	£85
1894	*	£3	£20	£35
1895	*	£3	£20	£35
1896	*	£3	£20	£35
1897	*	£3	£18	£30
1898	*	£3	£18	£30
1899	*	£3	£20	£35
1900	*	£3	£18	£30
1901	*	£3	£18	£30

EDWARD VII

	F	VF	EF	Unc
1902	*	£2	£10	£20
1902 matt proof	*	*	*	£25
1903	*	£5	£25	£50
1904	*	£6	£28	£65
1905	*	£6	£28	£55
1906	*	£3	£15	£45
1907	*	£5	£15	£45
1908	*	£7	£28	£65
1909	*	£4	£22	£50
1910	*	£4	£15	£30

GEORGE V

	F	VF	EF	Unc
1911	*	*	£8	£30
1911 proof	*	*	*	£40
1912	*	*	£15	£45
1913	*	*	£20	£45
1914	*	*	£8	£20
1915	*	*	£8	£20
1916	*	*	£8	£20
1917	*	*	£15	£40
1918	*	*	£7	£15
1919	*	*	£8	£20
1920	*	*	£10	£35
1920 debased	*	*	£10	£35
1921	*	*	£8	£30
1922	*	*	£8	£30
1923	*	*	£8	£40
1924	*	*	£8	£30
1925	*	*	£8	£30
1925 new rim	*	*	£8	£20
1926 new rim	*	*	£10	£30
1926 mod effigy	*	*	£8	£20
1927	*	*	£5	£20
1927 new rev prf	*	*	*	£20
1928	*	*	*	£10
1929	*	*	*	£10
1930	*	*	*	£10
1931	*	*	*	£10
1932	*	*	£6	£15
1933	*	*	*	£10
1934	*	*	£3	£10

George V 1929 sixpence

	F	VF	EF	Unc
1935	*	*	*	£8
1936	*	*	*	£8

GEORGE VI

	F	VF	EF	Unc
1937	*	*	*	£2
1937 proof	*	*	*	£4
1938	*	*	£2	£6
1939	*	*	*	£3
1940	*	*	*	£3
1941	*	*	*	£3
1942	*	*	*	£2
1943	*	*	*	£2
1944	*	*	*	£1
1945	*	*	*	£1
1946	*	*	*	£1
1947	*	*	*	£1
1948	*	*	*	£1
1949	*	*	*	£2
1950	*	*	*	£2
1950 proof	*	*	*	£3.50
1951	*	*	*	£2
1951 proof	*	*	*	£3.50
1952	*	£2	£8	£20

ELIZABETH II

	F	VF	EF	Unc
1953	*	*	*	£0.50
1953 proof	*	*	*	£2
1954	*	*	*	£2
1955	*	*	*	£0.60
1956	*	*	*	£0.60
1957	*	*	*	£0.30
1958	*	*	*	£2
1959	*	*	*	£0.20
1960	*	*	*	£1.50
1961	*	*	*	£1.50
1962	*	*	*	£0.25
1963	*	*	*	*
1964	*	*	*	*
1965	*	*	*	*
1966	*	*	*	*
1967	*	*	*	*

Groats (fourpences)

William IV 1836 groat
Earlier dates are included in Maundy sets

WILLIAM IV

	F	VF	EF	Unc
1836	*	*	£25	£50
1836 proof	*	*	*	£450
1837	*	£8	£35	£65

Victoria 1842 groat

VICTORIA

	F	VF	EF	Unc
1838	*	£5	£20	£50
1838 8 over 8 on side	*	£10	£35	£75
1839	*	£8	£25	£60
1839 proof	*	*	*	£150
1840	£2	£10	£30	£60
1840 narrow 0	*	£12	£40	*
1841	£3	£10	£35	£70
1841 I for last 1	*	*	*	*
1842	*	£8	£30	£50

	F	VF	EF	Unc
1842/1	£4	£15	£60	*
1843	*	£5	£25	£45
1844	*	£8	£35	£60
1845	*	£8	£35	£60
1846	*	£8	£35	£60
1847/6	£25	£50	£120	*
1848 small date ...	*	£8	£120	£50
1848 large date ...	*	£8	£25	£50
1848/6	*	£10	£35	*
1848/7	*	£8	£25	£55
1849	*	£8	£25	£60
1849/8	*	£8	£45	£80
1851	£15	£50	£150	*
1852	£40	£100	£250	*
1853	£35	£75	£200	*
1853 proof	*	*	*	£250
1854	*	£8	£25	£50
1854 5 over 3	*	£8	£30	£700
1855	*	£8	£25	£50
1857 proof	*	*	*	£700
1862 proof	*	*	*	£450
1888 JH	£5	£10	£30	£40

Silver threepences

Earlier dates are included in Maundy sets

WILLIAM IV

	F	VF	EF	Unc
1834	*	£6	£38	£80
1835	*	£6	£35	£80
1836	*	£6	£35	£80
1837	£5	£15	£45	£100

Victoria threepence of 1848

VICTORIA

	F	VF	EF	Unc
1838	*	£8	£35	£85
1839	*	£10	£45	£100
1840	*	£10	£50	£100
1841	*	£10	£45	£95
1842	*	£10	£45	£95
1843	*	£10	£45	£95
1844	*	£12	£55	£100
1845	*	£4	£35	£75
1846	*	£15	£85	£120
1847	*	*	£400	£800
1848	*	*	£400	£750
1849	*	£12	£50	£100
1850	*	£4	£30	£65
1851	*	£8	£40	£85
1852	*	*	£275	*
1853	*	£12	£55	£120
1854	*	£8	£40	£85
1855	*	£12	£55	£100
1856	*	£10	£50	£100
1857	*	£10	£50	£100
1858	*	£8	£35	£75
1858/6	*	*	*	*
1859	*	£4	£30	£65
1860	*	£8	£35	£75
1861	*	£4	£30	£65
1862	*	£8	£40	£80
1863	*	£10	£50	£100
1864	*	£8	£80	£80
1865	*	£10	£50	£100
1866	*	£8	£40	£80
1867	*	£8	£40	£85

SILVER THREEPENCES

	F	VF	EF	Unc
1868	*	£8	£40	£65
1868 RRITANNIAR	£20	£50	£200	*
1869	£10	£30	£100	*
1870	*	£6	£30	£65
1871	*	£7	£35	£70
1872	*	£5	£25	£60
1873	*	£5	£25	£60
1874	*	£5	£25	£55
1875	*	£5	£25	£55
1876	*	£5	£25	£55
1877	*	£5	£25	£55
1878	*	£5	£25	£55
1879	*	£5	£25	£55
1880	*	£6	£30	£60
1881	*	£6	£30	£60
1882	*	£8	£35	£80
1883	*	£5	£25	£55
1884	*	£5	£25	£55
1885	*	£5	£20	£50
1886	*	£5	£20	£50
1887 YH	*	£6	£25	£55
1887 JH	*	£2	£5	£8
1887 proof	*	*	*	£40
1888	*	£2	£7	£20
1889	*	£2	£6	£15
1890	*	£2	£6	£15
1891	*	£2	£6	£15
1892	*	£3	£10	£20
1893	£12	£40	£100	£225
1893 OH	*	*	£4	£15
1893 OH proof	*	*	*	£50
1894	*	£2	£8	£20
1895	*	£2	£8	£20
1896	*	£2	£6	£20
1897	*	*	£5	£20
1898	*	*	£5	£20
1899	*	*	£5	£20
1900	*	*	£5	£20
1901	*	*	£5	£15

EDWARD VII

	F	VF	EF	Unc
1902	*	*	£4	£10
1902 matt proof ...	*	*	*	£12
1903	*	£1.50	£6	£20
1904	*	£6	£14	£35
1905	*	£6	£14	£35
1906	*	£3	£10	£30
1907	*	£1.50	£5	£20
1908	*	£1.50	£6	£22
1909	*	£2	£6	£22
1910	*	£1.25	£4	£18

George V 1927 threepence, acorns on reverse

GEORGE V

	F	VF	EF	Unc
1911	*	*	£3	£12
1911 proof	*	*	*	£25
1912	*	*	£3	£12
1913	*	*	£3	£12
1914	*	*	£2	£10
1915	*	*	£2	£10
1916	*	*	£1.50	£8
1917	*	*	£1.50	£8
1918	*	*	£2	£8
1919	*	*	£2	£8

SILVER THREEPENCES

	F	VF	EF	Unc
1920	*	*	£2	£10
1920 debased	*	*	£2	£10
1921	*	*	£2	£12
1922	*	*	£2	£12
1925	*	£1	£6	£18
1926	*	£3	£10	£25
1926 mod effigy ...	*	£1	£6	£20
1927 new rev prf ...	*	*	*	£30
1928	*	£2	£6	£20
1930	*	£1.50	£5	£12
1931	*	*	£1	£6
1932	*	*	£1	£6
1933	*	*	£1	£6
1934	*	*	£1	£6
1935	*	*	£1	£6
1936	*	*	£1	£6

GEORGE VI

	F	VF	EF	Unc
1937	*	*	£0.75	£1.50
1937 proof	*	*	*	£5
1938	*	*	£0.50	£1
1939	*	£1	£3	£5
1940	*	*	£1	£2
1941	*	*	£1	£2
1942	£1	£2	£6	£8
1943	£1	£3	£7	£9
1944	£1.50	£5	£12	£20
1945[2]	*	*	*	*

[1]Threepences issued for use in the Colonies.
[2]All specimens of 1945 were thought to have been melted down but it appears that one or two still exist.

Small silver for Colonies

These tiny coins were struck for use in some of the Colonies – they were never issued for circulation in Britain. However, they are often included in collections of British coins and it is for this reason that prices for them are given here.

TWOPENCES

Other dates are included in Maundy sets.

VICTORIA	F	VF	EF	Unc
1838	*	£2	£15	£35
1838 2nd 8 like S ...	*	£6	£25	£75
1848	*	£2	£15	£35

THREEHALFPENCES

WILLIAM IV	F	VF	EF	Unc
1834	*	£5	£25	£50
1835	*	£5	£25	£50
1835/4	*	£10	£30	£85
1836	*	£5	£25	£50
1837	£10	£25	£100	£200

VICTORIA	F	VF	EF	Unc
1838	*	£2	£15	£30
1839	*	£1.25	£12	£25
1840	*	£5	£20	£50
1841	*	£2	£15	£40
1842	*	£2	£12	£35
1843	*	£1	£12	£30

George V threepence

	F	VF	EF	Unc
1843/34	£2	£10	£25	£75
1860	£1	£5	£20	£45
1862	£1	£5	£20	£45
1870 proof	*	*	*	£375

Maundy sets

EF prices are for evenly matched sets

Charles II 1677 Maundy set

CHARLES II	F	VF	EF
1670	£60	£120	£250
1671	£60	£120	£250
1672	£65	£125	£275
1673	£60	£120	£250
1674	£60	£120	£250
1675	£65	£150	£275
1676	£65	£150	£275
1677	£60	£120	£250
1678	£75	£175	£300
1679	£65	£150	£275
1680	£60	£125	£250
1681	£75	£175	£300
1682	£65	£150	£275
1683	£60	£125	£250
1684	£65	£150	£275

JAMES II	F	VF	EF
1686	£70	£150	£300
1687	£65	£150	£275
1688	£70	£150	£300

WILLIAM AND MARY	F	VF	EF
1689	£250	£450	£700
1691	£90	£150	£300
1692	£100	£175	£350
1693	£100	£175	£350
1694	£90	£150	£300

WILLIAM III	F	VF	EF
1698	£75	£125	£275
1699	£85	£175	£325
1700	£85	£175	£325
1701	£75	£130	£300

	F	VF	EF
ANNE			
703	£70	£120	£250
705	£70	£120	£250
706	£60	£100	£200
708	£75	£125	£275
709	£65	£110	£225
710	£75	£125	£275
713	£65	£110	£225
GEORGE I			
723	£75	£125	£275
727	£70	£120	£250
GEORGE II			
729	£60	£90	£180
731	£60	£90	£180
732	£55	£80	£160
735	£55	£80	£160
737	£55	£80	£160
739	£55	£80	£160
740	£55	£80	£160
743	£55	£90	£180
746	£50	£75	£150
760	£70	£100	£200

GEORGE III	F	VF	EF	Unc
1763	£50	£75	£140	£175
1766	£50	£80	£150	£175
1772	£50	£20	£150	£175
1780	£50	£80	£150	£175
1784	£50	£80	£150	£175
1786	£50	£80	£150	£175
1792 wire type	£75	£125	£200	£275

William and Mary 1694 Maundy set

	F	VF	EF	Unc
1795	*	£60	£90	£150
1800	*	£60	£90	£140
1817	*	£65	£100	£150
1818	*	£65	£100	£150
1820	*	£65	£100	£150
GEORGE IV				
1822	*	£60	£90	£130
1823	*	£55	£80	£120
1824	*	£55	£85	£125
1825	*	£55	£80	£120
1826	*	£55	£80	£120
1827	*	£55	£80	£120
1828	*	£55	£80	£120
1829	*	£55	£80	£120
1830	*	£55	£80	£120
WILLIAM IV				
1831	*	£65	£100	£175
1831 proof	*	*	*	£300
1832	*	£65	£100	£200
1833	*	£60	£90	£150
1834	*	£60	£90	£150
1835	*	£60	£90	£150

	F	VF	EF	Unc
1836	*	£65	£110	£220
1837	*	£65	£110	£220
VICTORIA				
1838			£60	£95
1839			£65	£100
1839 proof			*	£100
1840			£65	£100
1841			£70	£110
1842			£75	£125
1843			£70	£110
1844			£70	£110
1845			£60	£95
1846			£75	£125
1847			£7	£110

George IV 1825

	F	VF	EF	Unc
1848			£70	£110
1849			£75	£125
1850			£55	£90
1851			£55	£90
1852			£60	£95
1853			£60	£95
1853 proof			*	£400
1854			£55	£95
1855			£50	£90
1856			£50	£95
1857			£50	£95
1858			£50	£95
1859			£50	£95
1860			£50	£90
1861			£50	£90
1862			£50	£90
1863			£50	£90
1864			£50	£90
1865			£50	£90
1866			£50	£90
1867			£50	£90
1868			£50	£90
1869			£50	£90
1870			£45	£75
1871			£45	£75
1872			£45	£75
1873			£45	£75
1874			£45	£75
1875			£45	£75
1876			£45	£75
1877			£45	£75
1878			£45	£75
1879			£45	£75
1880			£45	£75
1881			£45	£75
1882			£45	£75
1883			£45	£75
1884			£45	£75
1885			£45	£75
1886			£45	£75
1887			£45	£75
1888 JH			£50	£80

MAUNDY SETS

	EF	Unc
1889	£50	£75
1890	£50	£75
1891	£50	£75
1892	£50	£75
1893 OH	£40	£55
1894	£45	£60
1895	£40	£55
1896	£40	£55
1897	£40	£55
1898	£40	£55
1899	£40	£55
1900	£40	£75
1901	£40	£55

EDWARD VII

	EF	Unc
1902	£40	£55
1902 matt proof	*	£50
1903	£35	£50
1904	£35	£50
1905	£35	£50
1906	£35	£50
1907	£35	£50
1908	£35	£50
1909	£50	£70
1910	£50	£70

GEORGE V

	EF	Unc
1911	£40	£70
1911 proof	*	£75
1912	£40	£70
1913	£40	£70
1914	£40	£75
1915	£40	£65
1916	£40	£65
1917	£40	£65
1918	£40	£65
1919	£40	£65
1920	£40	£65
1921	£40	£65
1922	£40	£65
1923	£40	£65
1924	£40	£65
1925	£40	£65
1926	£40	£65
1927	£40	£65
1928	£40	£65
1929	£40	£65
1930	£40	£65
1931	£40	£65
1932	£40	£65
1933	£40	£65
1934	£40	£65
1935	£45	£65
1936	£50	£65

GEORGE VI

	EF	Unc
1937	*	£55
1938	*	£55
1939	*	£60
1940	*	£60
1941	*	£60
1942	*	£60
1943	*	£60
1944	*	£60
1945	*	£60
1946	*	£60
1947	*	£65
1948	*	£65
1949	*	£65
1950	*	£65
1951	*	£65
1952	*	£65

ELIZABETH II

	EF	Unc
1953	£200	£30•
1954	*	£6•
1955	*	£6•
1956	*	£6•
1957	*	£6•
1958	*	£6•
1959	*	£6•
1960	*	£65
1961	*	£6•
1962	*	£6•
1963	*	£6•
1964	*	£6•
1965	*	£6
1966	*	£6•
1967	*	£6•
1968	*	£6
1969	*	£60
1970	*	£65
1971	*	£60
1972	*	£6•
1973	*	£6•
1974	*	£60
1975	*	£60
1976	*	£60
1977	*	£60
1978	*	£60
1979	*	£60
1980	*	£65
1981	*	£60
1982	*	£60
1983	*	£60
1984	*	£60
1985	*	£60
1986	*	£60
1987	*	£60
1988	*	£60
1989	*	£60
1990	*	£70
1991	*	£65
1992	*	£65
1993	*	£65
1994	*	£65
1995	*	£65
1996	*	£65
1997	*	£70
1998	*	£80
1999	*	£100
2000	*	£100

1925 Maundy (part set)

Nickel-brass threepences

1937 threepence of Edward VII, extremely rare

937-dated Edward VIII threepences, struck in 1936 ready for issue, were melted after Edward's abdication. A few, however, escaped into circulation to become highly prized collectors' pieces. George VI 937 threepences were struck in large numbers.

DWARD VIII	F	VF	EF	BU
937	*	*	£25000	*

GEORGE VI	F	VF	EF	BU
937	*	*	£1	£2
938	*	*	£3	£10
939	*	*	£4	£20
940	*	*	£2	£4
941	*	*	£1	£3
942	*	*	£1	£2
943	*	*	£1	£2
944	*	*	£1	£3
945	*	*	*	£3
946	£2	£10	£50	£150
948	*	*	£4	£6
949	£2	£10	£50	£125
950	*	*	£8	£25
951	*	*	£8	£25
952	*	*	*	£1.50

Elizabeth II 1953 nickel-brass threepence

ELIZABETH II	F	VF	EF	BU
953	*	*	*	£1
954	*	*	*	£2
955	*	*	*	£2
956	*	*	£1	£2
957	*	*	*	£2
958	*	*	£2	£4
959	*	*	*	£2
960	*	*	*	£1.25
961	*	*	*	*
962	*	*	*	*
963	*	*	*	*
964	*	*	*	*
965	*	*	*	*
966	*	*	*	*
967	*	*	*	*

Copper twopence

George III 1797 'cartwheel' twopence

GEORGE III	F	VF	EF	BU
1797	£8	£40	£200	£1000

Copper pennies

GEORGE III	F	VF	EF	BU
1797 10 leaves	£3	£10	£100	£450
1797 11 leaves	£3	£10	£100	£450

1797 'cartwheel' penny

	F	VF	EF	BU
1806	£3	£8	£60	£150
1806 no incuse curl	£3	£8	£60	£150
1807	£3	£8	£60	£150

1806 penny of George III

GEORGE IV	F	VF	EF	BU
1825	£5	£15	£90	£250
1826	£3	£12	£80	£300
1826 thin line down St Andrew's cross	£5	£15	£85	£225
1826 thick line	£5	£15	£85	£250
1827	£100	£400	£1000	*

COPPER PENNIES

William IV 1831 penny

WILLIAM IV	F	VF	EF	BU
1831	£10	£50	£225	*
1831.w.w incuse ...	£12	£60	£275	*
1831.w.w incuse ...	£15	£75	£300	*
1834	£15	£75	£275	*
1837	£20	£100	£350	*

Victoria 1841 copper penny

VICTORIA	F	VF	EF	Unc
1839 proof	*	*	£125	£225
1841	£12	£30	£75	*
1841 no colon after REG	£3	£15	£50	£120
1843	£12	£40	*	*
1843 no colon after REG	£15	*	*	*
1844	£3	£15	£50	£120
1845	£8	£20	£75	£175
1846 DEF far colon	£3	£15	£50	£120
1846 DEF close colon	£3	£15	£50	£120
1847 DEF close colon	£3	£15	£50	£120
1847 DEF far colon	£3	£15	£50	£120

	F	VF	EF	BU
1848	£3	£15	£50	£12(
1848/6	£15	£35	£100	£20(
1848/7	£3	£15	£50	£12(
1849	£30	£75	£250	£50(
1851 DEF far colon	£3	£15	£50	£12:
1851 DEF close colon	£4	£15	£50	£12(
1853 OT	£2	£10	£40	£10(
1853 colon nearer F	£3	£10	£50	£12(
1853 PT	£2	£10	£40	£9(
1854 PT	£2	£10	£40	£9(
1854/3	£15	£60	*	
1854 OT	£2	£10	£40	£9(
1855 OT	£2	£10	£40	£9(
1855 PT	£2	£10	£40	£9(
1856 PT	£25	£75	£175	£37!
1856 OT	£15	£45	£100	£30(
1857 OT	£2	£10	£40	£9(
1857 PT	£2	£10	£40	£9(
1857 small date ...	£2	£10	£40	£9(
1858	£2	£10	£40	£9(
1858 small date ...	£3	£10	£45	£10(
1858/3 now thought to be 1858 9/8 (see below)				
1858/7	£2	£5	£35	£9(
1858/6	£15	£35	£100	*
1858 no ww	£2	£5	£35	£9(
1858 no ww (large 1 and 5 small 8s)	£3	£8	£35	£10(
1858 9/8?	£12	£25	£50	£11(
1858 9/8? large rose	£12	£30	£65	£12!
1859	£3	£10	£35	£10(
1859 small date ...	£4	£15	£40	£11(
1860/59	*	£350	£1000	*

Bronze pennies

For fuller details of varieties in bronze pennies see English Copper, Tin and Bronze Coins in the British Museum 1558-1958 by C. W. Peck; The Bronze Coinage of Great Britain by M. J. Freeman and The British Bronze Penny 1860-1970 by Michael Gouby.

VICTORIA	F	VF	EF	BU
1860 RB, shield crossed with incuse treble lines	*	£10	£40	£75
1860 RB, shield crossed with close double raised lines	£8	£15	£45	£95
1860 RB, double lines, but farther apart, rock to left of lighthouse	£10	£50	£125	£300
1860 RB obv/TB rev	£45	£100	£500	*
1860 TB obv/RB rev	£40	£95	£450	*

1860 penny, toothed border on obverse

	F	VF	EF	BU
1860 TB, L.C. WYON on truncation, L.C.W. incuse below shield	*	£10	£40	£75

	F	VF	EF	BU
▌860 TB, same obv but L.C.W. incuse below foot	£20	£50	£250	£450
▌860 TB, as previous but heavy flan of 170 grains	*	£300	*	*
▌860 TB, LC, WYON below truncation, L.C.W. incuse below shield	*	£6	£40	£80
▌860 TB, no signature on obv. L.C.W. incuse below shield	*	£10	£60	£120
▌861 L.C. WYON on truncation, L.C.W. incuse below shield	£12	£35	£95	£225
▌861 same obv. no signature on rev	*	£6	£40	£80
▌861 L.C. WYON below truncation, L.C.W. incuse below shield	*	£6	£40	£80
1861 similar, but heavy flan (170 grains)	*	*	*	£500
▌861 same obv but no signature on rev	*	£6	£40	£95
1861 no signature on obv, L.C.W. incuse below shield	*	£8	£45	£85
▌861-6/8	£25	£75	£150	£500
1861 no signature either side	£2	£8	£40	£75
▌862	£2	£6	£35	£70
1862 sm date figs ...	£15	£50	*	*
1863	£2	£6	£40	£85
1863 slender 3	*	*	*	*
1863 die no. (2, 3 or 4) below date	£125	£250	*	*
1864 plain 4	£8	£40	£225	£650
1864 crossiet 4	£10	£45	£250	£750
1865	*	£10	£50	£85
1865/3	£15	£65	£275	£600
1866	*	£8	£40	£85
1867	*	£10	£45	£95
▌868	£6	£30	£100	£300
1869	£20	£125	£500	£1000
1870	£6	£30	£150	£250
1871	£8	£50	£200	£400
1872	*	£8	£40	£80
1873	*	£8	£40	£80
1874 (1873 type) ...	*	£8	£40	£80
1874 H (1873 type)	*	£8	£45	£85
1874 new rev, lighthouse tall and thin	£8	£15	£45	£85
1874 H as previous	£4	£10	£45	£75
1874 new obv/1873 rev	*	£6	£40	£70
1874 H as previous	*	£6	£40	£70
1874 new obv/new rev	*	£6	£40	£70
1874 H as previous	*	£6	£40	£60
1875	*	£8	£40	£65
1875 H	£20	£65	£275	£500
1876 H	*	£6	£25	£50
1877	*	£8	£25	£60
1878	*	£10	£30	£70
1879	*	*	£25	£60
1880	*	*	£30	£80
1881 (1880 obv)	*	*	£30	£60
1881 new obv	*	£15	£50	£100
1881 H	*	*	£25	£60
▌882 H	*	*	£25	£60
▌882 no H	£75	£300	£800	£2000
▌883	*	*	£20	£60
1884	*	*	£20	£50
1885	*	*	£20	£50
1886	*	*	£20	£50
▌887	*	*	£20	£50

BRONZE PENNIES

	F	VF	EF	BU
1888	*	*	£20	£50
1889 14 leaves	*	*	£20	£50
1889 15 leaves	*	*	£20	£50
1890	*	*	£20	£45
1891	*	*	£20	£45
1892	*	*	£20	£50
1893	*	*	£20	£50
1894	*	*	£35	£70
1895 2mm	*	£40	£175	£300

Victoria old head penny of 1895

	F	VF	EF	BU
1895	*	*	£5	£35
1896	*	*	£3	£30
1897	*	*	£2.50	£25
1897 higher horizon	£5	£25	£175	£350
1898	*	£1.25	£8	£35
1899	*	£1	£6	£30
1900	*	*	£5	£15
1901	*	*	£3	£12

Edward VII 1902, penny, low horizon

EDWARD VII

	F	VF	EF	BU
1902 low horizon ...	*	£8	£30	£50
1902	*	*	£10	£15
1903	*	*	£10	£25
1904	*	*	£12	£30
1905	*	*	£10	£28
1906	*	*	£10	£25
1907	*	*	£10	£25

BRONZE PENNIES

	F	VF	EF	BU
1908	*	*	£10	£30
1909	*	*	£10	£30
1910	*	*	£10	£25

GEORGE V

	F	VF	EF	BU
1911	*	*	£10	£25
1912	*	*	£10	£25
1912 H	*	*	£20	£50
1913	*	*	£15	£35
1914	*	*	£10	£25
1915	*	*	£10	£25
1916	*	*	£10	£25
1917	*	*	£10	£25
1918	*	*	£10	£25
1918 H	*	£15	£95	£175
1918 KN	*	£20	£120	£250
1919	*	*	£10	£25
1919 H	*	£5	£75	£200
1919 KN	*	£10	£150	£300
1920	*	*	£10	£25
1921	*	*	£10	£25
1922	*	*	£10	£25
1922 rev as 1927 ext. rare		*	*	£750
1926	*	*	£15	£40
1926 mod effigy ...	£5	£40	£350	£700
1927	*	*	£5	£15
1928	*	*	£3	£12
1929	*	*	£3	£12
1930	*	*	£5	£20
1931	*	*	£5	£20
1932	*	*	£8	£35
1933			highest rarity	
1934	*	*	£8	£25
1935	*	*	£2	£5
1936	*	*	*	£4

GEORGE VI

	F	VF	EF	BU
1937	*	*	*	£1
1938	*	*	*	£1
1939	*	*	*	£2
1940	*	*	*	£5
1944	*	*	*	£4
1945	*	*	*	£3
1945 9 double (2 dies)	£2	£5	£20	*
1946	*	*	*	£2
1947	*	*	*	£1
1948	*	*	*	£2
1949	*	*	*	£2

George VI 1948 penny

		F	VF	EF	BU
1950		£2	£5	£10	£20
1951		£2	£5	£8	£15

ELIZABETH II

	F	VF	EF	BU
1953	*	£1	£2	£3
1953 proof	*	*	*	£5

	Fair	F	VF	EF
1961	*	*	*	£0.50
1962	*	*	*	*
1963	*	*	*	*
1964	*	*	*	*
1965	*	*	*	*
1966	*	*	*	*
1967	*	*	*	*

Copper halfpennies

All copper unless otherwise stated

Charles II 1675 halfpenny

CHARLES II

1672	£5	£25	£80	£350
1672 CRAOLVS	£25	£100	£200	£750
1673	£5	£25	£80	£350
1673 CRAOLVS	£25	£90	£175	£500
1673 no stops on reverse	£10	£40	£100	£400
1673 no stops on obverse	£10	£40	£100	£400
1675	£10	£40	£100	£400
1675 no stops on obverse	£10	£50	£100	£400

James II 1685 tin halfpenny

JAMES II

1685 (tin)	£30	£75	£250	£800
1686 (tin)	£35	£90	£300	£850
1687 (tin)	£30	£75	£250	£800
1687 D over D	*	*	*	

WILLIAM AND MARY

1689 (tin) ET on right	£65	£150	£400	*
1689 (tin) ET on left	*	*	*	*
1690 (tin) dated on edge	£30	£75	£250	£900
1691 (tin) date in exergue and on edge	£30	£75	£250	£900

	Fair	F	VF	EF
1691/2 (tin) 1691 in exergue 1692 on edge	£30	£75	£250	£900
1692 (tin) date in exergue and on edge	£30	£75	£250	*
1694	£5	£25	£75	£375

William and Mary 1694 halfpenny

	Fair	F	VF	EF
1694 GVLIEMVS ...	*	*	*	*
1694 no stop after MARIA	£15	£45	£95	£400
1694 BRITANNIA with last I over A	£20	£60	*	*
1694 no stop on reverse	£10	£25	£80	£350

WILLIAM III
Type 1 (date in exergue)
	Fair	F	VF	EF
1695	£5	£25	£75	£400
1695 thick flan	£25	£75	£150	*
1695 BRITANNIA ...	£5	£25	£75	£400
1695 no stop on reverse	£5	£30	£80	*
1696	£5	£25	£75	£400
1696 GVLIEMVS, no stop on reverse ...	£25	£65	£125	*
1696 TERTVS	£15	£50	£120	*
1696 obv struck from doubled die	£15	£50	£120	*
1697	£5	£25	£80	*
1697 no stops either side	£5	£25	£80	*
1697 I of TERTIVS over E	£15	£50	£125	*
1697 GVLILMVS no stop on reverse ...	£15	£40	£120	*
1697 no stop after TERTIVS	£10	£25	£80	£400
1698	£10	£25	£80	£400

Type 2 (date in legend)
	Fair	F	VF	EF
1698	£5	£25	£100	£450
1699	£5	£15	£60	£350
1699 BRITANNIA ...	£5	£15	£60	£350
1699 GVLIEMVS ...	£5	£25	£100	£450

Type 3 (Britannia's hand on knee, date in exergue)
	Fair	F	VF	EF
1699	£5	£20	£75	£350
1699 stop after date	£10	£25	£100	£450
1699 BRITANNIA ...	£5	£20	£75	£350
1699 GVILELMVS ...	£10	£25	£100	£450
1699 TERTVS	£20	£50	£150	*
1699 no stop on reverse	£20	£50	£150	*
1699 no stops on obverse	£10	£30	£100	£450

COPPER HALFPENNIES

	FAIR	F	VF	EF
1699 no stops after GVLIELMVS	£5	£20	£75	£400
1700	£5	£15	£65	£400
1700 no stops on obverse	£5	£15	£75	*
1700 no stop after GVLIELMVS	£5	£15	£75	*
1700 BRITANNIA ...	£ 5	£15	£70	£400
1700 no stops on reverse	£5	£15	£75	*
1700 GVLIELMS ...	£5	£25	£85	*
1700 GVLIEEMVS ...	£5	£25	£85	*
1700 TER TIVS	£5	£15	£75	*
1700 1 of TERTIVS over V	£10	£25	£100	*
1701 BRITANNIA ...	£5	£15	£75	*
1701 no stops on obverse	£5	£15	£75	*
1701 GVLIELMVS TERTIVS	£5	£25	£100	*

GEORGE I
Type 1
	FAIR	F	VF	EF
1717	£5	£30	£150	£300
1717 no stops on obverse	£10	£40	£200	£40
1718	*	£35	£175	£350
1718 no stop on obverse	£10	£40	£200	£450
1719 on larger flan of type 2	£15	£50	£250	*
1719 – edge grained	£10	£40	*	*

Type 2
	FAIR	F	VF	EF
1719 both shoulder straps ornate	£5	£20	£85	£300
1719 – edge grained	£10	£40	*	*
1719 bust with left strap plain	£5	£20	£85	£350
1719 – edge grained	£10	£40	*	*
1720	£5	£20	£85	£300
1721	£5	£20	£85	£300
1721/0	£5	£20	£85	*
1721 stop after date	£5	£20	£85	£300
1722	£5	£20	£85	£300
1722 GEORGIVS ...	£5	£20	£85	*
1723	£5	£20	£85	£300
1723 no stop on reverse	£5	£20	£85	£350
1724	£5	£20	£85	£300

George II 1729 halfpenny

GEORGE II
Young Head
	FAIR	F	VF	EF
1729	£2	£10	£60	£175
1729 no stop on reverse	£2	£10	£50	£150

COPPER HALFPENNIES

	Fair	F	VF	EF
1730	*	£10	£60	£175
1730 GEOGIVS, no stop on reverse ...	£5	£20	£60	£175
1730 stop after date	£5	£20	£50	£175
1730 no stop after REX or on reverse	£5	£20	£75	£175
1731	*	£10	£60	£175
1731 no stop on reverse	*	£15	£50	£150
1732	*	£10	£40	£150
1732 no stop on reverse	*	£15	£50	£150
1733	*	£10	£50	£150
1733 only obverse stop before REX ...	*	£10	£50	£150
1734	*	£10	£50	£150
1734/3	*	£10	£40	£150
1734 no stops on obverse	*	£10	£50	£150
1735	*	£10	£50	£150
1736	*	£10	£50	£150
1737	*	£10	£50	£150
1738	*	£10	£50	£150
1739	*	£10	£50	£150

Old Head

	Fair	F	VF	EF
1740	*	£5	£40	£125
1742	*	£5	£40	£125
1742/0	*	£10	£60	£150
1743	*	£5	£40	£125
1744	*	£5	£40	£125
1745	*	£5	£40	£125
1746	*	£5	£40	£125
1747	*	£5	£40	£125
1748	*	£2	£40	£125
1749	*	£2	£40	£125
1750	*	£5	£40	£125
1751	*	£5	£40	£125
1752	*	£5	£40	£125
1753	*	£5	£40	£125
1754	*	£5	£40	£125

GEORGE III

	F	VF	EF	BU
1770	£1	£40	£125	£300
1771	£1	£40	£110	£250
1771 no stop on reverse	£2	£40	£110	£250
1771 ball below spear head	£2	£40	£110	£250
1772	£2	£40	£110	£250
1772 GEORIVS	£18	£100	£175	£350
1772 ball below spear head	£2	£40	£110	£250
1772 no stop on reverse	£2	£40	£110	£250
1773	£2	£40	£110	£250
1773 no stop after REX	£2	£40	£110	£250
1773 no stop on reverse	£2	£40	£110	£300
1774	£2	£40	£110	£250
1775	£3	£40	£110	£250
1799 5 incuse gunports	*	£5	£30	£75
1799 6 relief gunports	*	£5	£30	£75
1799 9 relief gunports	*	*	£30	£100
1799 no gunports ...	*	*	£30	£85
1799 no gunports and raised line along hull	*	£5	£35	£100
1806 no berries on olive branch	*	*	£25	£75

	F	VF	EF	BU
1806 line under SOHO 3 berries	*	*	£25	£7?
1807 similar but double-cut border bead between B and R	*	*	£30	£8?

GEORGE IV

	F	VF	EF	BU
1825	*	£2	£50	£11?

George IV 1826 halfpenny

	F	VF	EF	BU
1826 two incuse lines down cross	*	£5	£50	£12?
1826 raised line down centre of cross ...	*	£5	£50	£12?
1827	*	£5	£50	£12?

WILLIAM IV

	F	VF	EF	BU
1831	*	£5	£45	£12?
1834	*	£5	£45	£12?
1837	*	£4	£40	£125

VICTORIA

	F	VF	EF	BU
1838	*	£3	£20	£4?
1839 proof	*	*	*	£12?
1839 proof, rev inv	*	*	*	£15?
1841	*	£3	£20	£4?
1843	£3	£10	£50	£10?
1844	£1	£5	£40	£8?
1845	£18	£40	£250	£65?
1846	£2	£5	£40	£6?
1847	£1	£10	£40	£6?
1848	£1	£5	£40	£6?
1848/3	£15	£25	*	*
1848/7	£1	£3	£20	£5?
1851	£1	£3	£20	£6?
1851 7 incuse dots on and above shield	*	£3	£20	£6?
1852	*	£3	£20	£6?
1852 7 incuse dots on and above shield	*	£3	£20	£5?
1853	*	£3	£20	£4?
1853/2	£3	£10	£45	*
1854	*	£3	£15	£4?

Victoria 1853 copper halfpenny

	F	VF	EF	BU
1855	*	£3	£15	£4?
1856	*	£3	£20	£6?
1857	*	£3	£20	£4?

	F	VF	EF	BU
1857 7 incuse dots on and above shield	*	£5	£20	£55
1858	*	£5	£20	£55
1858/6	£2	£10	£30	£75
1858/7	£1	£5	£20	£55
1858 small date	£1	£5	£20	£55
1859	£1	£5	£20	£55
1859/8	£3	£10	£50	*
1860	*	*	*	£2000

Bronze halfpennies

VICTORIA	F	VF	EF	BU
1860	*	£5	£20	£50
1860 TB 7 berries in wreath	*	£5	£25	£60
1860 TB4 berries in wreath	*	£5	£25	£60
1860 TB similar but centres of four of leaves are double incuse lines	£5	£10	£35	£95
1861 obv 4 berries, 15 leaves, raised leaf centres, rev L.C.W. on rock	*	£5	£25	£75
1861 same obv, rev no signature			ext. rare	
1861 same but lighthouse has no vertical lines	£6	£10	£35	£95
1861 obv 4 berries, 4 double incuse leaf centres, rev L.C.W. on rock ...	*	£2	£25	£50
1861 same obv, rev no signature	£5	£8	£35	£100
1861 obv 7 double incuse leaf centres, rev L.C.W on rock	*	£2	£35	£65
1861 same obv, rev no signature	*	£2	£20	£45
1861 obv 16 leaves, rev lighthouse has rounded top	*	£2	£20	£45
1861 same obv, rev lighthouse has pointed top	*	£2	£20	£45
1861 no signature ...	*	£2	£20	£45
1862 L.C.W. on rock	*	£4	£20	£60
1862 letter (A,B or C) left of lighthouse base ...	£50	£125	£350	*
1863	*	£2	£20	£45
1864	*	£4	£25	£60
1865	*	£2	£25	£60
1865/3	£10	£50	£200	*
1866	*	£2	£20	£50
1867	*	£2	£25	£60
1868	*	£2	£25	£60

Victoria 1889 bronze halfpenny

BRONZE HALFPENNIES

	F	VF	EF	BU
1869	*	£5	£25	£85
1870	*	£4	£25	£60
1871	£10	£35	£125	£325
1872	*	£2	£20	£45
1873	*	£5	£25	£65
1874	*	£8	£30	£75
1874H	*	£2	£20	£40
1875	*	£2	£20	£40
1875H	*	£6	£25	£60
1876H	*	£2	£20	£45
1877	*	£2	£20	£45
1878	*	£15	£45	£175
1879	*	£2	£20	£40
1880	*	£2	£20	£40
1881	*	£2	£20	£40
1881H	*	£2	£20	£40
1882H	*	£2	£20	£40
1883	*	£2	£20	£40
1884	*	£2	£20	£40
1885	*	£2	£20	£40
1886	*	£1.50	£20	£40
1887	*	£1	£20	£40
1888	*	£1	£20	£40
1889	*	£1	£20	£40
1889/8	*	£8	£30	£85
1890	*	£1	£20	£50
1891	*	£1	£20	£40
1892	*	£1	£20	£40
1893	*	*	£20	£40
1894	*	£5	£25	£45
1895 OH	*	*	£2	£35
1896	*	*	£2	£30
1897 normal horizon	*	*	£2	£30
1897 higher horizon	*	*	£2	£30
1898	*	*	£5	£30
1899	*	*	£3	£30
1900	*	*	£15	£20
1901	*	*	£1	£10

EDWARD VII				
1902 low horizon ...	*	£5	£28	£65
1902	*	*	£5	£15
1903	*	*	£8	£25
1904	*	*	£10	£30
1905	*	*	£6	£20
1906	*	*	£6	£20
1907	*	*	£6	£20
1908	*	*	£6	£20
1909	*	*	£8	£25
1910	*	*	£8	£25

GEORGE V				
1911	*	*	£3	£15
1912	*	*	£3	£15

George V 1912 halfpenny

1913	*	*	£5	£20
1914	*	*	£3	£15
1915	*	*	£3	£15

BRONZE HALFPENNIES

	Fair	F	VF	EF
1916		*	£2	£15
1917	*	*	£2	£15
1918	*	*	£2	£15
1919	*	*	£2	£15
1920	*	*	£2	£15
1921	*	*	£2	£15
1922	*	*	£3	£15
1923	*	*	£2	£15
1924	*	*	£3	£15
1925	*	*	£4	£15
1925 mod effigy	*	*	£4	£20
1926	*	*	£4	£15
1927	*	*	£2.50	£12
1928	*	*	£2	£12
1929	*	*	£2	£12
1930	*	*	£2	£12
1931	*	*	£2	£12
1932	*	*	£2	£12
1933	*	*	£2	£15
1934	*	*	£2	£15
1935	*	*	£2	£10
1936	*	*	£2	£8

GEORGE VI

	Fair	F	VF	EF
1937	*	*	*	£1
1938	*	*	*	£2
1939	*	*	*	£2
1940	*	*	*	£3
1941	*	*	*	£3
1942	*	*	*	£1
1943	*	*	*	£1
1944	*	*	*	£2
1945	*	*	*	£1
1946	*	*	£2	£4
1947	*	*	*	£3
1948	*	*	*	£1
1949	*	*	*	£1
1950	*	*	*	£4
1951	*	*	*	£5
1952	*	*	*	£2

ELIZABETH II

	Fair	F	VF	EF
1953	*	*	*	£2
1954	*	*	*	£3
1955	*	*	*	£3
1956	*	*	*	£3
1957	*	*	*	£1
1958	*	*	*	£0.50
1959	*	*	*	£0.25
1960	*	*	*	£0.20
1962	*	*	*	*
1963	*	*	*	*
1964	*	*	*	*
1965	*	*	*	*
1966	*	*	*	*
1967	*	*	*	*

Copper farthings

Copper unless otherwise stated

OLIVER CROMWELL

	Fair	F	VF	EF
Patterns only	*	£1750	£3500	*

CHARLES II

	Fair	F	VF	EF
1671 patterns only	*	*	£100	£350
1672	£1	£4	£60	£250
1672 no stop on obverse	£2.75	£6	£75	£275
1672 loose drapery at Britannia's elbow	£2	£6	£75	£275
1673	£1	£5	£60	£250

Oliver Cromwell copper farthing

	Fair	F	VF	EF
1673 CAROLA	*	£35	*	*
1673 BRITANNIA	*	*	*	*
1673 no stops on obverse	£2	£5	£85	£300
1673 no stop on reverse	£2	£5	£85	£300
1674	£1	£4	£60	£250
1675	£1	£2.75	£60	£250
1675 no stop after CAROLVS	*	£35	*	£100
1676	*	*	*	*
1679	£1.50	£4	£60	£275
1679 no stop on reverse	*	*	*	*
1684 (tin) various edge readings	£12	£50	£250	£800
1685 (tin)	£15	£70	£275	£825

JAMES II

	Fair	F	VF	EF
1684 (tin)	£30	£80	£275	£800
1685 (tin) various edge readings	£20	£35	£200	*
1686 (tin) various edge readings	£20	£50	£200	*
1687 (tin)	*	*	*	*
1687 (tin) draped bust, various readings	*	*	*	*

WILLIAM AND MARY

	Fair	F	VF	EF
1689 (tin) date in exergue and on edge, many varieties	£15	£45	£200	*
1689/90 (tin) 1689 in exergue, 1690 on edge	*	*	*	*
1689/90 (tin) 1690 in exergue, 1689 on edge	*	*	*	*
1690 (tin) various types	£12	£30	£200	£800
1691 (tin) small and large figures	£12	£30	£200	£800
1692 (tin)	£15	£35	£200	£800
1694 many varieties	£2	£15	£75	£350

WILLIAM III
Type 1, date in exergue

	Fair	F	VF	EF
1695	£3	£7	£75	£350
1695 M over V	*	*	*	*
1696	£2	£5	£65	£350
1697	£2	£5	£60	£350

William III 1697 farthing

	Fair	F	VF	EF
1698	£5	£12	£75	*
1699	£2	£5	£65	£400
1700	£2	£5	£50	£375

	Fair	F	VF	EF
Type 2, date in legend				
1698	£4	£10	£60	£400
1699	£2	£10	£50	£400

Anne 1714 pattern farthing

ANNE

	Fair	F	VF	EF
1714 patterns (**F**) ...	£50	£150	£275	£350

George I 'dump' farthing of 1717

GEORGE I

'Dump Type'

	Fair	F	VF	EF
1717	£12	£50	£150	£300
1718 silver proof ...	*	*	*	£600
Larger flan				
1719 large lettering on obverse	£3	£10	£60	£250
1719 small lettering on obverse	£3	£10	£75	£275
1719 – last A of BRITANNIA over I	*	*	*	*

George I 1719 farthing

	Fair	F	VF	EF
1719 legend continuous over bust	£7	£25	*	*
1720 large lettering on obverse	£3	£10	£50	£250
1720 small lettering on obverse	£2	£5	£45	£250
1721	£2	£4	£40	£250
1721/0	£10	£30	*	*
1722 large lettering on obverse	£4	£10	£50	£250
1722 small lettering on obverse	£3	£8	£45	£250
1723	£2	£5	£40	£225
1723 R of REX over R	£8	*	*	*
1724	£5	£10	£50	£300

COPPER FARTHINGS

George II 1730 farthing

GEORGE II

	Fair	F	VF	EF
1730	*	£3	£20	£110
1731	*	£3	£25	£110
1732	*	£5	£25	£110
1733	*	£3	£20	£110
1734	*	£2	£20	£110
1734 no stops on obverse	*	£3	£30	£120
1735	*	£2	£20	£110
1735 3 over 3	*	£8	£35	£150
1736	*	£3	£20	£110
1736 triple tie-riband	*	*	*	*
1737 sm date	*	£2	£20	£110
1737 lge date	*	£3	£25	£110
1739	*	£2	£20	£80
1739/5	*	*	*	*
1741 Old Head	*	£3	£20	£50
1744	*	£2	£20	£45
1746	*	£2	£20	£45
1746 V over U	*	*	*	*
1749	*	£2	£20	£45
1750	*	£2	£20	£45
1754/0	*	£12	£35	£150
1754	*	£2	£20	£40

	F	VF	EF	BU
GEORGE III				
1771	*	£15	£65	£165
1773	*	£3	£35	£135
1774	*	£3	£35	£135
1775	*	£3	£40	£135
1799	*	*	£5	£40
1806	*	£1	£8	£50
1807	*	£2	£10	£45
GEORGE IV				
1821	*	£1	£30	£60
1822	*	£1	£30	£60
1823	*	£2	£30	£60
1825	*	£2	£30	£60
1825 D of DEI over U	£2	£5	£50	*
1826 date on rev ...	*	£1	£30	£60
1826 date on obv ...	*	£2	£35	£65
1826 I for 1 in date	*	*	*	*
1827	*	£2	£35	£65
1828	*	£2	£40	£90
1829	*	£3	£40	£90
1830	*	£2	£35	£75
WILLIAM IV				
1831	*	£2	£35	£90
1834	*	£2	£35	£90
1835	*	£2	£40	£110
1836	*	£2	£40	£110
1837	*	£2	£35	£90
VICTORIA				
1838	*	£2	£15	£40
1839	*	£2	£12	£35

COPPER FARTHINGS

	F	VF	EF	BU
1840	*	£2	£20	£40
1841	*	£2	£15	£30
1842	*	£4	£25	£45
1843	*	£2	£15	£35
1843 I for 1	*	£5	£35	£100
1844	£10	£50	£250	£650
1845	*	£3	£20	£50
1846	*	£5	£25	£60
1847	*	£2	£20	£50
1848	*	£3	£20	£55
1849	*	£7	£50	£200
1850	*	£2	£25	£50
1851	*	£6	£30	£90
1851 D over D	£10	£50	£250	£650
1852	*	£7	£30	£100
1853 w.w. raised ...	*	£1	£15	£35
1853 ww inc	*	£2	£20	£40
1854 ww inc	*	£2	£20	£40
1855 ww inc	*	£2	£20	£45
1855 ww raised ...	*	£4	£25	£50
1856	*	£3	£30	£60
1856 R over E	£10	£50	£250	£650
1857	*	£2	£15	£30
1858	*	£1	£15	£30
1859	*	£7	£30	£70
1860 proof	*	*	*	£3500

Bronze farthings

VICTORIA	F	VF	EF	BU
1860 RB	*	£2	£15	£30
1860 TB/RB (mule)	£25	£60	£100	*
1860 TB	*	£1	£15	£30
1861	*	£1	£12	£30
1862 small 8	*	£2	£12	£25
1862 large 8	*	£3	£15	£30
1863	£8.30	£20	£50	*
1864	*	£2	£12	£30
1865 large 8	*	£1	£12	£30
1865–5/2	*	£3	£15	£30
1865–5/3	*	£2	£18	£35
1865 small 8	*	£1	£10	£30
1865–5/3	*	£2	£18	£35
1866	*	*	£10	£25
1867	*	£1	£10	£25
1868	*	£2	£15	£28
1869	*	£2	£18	£35
1872	*	£2	£18	£28
1873	*	£1	£10	£38
1874 H	*	£2	£10	£25
1874 H both Gs over	£30	*	*	*
1875 5 berries/large date	£5	£10	£30	*
1875 5 berries/small date	*	*	*	*
1875 4 berries/small date	£6	£12	£35	*
1875 H 4 berries/small date	*	*	£10	£25
1876 H	*	£5	£20	£40
1877 proof	*	*	*	£1750
1878	*	*	£10	£25
1879	*	£1	£12	£25
1879 large 9	*	£2	£15	£25
1880 4 berries	*	£2	£15	£25
1880 3 berries	*	£5	£20	£40
1881 4 berries	*	£5	£20	£40
1881 3 berries	*	£2	£10	£18

	F	VF	EF	BU
1881 H 3 berries ...	*	£2	£10	£20
1882 H	*	£1	£8	£20
1883	*	£3	£12	£30
1884	*	*	£6	£20
1886	*	*	£6	£20
1887	*	*	£15	£22
1890	*	*	£10	£22
1891	*	*	£10	£22
1892	*	£3	£18	330
1893	*	*	£5	£18
1894	*	*	£5	£22
1895	*	£10	£35	£100
1895 OH	*	*	£3	£12

Victoria 1896, Old Head Farthing

	F	VF	EF	BU
1897 bright finish ...	*	*	£2	£15
1897 black finish higher horizon ...	*	*	£1	£12
1898	*	*	£2	£15
1899	*	*	£1	£12
1900	*	*	£1	£12
1901	*	*	£1	£10

Edward VII, 1907 Farthing

EDWARD VII				
1902	*	*	£1	£6
1903 low horizon ...	*	*	£2	£10
1904	*	*	£2	£10
1905	*	*	£2	£10
1906	*	*	£2	£10
1907	*	*	£2	£10
1908	*	*	£2	£10
1909	*	*	£2	£10
1910	*	*	£3	£12

GEORGE V				
1911	*	*	*	£4
1912	*	*	*	£4
1913	*	*	*	£4
1914	*	*	*	£4
1915	*	*	*	£4
1916	*	*	*	£4
1917	*	*	*	£4
1918 black finish ...	*	*	*	£6
1919 bright finish ...	*	*	*	£2
1919	*	*	*	£2
1920	*	*	*	£4
1921	*	*	*	£3
1922	*	*	*	£4
1923	*	*	*	£4
1924	*	*	*	£4
1925	*	*	*	£4

	F	VF	EF	BU
1926 modified effigy	*	*	*	£4
1927	*	*	*	£4
1928	*	*	*	£2
1929	*	*	*	£2
1930	*	*	*	£2
1931	*	*	*	£2
1932	*	*	*	£2
1933	*	*	*	£2
1934	*	*	*	£3
1935	*	*	£1.50	£5
1936	*	*	*	£1

George VI 1951 farthing (wren on reverse)

GEORGE VI
	F	VF	EF	BU
1937	*	*	*	£1
1938	*	*	*	£2
1939	*	*	*	£1
1940	*	*	*	£2
1941	*	*	*	£1
1942	*	*	*	£1
1943	*	*	*	£1
1944	*	*	*	£1
1945	*	*	*	£1
1946	*	*	*	£1
1947	*	*	*	£1
1948	*	*	*	£1
1949	*	*	*	£1
1950	*	*	*	£1
1951	*	*	*	£1
1952	*	*	*	£1

ELIZABETH II
	F	VF	EF	BU
1953	*	*	*	£0.50
1954	*	*	*	£0.35
1955	*	*	*	£0.35
1956	*	*	*	£1

Fractions of farthings

COPPER HALF FARTHINGS

GEORGE IV
	F	VF	EF	BU
1828 Britannia breaks legend	£5	£20	£75	£175
1828 Britannia below legend	£8	£35	£125	*
1830 lge date	£5	£25	£85	£200
1830 sm date	£6	£30	£100	*

WILLIAM IV
	F	VF	EF	BU
1837	*	£15	£75	£250

Victoria 1839 half farthing

BRONZE FARTHINGS
	F	VF	EF	BU
VICTORIA				
1839	*	£2	£15	£50
1842	*	£2	£10	£40
1843	*	*	£1	£10
1844	*	*	£1	£8
1844 E over N	£3	£12	£75	£250
1847	*	£3	£10	£40
1851	*	£3	£12	£45
1852	*	£3	£20	£50
1853	*	£4	£35	£75
1854	*	£4	£40	£95
1856	*	£5	£50	£110
1856 large date ...	£6	£25	*	*
1868 bronze proof	*	*	*	£150
1868 copper-nickel proof	*	*	*	£300

COPPER THIRD FARTHINGS
	F	VF	EF	BU
GEORGE IV				
1827	*	£5	£25	£100
WILLIAM IV				
1835	*	£5	£30	£100
VICTORIA				
1844	*	£8	£25	£75
1844 RE for REG ...	£20	£35	£95	*
1844 large G in REG	*	£8	£25	£75

BRONZE THIRD FARTHINGS
	F	VF	EF	BU
VICTORIA				
1866	*	*	£10	£30
1868	*	*	£10	£30
1876	*	*	£12	£35
1878	*	*	£10	£30
1881	*	*	£10	£30
1884	*	*	£5	£15
1885	*	*	£5	£15

Edward VII 1902 third farthing

	F	VF	EF	BU
EDWARD VIII				
1902	*	*	£6	£15
GEORGE V				
1913	*	*	£8	£20

COPPER QUARTER FARTHINGS
	F	VF	EF	BU
VICTORIA				
1839	£3	£10	£25	£50

Victoria 1839 quarter farthing

	F	VF	EF	BU
1851	£4	£12	£35	£60
1852	£3	£10	£25	£50
1853	£5	£12	£30	£60
1868 bronze-proof ...	*	*	*	£200
1868 copper-nickel proof	*	*	*	£350

Decimal coinage

f denotes face value

ELIZABETH II

BRITANNIAS

A United Kingdom gold bullion coin introduced in the autumn of 1987 contains one ounce of 22ct gold and has a face value of £100. There are also half ounce, quarter ounce and one-tenth ounce versions, with face values of £50, £25 and £10 respectively. All are legal tender.

The Britannia coins bear a portrait of The Queen on the obverse and the figure of Britannia on the reverse.

	BU
1987, 1988, 1989, 1991, 1992,	
1993, 1994, 1995, 1996, 1997 1oz, proof ...	**£550**
1987 to 1997 inclusive ½oz, proof	*
1987 to 1997 inclusive ¼oz, proof	*
1987 to 1997 inclusive ⅒oz, proof	**£65**
(½ and ¼ oz issued only in sets)	

To commemorate the 10th anniversary of the first Britannia issue, new reverse designs were introduced for the gold coins as well as a series of 4 silver coins with denominations from £2 to 20 pence. The silver coins were issued in Proof condition only for 1997.

1997. 1oz, ¼oz, ⅒oz issued individually (all coins issued in 4-coin sets)
1997. 1oz, ¼oz silver coins issued individually (all coins issued in 4-coin sets)
1998. Gold and silver coins issued with new portrait of HM the Queen and first reverse design.

FIVE POUNDS

1984 gold, BU	**£400**
1985 – –	**£425**
1986 – –	**£425**
1987 – new uncoupled effigy	**£425**
1988 – –	**£425**
1989 – BU, 500th anniversary of	
the sovereign	**£450**
1990 gold, BU	**£435**
1990 Queen Mother's 90th birthday, gold,	
proof	**£600**
1990 – silver, proof	**£35**
1990 – cu-ni, BU	**£10**
1991 gold, BU	**£450**
1992 gold, BU	**£450**
1993 40th Anniversary of The Coronation	
gold, proof	**£700**
1993 – silver, proof	**£32**
1993 – cu-ni, BU	**£10**
1993 gold BU	**£475**
1994 gold BU	**£500**
1995 gold BU	**£535**
1996 Queen's 70th birthday, gold, proof	**£645**
1996 – silver, proof	**£33**
1996 – cu-ni, BU	**£10**
1996 – gold, BU	**£575**
1997 Golden Wedding, gold, proof	**£650**
1997 – silver, proof	**£32**

(Gold versions also listed in FIVE POUNDS section of milled gold.) In 1984 the Royal Mint issued the first of an annual issue of Brilliant Uncirculated £5 coins. These bear the letter 'U' in a circle.

1997 – cu-ni, BU	**£10**
1997 – gold, BU	**£535**
1998 Prince Charles 50th Birthday, gold, proof	
... ...	**£600**
1998 – silver, proof	**£33**
1998 – cu-ni, BU	**£10**
1998 – gold, BU	**£535**
1999 Diana Memorial, gold, proof	**£600**
1999 – silver, proof	**£33**
1999 – cu-ni, BU	**£10**
1999 Millennium, gold, proof	**£600**
1999 – silver, proof	**£33**
1999 cu-ni, BU	**£10**
1999 gold, BU	**£480**
2000 Millennium, gold, proof	**£495**
2000 silver with 22 carat gold, proof	**£37**
2000 cu-ni, BU	**£10**
2000 Queen Mother commemorative,	
gold, proof	**£495**
2000 silver, proof	**£35**
2000 silver, piedfort	**£68**
2000 cu-ni, BU	**£10**
2000 gold, BU	**£480**

TWO POUNDS

1983 gold, proof	**£225**
1986 Commonwealth Games (nickel brass)	
... ...	**£4**
1986 –, in folder, BU	**£6**
1986 silver unc	**£15**
1986 – – proof	**£20**
1986 gold, proof	**£225**
1987 gold, proof	**£250**
1988 gold, proof	**£250**
1989 Bill of Rights (nickel brass)	**£4**
1989 –, in folder, BU	**£6**
1989 – silver, proof	**£23**
1989 Claim of Right (nickel brass)	**£4**
1989 Bill of Rights (nickel brass)	**£4**
1989 –, in folder, BU	**£6**
(For 1989 £2 piedforts see sets)	
1989 500th anniversary of the sovereign,	
gold, proof	**£275**
1990 gold, proof	**£250**
1991 gold, proof	**£250**
1993 gold, proof	**£250**
1994 Bank of England, gold, proof	**£425**
1994 –, gold 'mule', proof	**£600**
1994 –, silver, proof	**£30**
1994 –, silver piedfort, proof	**£50**
1994 –, in folder, BU	**£8**
1994	**£4**
1995 50th Anniverary of end of Second	
World War, silver, proof	**£27**
1995 ditto, in folder, BU	**£8**
1995 –, silver, piedfort, proof	**£50**
1995 –, gold, proof	**£375**
1995 50th Anniversary of United Nations,	
gold, proof	**£300**
1995 –, in folder, BU	**£6**
1995 –, silver, piedfort, proof	**£50**
1995 –, proof	**£30**
1995	**£4**

996 European Football, gold, proof	**£350**
996 –, silver, proof	**£27**
996 –, silver, piedfort	**£50**
996 –, in folder, BU	**£6**
996	**£4**
997 Bimetal, gold, proof	**£350**
997 –, silver, proof	**£29**
997 –, in folder, BU	**£6**
997 silver, piedfort	**£50**
997	**£4**
998 Bimetal, silver, proof	**£29**
998 – silver, piedfort	**£50**
998 – proof	**£6**
998 –, in folder, BU	**£6**
998	**£4**
1999 Rugby World Cup, gold, proof	**£300**
999 – silver, proof	**£30**
999 – silver, piedfort	**£75**
1999 –, in folder, BU	**£6**
1999	**£4**

(Gold versions are also listed in TWO POUNDS section of milled gold.)

ONE POUND

1983	**£2**
1983 Unc, in folder	**£5**
1983 silver, proof	**£30**
1983 – – piedfort	**£120**
1984 Scottish reverse	**£2**
1984 – Unc, in folder	**£5**
1984 – silver, proof	**£20**
1984 – – piedfort	**£50**
1985 New portrait, Welsh reverse	**£2**
1985 – – Unc, in folder	**£5**
1985 – – silver, proof	**£22**
1985 – – piedfort	**£50**
1986 Northern Ireland reverse	**£2**
1986 – Unc, in folder	**£5**
1986 – silver, proof	**£25**
1986 – – – piedfort	**£50**
1987 English reverse	**£2**
1987 – Unc, in folder	**£3**
1987 – silver, proof	**£20**
1987 – – – piedfort	**£50**
1988 Royal Arms reverse	**£2**
1988 – Unc, in folder	**£5**
1988 – silver, proof	**£30**
1988 – – – piedfort	**£50**
1989 Scottish rev as 1984,	
silver, proof	**£20**
1989 – – – silver, piedfort	**£50**
1990 Welsh reverse as 1985	**£2**
1990 – silver, proof	**£30**
1991 Northern Ireland rev as 1986,	
silver proof	**£25**
1992 English rev as 1987,	
silver, proof	**£25**
1993 Royal Coat of Arms (reverse as	
1983), silver, proof	**£30**
1993 – – – piedfort	**£50**
1994 Scottish Lion, silver, proof	**£35**
Ditto, Unc. in folder	**£5**
1994 – silver, piedfort	**£50**

1995 Welsh dragon, silver, proof	**£25**
Ditto, Unc in folder, Welsh version	**£5**
1995 – silver, piedfort	**£50**
1996 Northern Ireland Celtic Ring	
Unc in folder	**£5**
Silver, proof	**£27**
Silver, piedfort	**£50**
1997 English Lions Unc, in folder	**£5**
silver, proof	**£30**
silver, piedfort	**£45**
1998 Royal coat of arms/reverse as 1983,	
silver, proof	**£25**
silver, piedfort	**£45**
1999 Scottish Lion (reverse as 1984)	
new portrait, silver proof	**£25**
silver, piedfort	**£45**
2000 Welsh Dragon (reverse as 1995)	
new portrait, silver, proof	**£25**
silver, piedfort	**£47**

Note that the edge inscriptions on £2 and £1 appear either upright or inverted in relation to the obverse. (Sovereign and half sovereign prices are not listed here but in the main listings under milled gold.)

FIFTY PENCE

1969	**£1**
1970	**£1**
1973 EEC	**£1**
1973 – proof	**£3**
1976-1981	**f**
1982 rev changed to FIFTY PENCE	
instead of NEW PENCE	**f**
1983, 1985	**f**
1992 European Community	**f**
1992 – silver, proof	**£30**
1992 – silver, proof piedfort	**£55**
1992 – gold, proof	**£400**
1994 Normandy landing	**f**
1994 – silver, proof	**£28**
1994 – silver, piedfort	**£50**
1994 – gold, proof	**£400**
1997 new size (27.3mm diameter)	
silver, proof	**£27**
silver, piedfort	**£46**
1997 old and new size,	
silver proofs	**£50**
1998, 1998	**f**
1998 European Presidency	**£2**
1998 – silver, proof	**£25**
1998 – silver, piedfort	**£45**
1998 – gold, proof	**£250**
1998 National Health Service Commemorative £2	
1998 – silver, proof	**£25**
1998 – silver, piedfort	**£45**
1998 – gold, proof	**£250**
1999 Britannia reverse	*****
2000 Library Commemorative	**£2**
2000 –, in folder, BU	**£5**
2000 –, silver, proof	**£25**
2000 –, silver, piedfort	**£47**
2000 –, gold, proof	**£250**

TWENTY-FIVE PENCE

1972 Silver Wedding	**£1**
1972 – silver, proof	**£25**
1977 Jubilee	**£1**
1977 – silver, proof	**£20**
1980 Queen Mother's 80th birthday	**£1**
1980 – in blister pack	**£3**
1980 – silver, proof	**£32**
1981 Royal Wedding	**£1**
1981 – in folder	**£3**
1981 – silver, proof	**£30**

TWENTY PENCE

1982	f
1982 silver, proof piedfort	**£40**
1983, 1984, 1985, 1987, 1988-1999	f

TEN PENCE

1968	**£0.25**
1969	**£0.25**
1970	**£0.20**
1971	**£0.20**
1973	**£0.20**
1974-1977, 1979-1981	f
1992 new size (24.5mm diameter)	
silver, proof, piedfort	**£30**
1992 old and new size,	
silver, proofs	**£30**
1992, 1995, 1997 – cu-ni	f

FIVE PENCE

1968-1971	*
1975, 1977-1980, 1987, 1988, 1989	f
1990 silver, proof, old and new	**£26**
1990 silver, piedfort	**£30**
1990, 1991, 1992, 1994-1999 – cu-ni	f

TWO PENCE

1971	*
1973-1981	f
1985 new portrait, rev changed to	
TWO PENCE instead of NEW PENCE	*
1986-1999	f

ONE PENNY

1971	*
1973-1981	f
1982 rev changed to ONE PENNY	
instead of NEW PENNY	f
1983, 1984	f
1985 new portrait	f
1986-1999	f

HALF PENNY

1971	*
1973-81	*
1982 rev changed to HALFPENNY	
instead of 1/2 NEW PENNY	*
1983	*

Proof and Specimen Sets

Proof or specimen sets have been issued since 1887 by the Royal Mint in official cases. Prior to that date, sets were issued privately by the engraver. Some sets are of currency coins, easily distinguishable from proofs which have a vastly superior finish. The two 1887 sets frequently come on to the market, hence their place in this list. The 1953 'plastic' set, though made up of currency coins, is official. It was issued in a plastic packet, hence the name. Apart from the seats stated, as being uncirculated, currency or specimen, all those in the following listing are proof sets.

GEORGE IV   FDC
New issue, **1826**. Five pounds to farthing (11 coins) **£18000**

WILLIAM IV
Coronation, **1831**. Two pounds to farthing (14 coins) **£15000**

VICTORIA
Young head, **1839**. 'Una and the Lion' five pounds plus sovereign to farthing (15 coins) **£27500**
Young head, **1853**. Sovereign to half farthing, including 'Gothic' crown (16 coins) **£25000**
Jubilee head, Golden Jubilee, **1887**. Five pounds to Threepence ('full set' – 11 coins) **£5500**
As above, currency set (unofficial) **£1400**
Jubilee head, Golden Jubilee, **1887**. Crown to threepence ('short set' – 7 coins) **£950**
As above, currency set (unofficial) **£200**
Old head, **1893**. Five pounds to threepence ('full set') – 10 coins) **£6500**
Old head, **1893**. Crown to threepence ('short set' – 6 coins) **£1100**

EDWARD VII
Coronation, **1902**. Five pounds to Maundy penny – matt proofs (13 coins) **£1400**
Coronation, **1902**. Sovereign to Maundy penny – matt proofs (11 coins) ... ... · **£450**

GEORGE V
Coronation, **1911**. Five pounds to Maundy penny (12 coins) **£2250**
Coronation, **1911**. Sovereign to Maundy penny (10 coins) ... ... · **£750**
Coronation, **1911**. Halfcrown to Maundy penny (8 coins) ... ... · **£300**
New types, **1927**. Crown to threepence (6 coins) ... ... · **£225**

GEORGE VI
Coronation, **1937**. Gold set, five pounds to half sovereign (4 coins) **£1400**
Coronation, **1937**. Silver and bronze set, crown to farthing including Maundy money (15 coins) **£120**
Mid-century, **1950**. Halfcrown to farthing (9 coins) **£40**
Festival of Britain, **1951**. Crown to farthing (10 coins) **£50**

ELIZABETH II
Coronation, **1953**. Crown to farthing (10 coins) **£55**
Coronation, **1953**. Currency ('plastic') set, official, halfcrown to farthing (9 coins) **£15**
Specimen decimal set, **1968**. 10p, 5p; **1971** 2p, 1p, ½p in wallet (5 coins) **£1**
Last £sd coins, **1970**. (sets issued 1971-73). Halfcrown to Halfpenny (8 coins) **£15**
Proof decimal set, **1971**. (issued 1973), 50p, 10p, 5p, 2p, 1p, ½p (6 coins) **£15**
Proof decimal set, **1972**. 50p, Sliver Wedding, 25p, 10p, 5p, 2p, 1p, ½p (7 coins) **£15**
Proof decimal sets, **1973, 1974, 1975, 1976**. 50p, to ½p (6 coins) **£12**
Proof decimal set, **1977**. 50p to ½p, plus Jubilee crown (7 coins) **£13**
Proof decimal set, **1978**. 50p to ½p (6 coins) **£15**
Proof decimal set, **1979**. 50p to ½p (6 coins) **£15**
Proof decimal set, **1980**. 50p to ½p (6 coins) **£11**
Proof gold set, **1980**. Five pounds, two pounds, sovereign, half sovereign (4 coins) **£600**
Commemorative proof coin set, **1981**. Five pounds, sovereign, Royal Wedding Silver crown,
50p to ½p (9 coins) **£600**
Commemorative set, **1981**. Sovereign and Royal Wedding silver crown (2 coins) **£125**
Proof decimal set, **1981**. 50p to ½p (6 coins) **£11**
Proof gold set, **1982**. Five pounds, two pounds, sovereign, half sovereign (4 coins) **£725**
Proof decimal set, **1982**. 50p to ½p including 20p (7 coins) **£14**
Uncirculated decimal set, **1982**. 50p to ½p including 20p (7 coins) **£8**
Proof gold set, **1983**. Two pounds, sovereign, half sovereign (3 coins) **£325**
Proof decimal set, **1983**. £1 to ½p (8 coins) **£18**
Uncirculated decimal set, **1983**. £1 to ½p (8 coins) **£12**
Proof gold set, **1984**. Five pounds, sovereign, half sovereign (3 coins) **£575**
Proof decimal set, **1984**. £1 (Scottish rev) to ½p (8 coins) **£16**
Uncirculated decimal set, **1984**. £1 (Scottish rev) to ½p (8 coins) **£13**
Proof gold set, **1985**. new portrait. Five pounds, two pounds, sovereign, half sovereign (4 coins) **£750**
Proof decimal set, **1985**. new portrait. £1 (Welsh rev) to 1p (7 coins) in de luxe case **£20**
Proof decimal set, **1985**. As above, in standard case **£16**
Uncirculated decimal set, **1985**. £1 (Welsh rev) to 1p (7 coins) **£12**
Proof gold set, **1986**. Commonwealth Games two pounds, sovereign, half sovereign (3 coins) **£350**
Proof decimal set, **1986**. Commonwealth Games £2, Northern Ireland £1.50p to 1p (8 coins),
de luxe case **£25**
Proof decimal set, **1986**. As above in standard case **£20**
Uncirculated decimal set, **1986**. As above, in folder **£12**
Proof gold Britannia set, **1987**. One ounce, half ounce, quarter ounce tenth ounce (4 coins) **£650**
Proof decimal set, **1987**. Quarter ounce, tenth ounce (2 coins) **£150**

Proof gold set, **1987.** Two pounds, sovereign, half sovereign (3 coins) £325

Proof decimal set, **1987.** £1 (English rev) to 1p (7 coins) in de luxe case £23

Proof decimal set, **1987.** As above, in standing case £18

Uncirculated decimal set, **1987.** As above, in folder £10

Proof gold Britannia set, **1988.** One ounce, half ounce, quarter ounce, tenth ounce (4 coins) £615

Proof gold Britannia set, **1988.** Quarter ounce, tenth ounce (2 coins) £150

Proof gold set, **1988.** Two pounds, sovereign, half sovereign (3 coins) £325

Proof decimal set **1988.** £1 (Royal Arms rev) to 1p (7 coins) in de luxe case £26

Proof decimal set, **1988.** As above, in standard case £19

Uncirculated decimal set, **1988.** As above, in folder £11

Proof gold Britannia set, **1989.** One ounce, half ounce, quarter ounce, tenth ounce (4 coins) £700

Proof gold Britannia set, **1989.** Quarter ounce, tenth ounce (2 coins) £150

Proof gold set, **1989.** 500th anniversary of the sovereign. Five pounds, two pounds, sovereign,
half sovereign (4 coins) £900

Proof gold set, **1989.** 500th anniversary of the sovereign. Two pounds, sovereign, half sovereign (3 coins) £450

Proof decimal set, **1989.** Bill of Rights £2. Claim of Right £2,
£1 (Scottish rev as 1984), 50p to 1p (9 coins) in de luxe case £32

Proof decimal set, **1989.** As above, in standard case £27

Proof silver, Bill of Rights £2. Claim of Right £2. **1989.** (2 coins) £40

Proof silver piedfort, **1989.** £2 as above (2 coins) £80

Uncirculated. **1989.** As above (2 coins) in folder £10

Uncirculated decimal set, **1989.** £1 (Scottish rev as 1984) to 1p (7 coins) £15

Proof gold Britannia set, 199**0** £775

Proof gold set, **1990.** Five pounds, two pounds, sovereign, half-sovereign (4 coins) £800

Proof gold set, **1990.** Two pounds, sovereign, half sovereign (3 coins) £375

Proof silver set, **1990.** Five pence (23.59mm diam) and five pence (18mm diam, new size) £24

Proof decimal set, **1990.** £1 (Welsh rev as 1985) to 1p including large and small 5p (8 coins) in deluxe case £30

Proof decimal set, **1990.** As above, in standard case £25

Uncirculated decimal set, **1990.** £1 (Welsh rev as 1985) to 1p including large and small 5p (8 coins) £15

Proof gold Britannia set, **1991.** £700

Proof gold set, **1991.** Five pounds, two pounds, sovereign, half sovereign (4 coins) £750

Proof gold set, **1991.** Two pounds, sovereign, half sovereign (3 coins) £400

Proof decimal set, **1991.** £1 to 1p (7 coins) in deluxe case £30

Proof decimal set, **1991.** As above, in standard case £25

Uncirculated decimal set, **1991.** (7 coins) £15

Proof gold Britannia set, **1992.** £700

Proof gold set, **1992.** Five pounds, two pounds, sovereign, half sovereign (4 coins) £750

Proof gold set, **1992.** Two pounds, sovereign, half sovereign (3 coins) £400

Proof decimal set, **1992.** £1 (English rev as 1987) to 1p (two 50p, new 10p) (9 coins) in deluxe case £32

Proof decimal set, **1992.** As above, in standard case £28

Uncirculated decimal set, **1992.** £15

Proof gold Britannia set, **1993.** £700

Proof gold set, **1993.** Five pounds, two pounds, sovereign, half sovereign (4 coins) £800

Proof gold set, **1993.** Two pounds, sovereign, half sovereign (3 coins) £400

Proof decimal set, **1993.** Coronation Anniversary £5, £1 to 1p (8 coins) in deluxe case £35

Proof decimal set, **1993.** As above, in standard case £30

Uncirculated decimal set, **1993** (with two 50p, no £5) (8 coins) £12

Proof gold Britannia set, **1994.** £775

Proof gold set, **1994.** Five pounds, two pounds Bank of England, sovereign, half sovereign (4 coins) £850

Proof gold set, **1994.** Two pounds Bank of England, sovereign, half sovereign (3 coins) £400

Proof decimal set, **1994.** £2 Bank of England, £1 (Scottish rev), 50p D-Day to 1p (8 coins) in deluxe case £34

Proof decimal set, **1994.** As above, in standard case £28

Uncirculated decimal set, **1994.** £14

Proof gold Britannia set, **1995.** £850

Proof godl set, **1995.** Five pounds, two pounds Peace, sovereign, half sovereign (4 coins) £900

Proof gold set, **1995.** Two pounds Peace, sovereign, half sovereign (3 coins) £450

Proof decimal set, **1995.** Two pounds Peace, £1 (Welsh rev) to 1p (8 coins) in deluxe case £36

Proof decimal set, **1995.** As above, in standard case £29

Uncirculated decimal set, **1995.** £12

Proof gold Britannia set, **1996.** £900

Proof gold set, **1996.** Five pounds, two pounds, sovereign, half sovereign (4 coins) £900

Proof gold set, **1996.** Two pounds, sovereign, half sovereign (3 coins) £450

Proof silver decimal set, **1996.** £1 to 1p (7 coins) £100

Proof decimal set, **1996.** 60th Birthday £5, £2 Football, £1 Northern Irish rev) to 1p (9 coins) in deluxe case £38

Proof decimal set, **1996.** As above, in standard case **£32**
Proof gold Britannia set, **1997.** **£1000**
Uncirculated decimal sert, **1996.** £2 to 1p (8 coins) **£11**
Proof gold set, **1997.** Five pounds, two pounds (bimetal), sovereign, half sovereign (4 coins) **£900**
Proof gold set, **1997.** Two pounds (bimetal), sovereign, half sovereign **£450**
Proof silver Britannia set, **1997.** Two pounds to 20p **£85**
Proof decimal set, **1997.** Golden Wedding £5, £2 bimetal. £1 (English rev) to 1p, with new 50p in deluxe case ...**£40**
Proof decimal set, **1997.** As above, in standard case **£35**
Uncirculated decimal set, **1997.** As above but no £5 (9 coins) **£11**
Proof gold Britannia set, **1998.** **£1000**
Proof gold set, **1998,** £5 to half sovereign **£900**
Proof gold set, **1998,** £2 to half sovereign **£450**
Proof silver set, Britannia **1998,** £2 to 20p **£85**
Proof decimal set, **1998,** Prince Charles, £5 to 1p in deluxe case **£40**
Proof decimal set, **1998,** as above, in standard case **£33**
Uncirculated set, **1998,** as above but no £5 (9 coins) **£11**
Proof silver set, **1998,** 'EU' and 'NHS' 60p (2 coins) **£50**
Proof gold Britannia set, **1999.** **£1000**
Proof gold set, **1999,** £5, £2 Rugby World Cup, sovereign, half sovereign **£1000**
Proof gold set, **1999,** £2 Rugby World Cup, sovereign, half sovereign **£450**
Proof decimal set, **1999,** Diana £5 to 1p in deluxe case **£40**
Proof decimal set, **1999,** as above, in standard case **£35**
Uncirculated set, **1999,** as above but no £5 (8 coins) **£11**
Uncirculated set, **1999,** as above but no £5 (8 coins) **£11**
Proof gold, Britannia set, 2000 ... ...**£900**
Proof gold, 2000, £5 to half sovereign **£950**
Proof gold, 2000, £2 to half sovereign **£395**
Proof silver decimal set, 2000, £5 to 1p plus Maundy coins (13 coins) **£245**
Proof decimal set, 2000, Executive (10 coins) **£70**
Proof decimal set, 2000, Deluxe (10 coins) **£40**
Proof decimal set, 2000, Standard (10 coins) **£30**
Uncirculated set, 2000, as above but no £5 (9 coins) **£12**

Scottish Coins

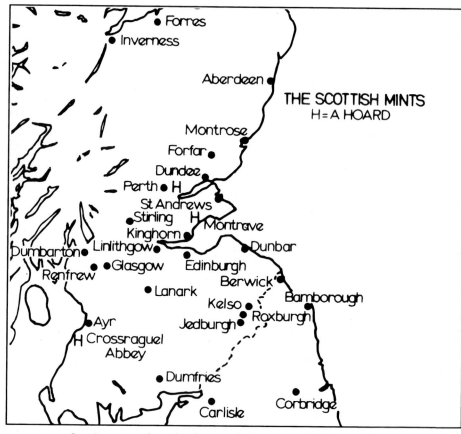

THE SCOTTISH MINTS
H = A HOARD

Based on a map of actual and supposed mints prepared by Spink and Son Ltd.

The number of mints which have been in operation in Scotland can be seen from the map above. The mints of the first coinage of Alexander III are the greatest number ever working together in Scotland, and it is this area that really attracts the collector of the different mint issues. For this reason, when we deal with this reign later on, we give a price for issues of each mint town, but not for any other reign.

MINT TOWN	KING(S)
ABERDEEN	Alexander III, David II
	Robert III, James I, II, III
AYR	Alexander III
BAMBOROUGH	Henry
BERWICK	David I, Malcom IV,
	William I, Alexander II, III
	Robert Bruce, James III
CARLISLE	David I, Henry
CORBRIDGE	Henry
DUMBARTON	Robert III
DUMFRIES	Alexander III
DUNBAR	William I ?, Alexander III
DUNDEE	William I ?, Alexander III
DUNFERMLINE	William I
FORFAR	Alexander III
FORRES	Alexander III
GLASGOW	Alexander III
INVERNESS	Alexander III
JEDBURGH	Malcom IV
KELSO	Alexander II
KINGHORN	Alexander III
LANARK	Alexander III
LINLITHGOW	James I, II
MONTROSE	Alexander III
PERTH	William I, Alexander III,
	Robert II to James II
RENFREW	Alexander III
ROXBURGH	Alexander III
ST ANDREWS	Alexander III
STIRLING	Alexander III, James I, II
	Mary Stuart

Prices are for the commonest coins in each case. Collectors should expect to pay these amounts and upwards. For further details see The Scottish Coinage, by I. Stewart (Spink, 1967, reprint 1975) and Standard Catalogue, Volume 2 (Seaby, 1984). Gold coins are indicated. All other coins are silver unless another metal is stated.

	F	VF
DAVID I 1124-53		
Pennies	£500	£1000

Four different groups; struck at the mints of Berwick, Carlisle, Roxburgh and Edinburgh

This superb David I penny of Carlisle realised £1,210 in Spink's Douglas auction in 1997

HENRY 1136-52
(Earl of Huntingdon and Northumberland)
Pennies ... ... £1250   *
Three types; struck at the mints of Corbridge, Carlisle and Barnborough.

MALCOLM IV 1153-65
Pennies ... ... £3250   *
Five types; struck at the mints of Roxburgh and Berwick.

WILLIAM THE LION 1165-1214
Pennies £65   £140
Three issues; struck at the mints of Roxburgh, Berwick, Edinburgh, Dun (Dunfermline?), Perth

ALEXANDER II 1214-49
Pennies £650   £1500
Mints of Berwick and Roxburgh, varieties of bust.

Halfpenny and farthing of Alexander III and penny of Robert Bruce

ALEXANDER III 1249-86
1st coinage pennies 1250-80
Mints

		F	VF
Aberdeen	... ...	£90	£225
Ayr	... ...	£135	£375
Berwick	... ...	£40	£110
'DUN'	... ...	£125	£350
Edinburgh	... ...	£40	£120
Forfar	... ...	£125	£350
Fres	... ...	£135	£375
Glasgow	... ...	£125	£350
Inverness	... ...	£150	£400
Kinghorn	... ...	£150	£375
Lanark	... ...	£135	£375
Montrose	... ...	£250	*
Perth	... ...	£50	£130

SCOTTISH COINS

	F	VF
Renfrew	£200	*
Roxburgh	£45	£140
St. Andrews	£90	£225
Stirling	£120	£325
'TERWILANER' (uncertain name)	£200	*

2nd coinage c. 1280 –
Many types and varieties

	F	VF
Pennies	£18	£45
Halfpennies	£75	£175
Farthings	£150	£400

JOHN BALIOL 1292-6
1st coinage (rough surface issue)

	F	VF
Pennies	£90	£225
Halfpennies	ext. rare	

2nd coinage (smooth surface issue)

	F	VF
Pennies	£100	£285
Halfpennies	£175	£425

Robert Bruce Penny

ROBERT BRUCE 1306-29

	F	VF
Pennies	£300	£650
Halfpennies	£400	£825
Farthings	ext. rare	

Probably all struck at Berwick.

David II Groat, Edinburgh Mint

DAVID II 1329-71

	F	VF
Nobles (gold)	ext. rare	
Groats ... ... ,..	£70	£200
Halfgroats	£60	£175
Pennies	£35	£80
Halfpennies	£200	£450
Farthings	£500	*

Three issues, but these denominations were not struck for all issues. Edinburgh and Aberdeen mints.

ROBERT II 1371-90

	F	VF
Groats	£60	£180
Halfgroats	£75	£200
Pennies	£65	£150
Halfpennies	£135	£375

Some varieties. Struck at mints of Dundee, Edinburgh, Perth.

SCOTTISH COINS

ROBERT III 1390-1406	F	VF
Lion or crowns (gold)	£450	£1000
Demy lions or halfcrowns (gold) ...	£425	£925
Groats	£60	£150
Halfgroats	£125	£350
Pennies	£160	£350
Halfpennies	£250	*

Three issues, many varieties. Struck at mints of Edinburgh, Aberdeen, Perth, Dumbarton.

James I Demy or Nine Shilling Piece

JAMES I 1406-37

	F	VF
Demies (gold)	£375	£675
Half demies (gold)	£475	£900
Groats	£100	£160
Billon pennies	£125	*
Billon halfpennies	£150	*

Mints, Aberdeen, Edinburgh, Inverness, Linlithgow, Perth, Stirling.

JAMES II 1437-60

	F	VF
Demies (gold) from	£425	£850
Lions (gold) from	£550	£1350
Half lions (gold) from		Very rare
Groats	£185	£600
Halfgroats	£425	*
Billon pennies	£175	*

Two issues, many varieties. Mints: Aberdeen, Edinburgh, Linlithgow, Perth, Roxburgh, Stirling.

ECCLESIASTICAL ISSUES C 1452-80

	F	VF
Bishop Kennedy copper pennies ...	£75	£200
Copper farthings	£175	*

Different types, varieties

JAMES III 1460-88

	F	VF
Riders (gold) from	£750	£1600
Half riders (gold)	£950	£2000
Quarter riders (gold)	£1000	£2250
Unicorns (gold)	£850	£1800
Groats ... ...from	£165	£400

*James III groat and
James V one-third groat*

	F	VF
Halfgroats from	£350	*
Pennies from	£125	£325
Billon placks from	£65	*
Billon half placks from		Very rare

	F	VF
Billon pennies from	£70	*
Copper farthings from	£165	*

Many varieties. Mints: Edinburgh, Berwick, Aberdeen.

James IV Unicorn

JAMES IV 1488-1513

	F	VF
Unicorns (gold)	£700	£1650
Half unicorns (gold)	£600	£1200
Lions or crowns (gold)	£900	£2250
Half lions (gold)	£1500	£3500
Pattern angel (gold)		unique
Groats	£350	£800
Halfgroats	£400	*
Pennies (light coinage) ... ...ext rare		*
Billon placks	£35	£80
Billon half placks	£120	*
Billon pennies	£50	£100

Different types, varieties. Mint: Edinburgh only.

James V 'Bonnet' piece of 1540

JAMES V 1513-42	F	VF
Unicorns (gold)	£800	£1850
Half unicorns (gold)	£1500	£4000
Crowns (gold)	£550	£1250
'Bonnet' pieces or ducats (gold) ...	£1750	£3750
Two-thirds ducats (gold)	£1850	£3500
One-third ducats (gold)	£2350	£5250
Groats from	£100	£250
One-third groats	£165	£400

James V groat

	F	VF
Billon placks	£30	£100
Billon bawbees	£25	£80
Billon half bawbees	£75	£200
Billon quarter bawbees		unique

Different issues, varieties. Edinburgh mint.

Note: from here on all Scottish coins were struck at Edinburgh.

MARY 1542-67

1st Period 1542-58

	F	VF
Crown (gold)	£950	£2400
Twenty shillings (gold)	£1800	*
Lions or forty-four shillings (gold)	£850	£2100

Extremely rare Francis and Mary ducat which realised £77,000 at a Spink auction in March 1997

	F	VF
Half lions or twenty-two shillings (gold)	£525	£1450
Ryals or £3 pieces (gold)		
1555, 1557, 1558	£1850	£4750
Half ryals (gold) 1555,1557,1558 ...	£2750	*
Portrait testoons, 1553	£1250	£3750

Mary, Queen of Scots Half Testoon, 1560, Francis and Mary

	F	VF
Non-portrait testoons, 1555-8	£150	£450
– half testoons, 1555-8	£175	£450
Billon bawbees	£30	£80
– half bawbees	£75	£200
– pennies (facing bust)	£175	£475
– pennies (no bust) 1556	£125	£400
– lions, 1555, 1558	£25	£75
– placks, 1557	£25	£75

2nd period (Francis and Mary) 1558-60

	F	VF
Ducats or sixty shillings (gold) ...	ext. rare	
Non-portrait testoons, 1558-61 ...	£150	£400
– half testoons, 1558-60	£185	£500
Twelvepenny groats (Nonsunt) 1558-9	£90	£250
– lions, 1559-60	£25	£80

3rd period (widowhood) 1560-5

	F	VF
Crown (gold) 1562		
Portrait testoons, 1561-2	£800	£2500
– half testoons, 1561-2	£850	*

4th period (Henry and Mary) 1565-7

	F	VF
Portrait ryals, 1565	ext. rare	
Non-portrait ryals, 1565-7	£225	£575

Mary and Henry 1565 two thirds ryal

	F	VF
– two thirds ryals, 1565-7	£200	£575
– – undated	£450	£1000
– one-third ryals, 1565-6	£200	£475
– testoons, 1565	ext. rare	

5th period (2nd widowhood) 1567

	F	VF
_ Non portrait ryals, 1567	£210	£500
– two thirds ryals, 1567	£225	£550
– one-third ryals, 1566-7	£275	£625

Mints: Edinburgh, Stirling (but only for some bawbees)

JAMES VI

Before English accession 1567-1603

1st coinage 1567-71

	F	VF
Ryals 1567-71	£200	£475
Two-third ryals –	£190	£450
One-third ryals –	£200	£475

Superb gold £20 piece of 1575 realised £30,800 in Spink auction in March 1997

2nd coinage 1571-80

	F	VF
Twenty pounds (gold)	£9500	£22000
Nobles, 1572-7, 1580	£60	£275
Half nobles –	£70	£200
Two merks, 1578-80 –	£900	*
Merks, 1579-80	£1000	*

3rd coinage 1580-81

	F	VF
Ducats (gold), 1580	£2750	£5500
Sixteen shillings, 1581	£900	£3000
Eight shillings, 1581	£850	*
Four shillings, 1581	£800	*
Two shillings, 1581	ext. rare	

SCOTTISH COINS

	F	VF
4th coinage 1582-88		
Lion nobles (gold)	£2500	£5000
Two-third lion nobles (gold)	£2750	£6250
One-third lion nobles (gold)	£3250	£7500
Forty shillings, 1582	£25000	£7500
Thirty shillings, 1582-6	£180	£650
Twenty shillings, 1582-5	£135	£375
Ten shillings, 1582-4	£110	£300

James VI twenty shillings, 1582

	F	VF
5th coinage 1588		
Thistle nobles (gold)	£1200	£2500
6th coinage 1591-93		
Hat pieces (gold) 1591-3	£2350	£4750
Balance half merks, 1591-3	£170	£400
Balance quarter merks, 1591	£275	£625
7th coinage 1594-1601		
Riders (gold)	£450	£900
Half riders (gold)	£375	£800
Ten shillings, 1593-5, 1598-1601 ...	£90	£275
Five shillings, 1593-5, 1598-1601 ...	£100	£275
Thirty pennies, 1595-6, 1598-9, 1601	£75	£200
Twelve pennies, 1594-6	£75	£200

James VI Sword and Sceptre piece, 1601

	F	VF
8th coinage 1601-4		
Sword and sceptre pieces (gold) ...	£265	£525
Half sword and sceptre pieces (gold)	£225	£425
Thistle-merks, 1601-4	£60	£165
Half thistle merks –	£40	£125
Quarter thistle-merks –	£35	£110
Eighth thistle-merks, 1601-3	£35	£120
Billon and copper issues		
Billon placks or eight penny groats	£20	£75
Billon half packs	£100	*
Billon hardheads	£25	£85
Billon saltire placks	£140	*

	F	VF
Copper twopence 1597	£100	*
Copper penny 1597	£150	*
After English accession 1603-25		
Units (gold)	£375	£800
Double crowns (gold)	£475	£1200
Britain crowns (gold)	£375	£900
Halfcrowns (gold)	£350	£750
Thistle crowns (gold)	£275	£650
Sixty shillings	£250	£650
Thirty shillings	£70	£220
Twelve shillings	£80	£185
Six shillings	£125	*
Two shillings	£40	£100
One shilling	£65	£175

*James VI Gold Unit
(after English accession)*

	F	VF
Sixpences	*	*
Copper twopences	£20	£50
Copper pennies	£35	£90

Charles I Briot Unit, 3rd coinage

	F	VF
CHARLES 1652-49		
1st coinage 1625-36		
Units (gold)	£475	£950
Double crowns (gold)	£950	*
Britain crowns (gold)	ext. rare	
Sixty shillings	£325	£850
Thirty shillings	£85	£225
Twelve shillings	£75	£180
Six shillings	£200	*
Two shillings	£75	*
One shilling	ext. rare	
2nd coinage 1636		
Half merks	£60	£180
Forty penny pieces	£50	£130
Twenty penny pieces	£60	*

	F	VF
3rd coinage 1580-81		
Units (gold)	£500	£1100
Half units (gold)	£750	£1850
Britain crowns (gold)	£625	£1500
Britain half crowns (gold)	£400	£1000
Sixty shilling	£250	£800
Thirty shilling	£65	£165

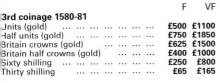

Charles I Twelve Shillings, 3rd coinage; Falconer's issue.

	F	VF
Twelve shillings	£60	£175
Six shillings	£50	£150
Half Merks	£50	£170
Forty pennies	£30	£80
Twenty pennies	£25	£60
Three shillings	£50	£140
Two shillings	£50	£120
Copper twopences (lion)	£20	£80
– pennies –	£75	*
– twopences (CR crowned)	£15	£60
– twopences (Stirling turners) ...	£15	£50

CHARLES II 1660-85	F	VF
1st coinage		
Four merks		
1664 thistle above bust	£300	*
1664 thistle below bust	£300	*
1665	*	*
1670	£325	*
1673	£250	£600
1674 F below bust	£275	£650
1675	£275	£600

Two merks		
1664 thistle above bust	£200	£500

Charles II silver
two merks 1664

1664 thistle below bust	£200	£500
1670	£225	*
1673	£200	£500
1673 F below bust	£275	*
1674	£250	*
1674 F below bust	£225	*
1675	£175	£450

Charles II, Merk 1669

Merks		
1664	£50	£175
1665	£75	£225
1666	£150	*
1668	£75	£225
1669	£40	£150
1670	£50	£175
1671	£40	£150
1672	£40	£140
1673	£40	£150
1674	£75	£225
1674 F below bust	£50	£185
1675 F below bust	£50	£185
1675	£100	£250

Half merks		
1664	£75	£200
1665	£90	£250
1666	£125	*
1667	£90	£250
1668	£80	£225
1669	£50	£150
1670	£65	£170
1671	£50	£150
1672	£70	£180
1673	£70	£180
1675 F below bust	£60	£170
1675	£60	£170

2nd coinage		
Dollars		
1676	£200	£450
1679	£200	£500
1680	£250	*
1681	£200	£450
1682	£150	£350

Half dollars		
1675	£200	£450
1676	£250	£500
1681	£200	£450

Quarter dollars		
1675	£75	£225
1676	£50	£175
1677	£60	£200
1678	£75	£225
1679	£90	£250
1680	£70	£220
1681	£70	£220
1682	£75	£225

Eighth dollars		
1676	£60	£150
1677	£60	£160
1678/7	£90	*
1679	*	*
1680	£75	£175
1682	£100	£275

Sixteenth dollars

1677	£35	£90
1678/7	£65	£150
1679/7	£100	*
1680	£65	£150
1681	£50	£125

Charles II 1678 Bawbee

Copper twopence CR" crowned	£20	£65
Copper bawbees, 1677-9	£35	£90
Copper turners, 1677-9	£25	£85

JAMES VII 1685-9

Sixty shillings 1688 proof only[1]	FDC	£950
– gold proof only[1]	FDC	*

([1]Struck in 1828, not contemporary)

Forty shillings

1887	£90	£350
1688	£150	£450

James VII 1687 ten shillings

Ten shillings

1687	£90	£300
1688	£110	£350

WILLIAM AND MARY 1689-94

Sixty shillings

1691	£150	£550
1692	£150	£500

Forty shillings

1689	£100	£325
1690	£90	£300
1691	£70	£250
1692	£85	£270
1693	£100	£375
1694	£90	£300

Twenty shillings

1693	£100	£350
1694	£200	*

Ten shillings

1689	*	*
1690	£100	£275
1691	£80	£200
1692	£65	£150
1694	£150	£400

William and Mary 1694 five shillings

Five shillings	F	VF
1691	£75	£250
1694	£65	£200
Copper bawbee 1691-4	£50	£140
Copper bodle 1691-4	£35	£85

WILLIAM II 1694-1702	F	VF
Pistole (gold) 1701	£1750	£4000
Half pistole (gold) 1701	£1750	£4000

Sixty shillings

1699	*	*

Forty shillings

1695	£70	£265
1696	£75	£275
1697	£70	£265
1698	£80	£300
1699	£100	£350
1700	£200	*

Twenty shillings

1695	£70	£200
1696	£70	£200
1697	*	*
1698	£75	£220
1699	*	*

Ten shillings

1695	£65	£150
1696	£65	£150
1697	£75	£175
1698	£80	£185
1699	£125	£350

Five shillings

1695	£40	£90
1696	£40	£90
1697	£30	£85
1699	£65	£135
1700	£65	£135
1701	£80	*
1702	£70	£200
Copper bawbee 1695-7	£25	£100
Copper bodle 1695-7	£30	£120

ANNE 1702-14
Pre-Union 1702-7

Ten shillings

1705	£75	£200
1706	£100	£300

Five shillings

1705	£20	£80
1706	£25	£90

Post-Union 1707-14
see under British milled series

JAMES VIII 1688-1766 (The Old Pretender)

Guinea 1716, gold	FDC	£3000
– silver	FDC	£800
– bronze	FDC	£1000
Crown 1709		unique
Crown 1716, silver	FDC	£900
– gold		ext. rare
– bronze		ext. rare

NB: All the 1716-dated pieces were struck in 1828 from original dies.

Irish Coins

Hammered Issues 995-1661

Prices are for the commonest coins in each case. It should be remembered that most of the Irish coins of these times are in fairly poor condition and it is difficult to find specimens in VF condition upwards. For more details see The Guide Book to the Coinage of Ireland AD 995 to the present day, by Anthony Dowle and Patrick Finn (ref. DF in the following lists): Seaby's Coins of Scotland, Ireland and the Islands, which is volume Two of Seaby's Standard Catalogue (ref Sby in price list): and also Patrick Finn's Irish Coin Values.

All coins are silver unlesss otherwise stated

HIBERNO-NORSEMEN OF DUBLIN 995-1150

	F	VF
Pennies, imitative of English coins, many types and varieties ...from	£90	£160

Hiberno-Norse penny, c 1015-1035

Hiberno-Norseman of Dublin Penny c1035-1055

JOHN, as Lord of Ireland c 1185-1199

Halfpennies, with profile portrait	£1250	*
Halfpennies, with facing head	£45	£95
Farthings	£250	£500
Different types,varieties, mints, moneyers.		

JOHN DE COURCY Lord of Ulster 1177-1205

Halfpenny		unique
Farthings	£450	£1000
Different types,varieties, mints, moneyers.		

John as King of England, Rex/Triangle Penny

JOHN as King of England and Lord of Ireland c 1199-1216

Rex/Triangle types	F	VF
Pennies ... ...from	£40	£90
Halfpennies	£70	£160
Farthings	£400	£950
Different types,varieties, mints, moneyers.		

HENRY III 1216-1272

Pennies (c 1251-1254) ... ...from	£35	£80

Dublin only, moneyers DAVI and RICHARD. many varieties.

Edward I Waterford penny

EDWARD I 1272-1307

Pennies ... ...from	£35	£50
Halfpennies	£45	£100

Edward I Farthing, Dublin

Farthings	£95	£250

Dublin,Waterford and Cork. Many different issues.

EDWARD III 1327-1377

Halfpennies Dublin mint	ext. rare

There were no Irish coins struck for Edward II, Richard II, Henry IV or Henry V.

HENRY VI 1422-1461

Pennies, Dublin mint	very rare

Edward IV untitled crown groats

EDWARD IV 1461-1483

Untitled crown groats ... ...from	£300	£650
– pennies	£600	*
Titled crown groats	£950	*
– halfgroats		ext. rare
– pennies		ext. rare
Cross on rose/-sun groats	£950	*

IRISH COINS

	F	VF
Bust/rose-sun double groats	£1500	£3500
– – groats	£1750	*
– – halfgroats		ext.rare
– – pennies		ext.rare
'English style' groats	£65	£160
– halfgroats	£375	£700
– pennies	£60	£125
– halfpennies		ext.rare
Bust/rose groats	£350	£750
– – pennies	£75	£175
copper issues		
Crown/cross farthing	£850	*
– – half farthing	£700	*
PATRICIUS/SALVATOR		
Farthing	£600	£1250
3 crowns/sun half-farthing		very rare

This is, of course, a very abbreviated listing of the issues of Edward IV which are numerous and complicated, and still pose numismatics many problems. There are also many varieties and different mints.

RICHARD III 1483-1485

	F	VF
Bust/rose-cross groats	£750	£2000
— halfgroat		unique
— penny		unique
Cross and Pellet Penny	£700	*
Three-crown groats	£425	£850
Different mints, varieties, etc.		

HENRY VII 1485-1509
Early issues

	F	VF
Three-crown groats	£70	£175
— halfgroats	£135	£300
— pennies	£375	£750
— halfpennies		ext. rare
Different mints, varieties, etc.		

LAMBERT SIMNEL (pretender) 1487

	F	VF
Three-crown groats	£850	£2000
Different mints, varieties.		

HENRY VII 1485-1509

Henry VII facing bust Groat, Dublin

Later issues

	F	VF
Facing bust groats	£90	£200
— halfgroats	£750	*
— pennies	£650	*
Crowned H pennies		very rare
Many varieties. Mainly Dublin. Waterford is extemely rare.		

HENRY VIII 1509-1547

	F	VF
'Harp' groats	£40	£90
— halfgroat	£275	£650

Henry VIII harp groats (with initials HA and HI)

These harp coins carry crowned initials, e.g., HA (Henry and Anne Boleyn), HI (Henry and Jane Seymour), HK (Henry and Katherine Howard), HR (Henricus Rex).

Henry VIII portrait groat

Posthumous issues	F	VF
Portrait groats current for 6 pence	£70	£175
— halfgroats ...current for 3 pence	£90	£200
— pennies current for 3 halfpence	£325	£850
— halfpennies current for 3 farthings	£400	£1000
Different busts, mintmarks etc.		

EDWARD VI 1547-1553

	F	VF
Base shillings 1552 (MDLII)	£600	£1250
— contemporary copy	£50	£175

Mary 1553 shilling

MARY 1553-1558

	F	VF
Shillings 1553 (MDLIII)	£475	£1100
Shillings 1554 (MDLIIII)		ext. rare
Groats		very rare
Halfgroats		ext. rare
Pennies		ext. rare
Several varieties of the shillings and groats.		

PHILIP AND MARY 1554-1558

	F	VF
Base shillings	£200	£650
— groats	£55	£150
Several minor varieties.		

ELIZABETH I 1558-1603

	F	VF
Base portrait shillings	£175	£650
— groats	£100	£325

Elizabeth I 1561 portrait shilling

	F	VF
Fine silver portrait shillings 1561	£125	£475
— groats –	£225	£525
Base shillings arms-harp	£100	£375
— sixpences –	£80	£200
— threepences –	£125	£350
— pennies –	£20	£80
— halfpennies –	£50	£150

JAMES I 1603-1625
Shillings	£60	£150
— Sixpences	£45	£125

Different issues, busts and mintmarks.

CHARLES I 1625-1649
Siege money of the Irish Rebellion 1642-1649
Siege coins are rather irregular in size and shape.

Kilkenny Money 1642
Copper halfpennies (F)	£175	£475
Copper farthings (F)	£175	£550

Inchiquin Money 1642-1646
(The only gold coins struck in Ireland)
Gold double pistoles	ext. rare	
Gold pistoles (F)	ext. rare	
Crowns	£950	£2250

Inchiquin shilling

Halfcrowns	£950	£2250
Shillings	£1250	*
Ninepences	£2500	*
Sixpences	*	*
Groats (F)	£2000	*
Threepences ... ... ext. rare		*

Three issues and many varieties.

Ormonde Money 1643
Crowns (F)	£300	£650
Halfcrowns (F)	£225	£525
Shillings	£100	£250

Ormonde Money, Halfcrown

Ormonde sixpence

Sixpences (F)	£90	£200
Groats (F)	£75	£175
Threepences	£65	£150
Halfgroats (F)	£275	£600

Many varieties.

Rebel Money 1643
Crowns	£1250	£2500
Halfcrowns	£1500	£3000

Town Pieces 1645-1647
Bandon
Copper farthings (F)	£200	*

Kinsale copper farthing

Kinsale
Copper farthings (F)	£250	*

Youghal
Copper farthings (F)	£300	£800
Brass twopences	ext. rare	
Pewter threepences	ext. rare	

IRISH COINS

	F	VF
Cork		
Shillings **(F)**	£1000	£2500
Sixpences **(F)**	£475	£950
Copper halfpennies		ext. rare
Copper farthings **(F)**	£275	*
Elizabeth I shillings countermarked		
CORKE **(F)**		ext. rare

Youghal farthing

'Blacksmith's' Money 1649
(Based on English Tower halfcrown)

	F	VF
Halfcrown, varieties	£375	£1100

Dublin Money 1649

	F	VF
Crowns	£1750	£4500
Halfcrowns	£1250	£2750

Charles II Armstrong Issue, Farthing

CHARLES II 1660-1685
Armstrong issues 1660-1661

	F	VF
Copper farthings	£30	£100

Charles II to George IV

This series, of which all the issues except Bank of Ireland tokens were struck in base metal, features a large number of varieties, many of which are unpublished, but there is space here for only the main types and best-known variants. A number of rare proofs have also been omitted.

Except for the 'gunmoney' of James II, Irish copper coins are notably hard to find in the top grades, especially the so-called 'Voce populi' issues and specimens of Wood's coinage (which are reasonably common in the lower grades, apart from the rarities).

We have listed some of the 'gunmoney' of James II in only three grades – Fair, Fine and VF. The majority of these hastily produced coins were not well struck and many pieces with little substantial wear are, arguably, not EF in the strictest sense.

Finally, a note on the dating of gunmoney. In the calendar used up to 1723 the legal or civil year commenced on March 25 in Great Britain and Ireland, so December 1689 came before, not after January, February and March 1689. Coins dated March 1689 and March 1690 were struck in the same month.

CHARLES II	Fair	F	VF	EF
St Patrick's coinage				
Halfpenny	£60	£125	*	*
— star in rev legend	£90	£250	*	*
Farthing	£50	£110	£350	*
— stars in rev legend	£60	£125	£400	*
— cloud around				
St Patrick	*	*	*	*
— martlet below king	£75	£200	£500	*
— annulet below king	£50	£100	*	*

Charles II St Patrick's Farthing

Regal coinage
Halfpennies

	Fair	F	VF	EF
1680 large letters				
small cross	£20	£60	£140	*
1680 large letters,	£5	£30	£125	*
pellets	£5	£30	£120	£275
1681 large letters	*	£125	£400	*
1681 small letters	*	*	*	*
1682 large letters	*	*	*	*
1682 small letters	£4	£15	£100	£275
1683	£4	£15	£100	£275
1684	£25	£75	£300	*

JAMES II
Regular coinage
Halfpennies

	Fair	F	VF	EF
1685	£5	£35	£175	£350
1686	£3	£25	£110	£250
1687	£80	£250	£700	*
1688	£10	£35	£180	*

Emergency coinage
Gunmoney
Crowns

	Fair	F	VF	EF
1690	£15	£35	£95	*
1690 'chubby'				
horseman, sword				
to E (Sby 6577)	£30	£70	£175	*
1690 similar (DF 373)	£30	£70	£175	*

James II Gunmoney Crown

	Fair	F	VF	EF
Large halfcrowns				
1689 July	£4	£30	£95	*
1689 August	£2	£20	£55	*
1689 September ...	£2	£20	£65	*
1689 October	£2	£20	£50	*
1689 November ...	£2	£20	£55	*
1689 December ...	£2	£20	£55	*
1689 January	£2	£20	£55	*
1689 February	£2	£20	£55	*
1689 March	£2	£20	£60	*
1690 March	£2	£20	£55	*
1690 April	£3	£20	£60	*
1690 May	£3	£25	£80	*
Small halfcrowns				
1690 April	£35	£125	*	*
1690 May	£2	£15	£35	£80
1690 June	£2	£15	£40	*
1690 July	£2	£15	£40	*
1690 August	£3	£20	£55	*
1690 September	*	*	*	*
1690 October	£75	£250	*	*
Large shillings				
1689 July	£2	£12	£40	£100
1689 August	£2	£10	£35	£90
1689 September ...	£2	£10	£35	£90
1689 October	£3	£15	£50	£120
1689 November ...	£2	£10	£40	£100
1689 December ...	£2	£10	£40	£100
1689 January	£2	£10	£35	£90
1689 February	£2	£10	£40	£100
1689 March	£2	£10	£40	£100
1690 March	£2	£10	£40	£100
1690 April	£3	£10	£40	£100
Small shillings				
1690 April	£3	£15	£45	£120
1690 May	£2	£10	£35	£90
1690 June	£2	£10	£35	£90
1690 July	*	*	*	*
1690 August	*	*	*	*
1690 September ...	£20	£50	*	*

James II

Gunmoney, halfcrown, May 1690

	Fair	F	VF	EF
Sixpences				
1689 June	£1	£10	£35	£90
1689 July	£1	£10	£30	£85
1689 August	£1	£10	£35	£90
1689 September ...	£4	£18	£60	*
1689 October	*	*	*	*
1689 November ...	£3	£12	£45	£100
1689 December ...	£1	£10	£35	£90
1689 January	£1	£10	£35	£90
1689 February	£2	£12	£40	£100
1689 March	*	*	*	*
1690 March	*	*	*	*
1690 April	*	*	*	*
1690 May	£15	£35	£100	*
1690 June	*	*	*	*
1690 October	*	*	*	*
Pewter Money				
Crown	£175	£400	£1200	*
Groat	£150	£350	£950	*
Penny large bust ...	£150	£350	*	*
Penny small bust	£100	£225	£500	*

	Fair	F	VF	EF

James II Pewter Money, Halfpenny, 1690

	Fair	F	VF	EF
Halfpenny large bust	£45	£125	£325	*
Halfpenny small bust	£50	£135	£350	*

Limerick Money halfpenny

Limerick Money				
Halfpenny	£8	£45	£90	*
Farthing reversed N	£10	£50	£95	*
— normal N	£12	£60	£125	*

1693 halfpenny

WILLIAM AND MARY
Halfpennies

	Fair	F	VF	EF
1692	£2	£15	£75	*
1693	£2	£15	£70	*
1694	£2	£20	£80	*

WILLIAM III

	Fair	F	VF	EF
1696 Halfpenny draped bust ... ... :	£10	£30	£95	*
1696 Halfpenny crude undraped bust ... :	£30	£100	£250	*

GEORGE I
Wood's coinage

	Fair	F	VF	EF
1722 harp left ... ... :	£15	£50	£175	*
1722 harp right ...	£3	£12	£80	£350
1723	£2	£8	£60	£250
1723 obv Rs altered Bs	£2	£10	£70	£275
1723 no stop after date	£2	£8	£65	£250
1723/2	£5	£20	£100	*
1723 star in rev legend	*	*	*	*

IRISH COINS

	Fair	F	VF	EF
1723 no stop before HIBERNIA	£3	£12	£80	£250
1724 head divides rev legend	£4	£20	£100	*
1724 legend continuous over head	£5	£25	£125	*

George I Wood's farthing, 1723

Farthings

	Fair	F	VF	EF
1722 harp left	£25	£100	£450	*
1723 D: G:	£10	£30	£125	*
1723 DEI GRATIA ...	£3	£12	£80	£250
1724	£10	£30	£160	*

GEORGE II
halfpennies

	Fair	F	VF	EF
1736	*	£5	£35	£130
1737	*	£5	£35	£130
1738	*	£6	£45	£140
1741	*	£5	£35	£130
1742	*	£5	£35	£130
1743	*	£7	£55	£160
1744	*	£7	£55	£160
1744/43	*	£7	£60	£175
1746	*	£6	£45	£140
1747	*	£5	£40	£140
1748	*	£7	£55	£160
1749	*	£5	£40	£140
1750	*	£5	£40	£140
1751	*	£6	£45	£140
1752	*	£6	£45	£140
1753	*	£6	£45	£140
1755	£1	£10	£100	£300
1765	*	£5	£35	£130

Farthings

	Fair	F	VF	EF
1737	*	£5	£45	£125
1738	*	£2	£25	£90
1744	*	£5	£45	£120
1760	*	£4	£35	£800

George III, Voce Populi Halfpenny 1760

GEORGE III
Voce populi coinage
Halfpennies (1760)

	Fair	F	VF	EF
Type 1 (DF 565) ...	£40	£125	£300	*

	Fair	F	VF	EF
Type 2(DF 566)	£20	£50	£175	*
Type 3(DF 567)	£35	£100	£250	*
Type 4(DF 569)	£25	£75	£200	*
Type 5(DF 570)	£15	£40	£160	£400
Type 6(DF 571)	£20	£50	£175	£425
Type 7(DF 572)	£15	£40	£160	£400
Type 8(DF 573)	£15	£40	£150	£400
Type 9(DF 575)	£35	£100	£275	*
Type 9, P before head (DF 576)	£20	£50	£180	£425
Type 9, P under head (DF 577)	£20	£60	£200	*

Farthings (1760)

	Fair	F	VF	EF
Type 1 loop to truncation	£45	£100	£375	*
Type 2 no loop ...	*	*	*	*

London coinage
Halfpennies

	Fair	F	VF	EF
1766	*	£5	£35	£125
1769	*	£5	£35	£125
1769 2nd type	*	£6	£40	£200
1775	*	£10	£60	£200
1776	£5	£25	£100	£250
1781	*	£5	£35	£120
1782	*	£5	£35	£120

George III Halfpenny, 1805

Soho coinage

	Fair	F	VF	EF
Penny 1805	£3	£30	£100	*
Halfpenny 1805 ...	£2	£25	£95	*
Farthing 1806	£1	£20	£90	*

Bank of Ireland token coinage

	Fair	F	VF	EF
Six shillings 1804 ...	£8	£60	£200	£500

1804 six shilling Bank of Ireland

MALCOLM BORD

GOLD COIN EXCHANGE

16 CHARING CROSS ROAD,
LONDON WC2H 0HR

TELEPHONE: 020 7240 0479

FAX: 020 7240 1920

As one of London's leading dealers in most branches of Numismatics we are able to offer you unrivalled advice when it comes to both the buying or selling of coins or whether you wish to buy or sell coins or medals, we will endeavour to offer the most competitive price.

REMEMBER

That any offer we make is not subject to commission and we offer immediate payment.

A comprehensive selection of coins and medals is always available for viewing at our showroom.

IRISH COINS

	Fair	F	VF	EF
Thirty pence 1808	£2	£25	£100	£250
Ten pence 1805 ...	£1	£10	£45	£120
Ten pence 1806 ...	£1	£6	£30	£75
Ten pence 1813 ...	£1	£5	£20	£70
Five pence 1805 ...	£1	£5	£15	£60
Five pence 1806 ...	£2	£8	£25	£80

Bank of Ireland ten pence token, 1813

GEORGE IV

Penny 1822...	*	£5	£50	£140
Penny 1823...	*	£5	£50	£180
Halfpenny 1822 ...	*	£4	£40	£120
Halfpenny 1823 ...	*	£4	£40	£150

Free State and Republic

Proofs exist for nearly all dates of the modern Irish coinage. However, only a few dates have become available to collectors or dealers and apart from the 1928 proofs, are all very rare. They have therefore been omitted from the list.

TEN SHILLINGS

	F	VF	EF	Unc
1966	*	£2.50	£5	£7.50
1966	*	*	*	£15

HALFCROWNS

	F	VF	EF	Unc
1928	£3	£6	£12	£25
1928 proof	*	*	*	£30

Reverse of halfcrown

	F	VF	EF	Unc
1930	£3	£10	£75	£250
1931	£6	£20	£100	£300
1933	£3	£15	£80	£250
1934	£5	£20	£40	£150
1937	£30	£75	£300	£750
1939	£3	£6	£15	£50
1940	£3	£5	£10	£40
1941	£4	£6	£20	£50
1942	£4	£6	£20	£45
1943	£70	£150	£600	£1750
1951	*	£1	£5	£30
1954	*	£1	£5	£30
1955	*	£1	£5	£20
1959	*	£1	£5	£15
1961	*	£1	£5	£20

	F	VF	EF	Un
1961 mule (normal) obv/pre-1939 rev)	£5	£12	£250	
1962	*	*	*	£
1963	*	*	*	£
1964	*	*	*	£
1966	*	*	*	£
1967	*	*	*	£

1937 florin

FLORINS

	F	VF	EF	Un
1928	£2	£4	£8	£2
1928 proof	*	*	*	£3
1930	£3	£6	£50	£25
1931	£3	£10	£80	£25
1933	£10	£30	£80	
1934	£15	£35	£120	
1935	£3	£10	£35	£20
1937	£3	£15	£70	£25
1939	£2	£4	£10	£2
1940	£2	£5	£12	£2
1941	£2	£5	£12	£3
1942	£2	£5	£12	£3
1943	£2500	£5000	£7500	£1500
1951	*	*	£3	£1
1954	*	*	£3	£1
1955	*	*	£3	£1
1959	*	*	£3	£1
1961	*	£3	£6	£2
1962	*	*	£3	£1
1963	*	*	£3	£1
1964	*	*	*	£
1965	*	*	*	£
1966	*	*	*	£
1968	*	*	*	£

SHILLINGS

	F	VF	EF	Un
1928	*	£3	£8	£1
1928 proof	*	*	*	£2
1930	£2	£10	£50	£20
1931	£2	£10	£50	£20
1933	£3	£10	£20	£20
1935	£2	£5	£20	£7
1937	£5	£25	£150	£50
1939	*	£3	£6	£2
1940	*	£3	£8	£2
1941	£2	£5	£8	£2
1942	£2	£5	£8	£2
1951	*	£1	£3	£1
1954	*	*	£3	£1
1955	*	£2	£5	£2
1959	*	*	£3	£1
1962	*	*	*	£
1963	*	*	*	£
1964	*	*	*	£
1966	*	*	*	£
1968	*	*	*	£

SIXPENCES

	F	VF	EF	Un
1928	*	£1	£3	£1
1928 proof	*	*	*	£2
1934	*	£1	£8	£3
1935	*	£3	£12	£6
1939	*	£1	£5	£2

	F	VF	EF	Unc
1940	*	£1	£5	£20
1942	*	*	£5	£20
1945	*	£5	£25	£60
1946	£1	£5	£50	£170
1947	*	£2	£20	£50
1948	*	£2	£8	£25
1949	*	*	£5	£25
1950	*	£2	£15	£60
1952	*	£1	£4	£15
1953	*	£1	£4	£15
1955	*	£1	£4	£15
1956	*	*	£3	£10
1958	*	£1	£5	£35
1959	*	*	£2	£6
1960	*	*	£2	£6
1961	*	*	£2	£6
1962	*	*	£3	£30
1963	*	*	*	£3
1964	*	*	*	£3
1966	*	*	*	£3
1967	*	*	*	£3

1968 sixpence

1968	*	*	*	£2
1969	*	*	*	£3

THREEPENCES

1928	*	£1	£3	£8
1928 proof	*	*	*	£12
1933	£1	£3	£20	£150
1934	*	£1	£5	£30
1935	£1	£3	£15	£65
1939	£1	£5	£50	£200
1940	*	*	£5	£25
1942	*	*	£5	£20
1943	*	*	£5	£40
1946	*	*	£5	£15
1948	*	£2	£15	£50
1949	*	*	£5	£20
1950	*	*	£2	£6
1953	*	*	£2	£5
1956	*	*	£1	£4
1961	*	*	*	£3
1962	*	*	*	£3
1963	*	*	*	£3
1964	*	*	*	£3
1965	*	*	*	£3
1966	*	*	*	£3

1967 threepence

1967	*	*	*	*
1968	*	*	*	*

PENNIES

1928	*	*	£3	£10
1928 proof	*	*	*	£30
1931	*	£2	£10	£50

	F	VF	EF	Unc
1933	*	£3	£15	£70
1935	*	*	£6	£20
1937	*	*	£9	£60
1938 (unique?)	*	*	*	*
1940	£2	£6	£60	*
1941	*	£1	£6	£15
1942	*	*	£3	£10
1943	*	*	£5	£15
1946	*	*	£3	£10
1948	*	*	£3	£10
1949	*	*	£3	£10
1950	*	*	£3	£10
1952	*	*	£2	£5
1962	*	*	£2	£4
1963	*	*	*	£2
1964	*	*	*	£2
1965	*	*	*	£1
1966	*	*	*	£1
1967	*	*	*	£1
1968	*	*	*	£1

HALFPENNIES

1928	*	£3	£6	£20
1928 proof	*	*	*	£20
1933	£1	£10	£40	£200
1935	*	£5	£15	£50
1937	*	*	£15	£30
1939	£4	£10	£25	£60
1940	*	£3	£20	£35
1941	*	*	£5	£10
1942	*	*	£2	£10
1943	*	*	£3	£10
1946	*	*	£5	£20
1949	*	*	£3	£5
1953	*	*	*	£3
1964	*	*	*	£2
1965	*	*	*	£2
1966	*	*	*	£2
1967	*	*	*	£1.50

FARTHINGS

1928	*	*	£3	£6
1928 proof	*	*	*	£10
1930	*	*	£5	£8
1931	£1	£3	£8	£18
1932	£1	£3	£10	£20
1933	*	£2	£5	£10
1935	*	£5	£12	£25
1936	*	£6	£15	£30
1937	*	£2	£5	£12
1939	*	*	£3	£5
1940	*	£3	£6	£20
1941	*	£1	£3	£5
1943	*	£1	£3	£6
1944	*	£1	£3	£6
1946	*	£1	£3	£5
1949	*	£2	£5	£8
1953	*	*	£3	£5
1959	*	*	£1	£3
1966	*	*	£2	£5

DECIMAL COINAGE
50p, 10p, 5p, 2p, 1p, ½p
All issues face value only.

SETS

1928 (in card case)	*	*	FDC	£120
1928 (in leather case)	*	*	FDC	£200
1966 unc. set	*	*	*	£10
1971 specimen set in folder	*	*	*	£5
1971 proof set	*	*	*	£9

The Anglo-Gallic Series

Chronological table of the Kings of England and France in the period 1154-1453

Henry II 1154-89
He was Duke of Normandy and Count of Anjou, Maine and Touraine. Through his marriage in 1152 with Eleanor of Aquitaine he became Duke of Aquitaine and Count of Poitou. He relinquished both these titles to his son Richard who in 1169 did homage to Louis VII of France. In 1185 he forced Richard to surrender Aquitaine and Poitou to ELEANOR who later – during Richard's absence – actually governed her provinces.

Richard I (Coeur de Lion) 1189-99
After his homage to the French King, he was, in 1172, formally installed as Duke of Aquitaine and Count of Poitou. Although his father forced him in 1185 to surrender Aquitaine and Poitou to his mother he retained actual government. Later Eleanor ruled in his absence.

John 1199-1216
He lost all provinces of the Angevin Empire except Aquitaine and part of Poitou.

Henry III 1216-72
In 1252 he ceded Aquitaine to his son Edward.

Edward I 1272-1307
He governed Aquitaine since 1252. In 1279 he became Count of Ponthieu in the right of his wife, Eleanor of Castile. When she died in 1290 the county went to his son Edward.

Edward II 1307-27
He was Count of Ponthieu as from 1290. In 1325 he relinquished the county of Ponthieu and the Duchy of Aquitaine to his son Edward.

Edward III 1327-77
He was Count of Ponthieu and Duke of Aquitaine as from 1325. At the outbreak of the war in 1337 he lost Ponthieu which was restored to him in 1360. In 1340 he assumed the title of King of France, which he abandoned again in 1360 as a result of the Treaty of Calais. He then obtained Aquitaine in full sovereignty and consequently changed his Aquitanian title from Duke (dux) to Lord (dominus) as the first one implied the overlordship of the French King. He gave Aquitaine as an apanage to his son, the Prince of Wales, better known as Edward The Black Prince, b.1330, d.1376, who was Prince of Aquitaine from 1362 till 1372, although he actually ruled from 1363 till 1371. In 1369, after war broke out again Edward reassumed the French title, which was henceforth used by the Kings of England until the Treaty of Amiens in 1802.

Richard II 1377-99
The son of The Black Prince succeeded his grandfather, Edward III, as King of England and as Lord of Aquitaine.

Henry IV 1399-1413
He adopted the same titles Richard II had, whom he ousted from the throne.

Henry V 1413-22
From 1417 until 1420 he used the title 'King of the French' on his 'Royal' French coins. After the Treaty of Troyes in 1420 he styled himself 'heir of France'.

Henry VI 1422-61
He inherited the title 'King of the French' from his grandfather Charles VI. He lost actual rule in Northern France in 1450 and in Aquitaine in 1453.

Louis VII 1137-80

Philip II (Augustus) 1180-1223

Louis VIII 1223-26
Louis IX (Saint Louis) 1226-70
Philip III 1270-85

Philip IV 1285-1314

Louis X 1314-16
Philip V 1316-22
Charles IV 1322-28

Philip VI (de Valois) 1328-50

John II (The Good) 1350-64

Charles V 1364-80

Charles VI 1380-1422

Charles VII 1422-61

...ll Kings of England in the period 1154-1453 had
...terests in France. They were Dukes or Lords of
...quitaine, Counts of Poitou or Ponthieu, Lords of
...soudun or they were even or pretended to be,
...ings of France itself, and, in those various capaci-
...es, struck coins. These coins, together with the
...rench coins of their sons, and of their English
...assals, are called Anglo-Gallic coins'.
    So starts the introduction of the Bourgey-Spink
...ook by E.R. Duncan Elias on this series. We would
...lso like to thank Messrs Bourgey and Spink for
...llowing us to use some of the illustrations from
...e book, as well as the chronological table of the
...ings of England and France during the period.
    The Anglo-Gallic Coins by E.R.D. Elias is still
...vailable from Spink and Son Ltd, London (see
...ome Useful Books on page 11).

Henry II
Denier,
Aquitaine

HENRY II 1152-68	F	VF
...enier	£40	£120
...bole	£80	£225
RICHARD THE LIONHEART 1168-99		
...quitaine		
...enier	£40	£125
...bole	£45	£150
...oitou		
...enier	£30	£80
...bole	£60	£200
...soudun		
...enier	£200	*
ELEANOR 1199-1204		
...enier	£40	£120
...bole	£300	*

Edward I
Denier au lion,
during his
father's
lifetime

EDWARD I
During the lifetime of his father 1252-72

	F	VF
...enier au lion	£35	£95
...bole au lion	£50	£135
After succession to the English throne 1272-1307		
...enier au lion	£100	£250
...bole au lion	£160	*

Edward I
Obole au lion,
after succession

...enier á la croix longue	£100	£250
...enier au léopard, first type	£35	£75
...bole au léopard, first type	£60	£125
...enier á la couronne	£350	*

The coinage of PONTHIEU (Northern France) under the Edwards

Edward I	F	VF
Denier	£125	£300
Obole	£125	£300
Edward III		
Denier	£150	*
Obole	£300	*

EDWARD II

Gros Turonus Regem	ext. rare	
Maille blanche	ext. rare	
Maille blanche Hibernie	£60	£125

EDWARD III

Gold coins

Ecu d'or	£850	£2250
Florin	£2500	£6500
Léopard d'or, 1st issue	ext. rare	
Léopard d'or, 2nd issue	£800	£1750

Edward III Léopard d'or, 2nd issue

Léopard d'or, 3rd issue	£750	£1650
Léopard d'or, 4th issue	£1250	*
Guyennois d'or, 1st type	£4000	£9000
Guyennois d'or, 2nd type	£1750	£4000
Guyennois d'or, 3rd type	£900	£2000

Silver coins

Gros aquitainique au léopard	£150	£400
Gros tournois à la crois mi-longue	£200	£550
Gros tournois à la croix longue	£120	£300
Sterling	£75	£200
Demi-sterling	£125	£300
Gros au léopard passant	£450	*
Gros à la couronne	£150	£400
Gros au châtel aquitainique	£150	£400
Gros tournois au léopard au-dessus	£75	£200
Gros à la porte	£75	£180
Gros acquitainique au léopard au-dessous	£200	*
Blanc au léopard sous couronne	£60	£150
Gros au léopard sous couronne	£250	£600
Gros à la couronne avec léopard	£175	£450
Sterling à la tête barbue	£325	£950
Petit gros de Bordeaux	ext. rare	
Gros au lion	£160	£450
Demi-gros au lion	£140	£350
Guyennois of argent (sterling)	£125	£275
Gros au buste	£750	*
Demi-gros au buste	£500	£1250

Black coins

Double à la couronne, 1st type	£100	*
Double à la couronne, 2nd type	£100	£200
Double à la couronne, 3rd type	£100	*
Double au léopard	£90	£180
Double au léopard sous couronne	£35	£95
Double guyennois	ext. rare	
Denier au léopard, 2nd type	£35	£100
Obole au léopard, 2nd type	ext. rare	
Denier au léopard, 3rd type	£45	£120
Denier au léopard, 4th type	£50	£150

THE ANGLO-GALLIC SERIES

	F	VF
Obole au léopard, 4th type	£50	£125
Denier au lion	£35	£90

N.B. Some issues of the deniers au léopard of the 2nd and 3rd type are very rare to extremely rare and therefore considerably more valuable.

The coinage of BERGERAC
Henry, Earl of Lancaster 1347-51

Gros tournois à la croix longue ...	£800	£1600
Gros tournois à la couronne	£500	*
Gros au châtel aquitainque	£750	£1500
Gros tournois au léopard au-dessus	£400	£800
Gros à la couronne		ext. rare
Gros à fleur-de-lis		ext. rare
Gros au léopard passant		ext. rare
Double		ext. rare
Denier au léopard		£500

Henry, Duke of Lancaster 1351-61

Gros tournois à la couronne avec léopard	£600	*
Gros au léopard couchant	£700	*
Sterling à la tête barbue	£350	*
Gros au lion		ext. rare

EDWARD THE BLACK PRINCE 1362-72
Gold Coins

Léopard d'or	£750	£1650
Guyennois d'or	£1250	*
Chaise d'or	£250	£2500
Pavillon d'or 1st issue	£950	£2000
Pavillon d'or 2nd issue	£950	£2000
Demi-pavillon d'or		ext. rare
Hardi d'or	£1000	£2250

*Edward the Black Prince
Hardi d'or of Bordeaux*

Silver Coins

Gros	£750	£1500

Edward the Black Prince Demi-Gros

Demi-gros	£85	£175
Sterling	£65	£130
Hardi d'argent...	£40	£90

Edward the Black Prince Hardi d'argent

Black Coins

Double guyennois	£100	£250
Denier au lion	£50	£125
Denier	£60	£150

RICHARD II 1377-99
Gold Coins

Hardi d'or	£1000	£2750
Demi-hardi d'or		ext. rare

Silver Coins

Double Hardi d'argent	£500	*
Hardi d'argent...	£70	£160

Black Coins

Denier	£90	£200

HENRY IV 1399-1413
Silver Coins

Double Hardi d'argent	£500	*

Henry IV Double Hardi d'argent

	F	VF
Hardi d'argent...	£50	£120
Hardi aux genêts...	£300	*

Black Coins

Denier	£40	£120
Denier aux genêts	£100	£300

HENRY V 1413-22
Gold Coins

Agnel d' or	£4500	£9500
Salut d' or	£5500	£15000

Silver Coins

Florette, 1st issue	£90	£200
Florette, 2nd issue	£140	£300
Florette, 3rd issue	**£70**	**£150**
Florette, 4th issue	**£70**	**£150**
Guénar	**£250**	**£500**
Gros au léopard	£350	*

Black Coins

Mansiois		ext. rare
Niquet	£50	£135
Denier tournois	£60	£150

HENRY VI 1422-53
Gold Coins

Salut d' or	£325	£650
Angelot	£1250	£30000

Henry VI Salut d'or, Paris Mint

Silver Coins

Grand Blanc aux ècus	£40	£125
Petit Blanc	£125	£275
Trésin...		ext. rare

Henry V Grand Blanc, Paris Mint

Black Coins

Denier Parisis, 1st issue	£60	£150
Denier Parisis, 2nd issue	£60	£150
Denier tournois	£60	£160
Maille tournois	£70	£160

N.B. *The prices of the saluts and grand blancs are for the mints of Paris, Rouen and Saint Lô; coins of other mints are rare to very rare and consequently more valuable.*

Island Coinages

CHANNEL ISLANDS

From the date of their introduction onwards, proofs have been struck for a large number of Channel Islands coins, particularly in the case of Jersey. Except for those included in the modern proof sets these are mostly at least very rare and in the majority of cases have been omitted from the list. A number of die varieties which exist for several dates of the earlier 19th century Guernsey eight doubles have also been excluded. For further information in both cases the reader is referred to The Coins of the British Commonwealth of Nations, Part I, European Territories by F. Pridmore, published by Spink and Son Ltd.

GUERNSEY

TEN SHILLINGS

	F	VF	EF	BU
1966	*	*	*	£1

THREEPENCE

	F	VF	EF	BU
1956	*	*	*	£1
1959	*	*	*	£1
1966 proof only	*	*	*	£1

EIGHT DOUBLES

	F	VF	EF	BU
1834	*	£12	£30	£100
1858	*	£12	£30	£100
1864	*	£15	£40	*
1868	*	£10	£30	*
1874	*	£10	£30	*
1885 H	*	*	£12	£25
1889 H	*	*	£10	£20
1893 H	*	*	£10	£20
1902 H	*	*	£10	£20
1903 H	*	*	£10	£20
1910 H	*	*	£12	£25
1911 H	*	*	£12	£30
1914 H	*	*	£12	£25
1918 H	*	*	£10	£30
1920 H	*	*	£8	£10
1934 H	*	*	£8	£10
1934 H prooflike	*	*	*	£50
1938 H	*	*	*	£5
1945 H	*	*	*	£5
1947 H	*	*	*	£4
1949 H	*	*	*	£4
1956	*	*	*	£1
1959	*	*	*	£1
1966 proof only	*	*	*	£3

FOUR DOUBLES

	F	VF	EF	BU
1830	*	*	£20	£60
1858	*	*	£25	£70

Guernsey 1864 four doubles

	F	VF	EF	BU
1864	*	£5	£35	*
1868	*	£5	£35	*

EIGHT DOUBLES (continued)

	F	VF	EF	BU
1874	*	*	£30	*
1885 H	*	*	£8	£25
1889 H	*	*	£5	£20
1893 H	*	*	£4	£15
1902 H	*	*	£4	£15
1903 H	*	*	£4	£15
1906 H	*	*	£4	£15
1908 H	*	*	£4	£15
1910 H	*	*	£3	£15
1911 H	*	*	£3	£15
1914 H	*	*	£3	£15
1918 H	*	*	£3	£15
1920 H	*	*	*	£10
1945 H	*	*	*	£4
1949 H	*	*	*	£5
1956	*	*	*	£1
1966 proof only	*	*	*	£1

TWO DOUBLES

	F	VF	EF	BU
1858	*	£4	£25	*
1868	*	£4	£30	*
1874	*	£4	£20	*
1885 H	*	*	£6	£15
1889 H	*	*	£4	£10
1899 H	*	*	£4	£10
1902 H	*	*	£5	£10
1903 H	*	*	£5	£15
1906 H	*	*	£4	£15
1908 H	*	*	£4	£20
1911 H	*	*	£4	£15
1914 H	*	*	£4	£18
1917 H	*	£10	£30	£60
1918 H	*	*	£2	£6
1920 H	*	*	£3	£8
1929 H	*	*	£2	£5

ONE DOUBLE

	F	VF	EF	BU
1830	*	*	£10	£25
1868	*	£5	£20	*
1868/30	*	£5	£20	*
1885 H	*	*	£4	£10
1889 H	*	*	£2	£5
1893 H	*	*	£2	£5
1899 H	*	*	£2	£5
1902 H	*	*	£2	£5
1903 H	*	*	£2	£5
1911 H	*	*	£2	£8
1911 H new type	*	*	£2	£8
1914 H	*	*	£3	£8
1929 H	*	*	£1	£2
1933 H	*	*	£1	£2
1938 H	*	*	£1	£2

ISLAND COINAGES

DECIMAL COINAGE

The word 'NEW' was omitted from coins issued after December 1976, being replaced by the word for the denomination.

f denotes face value

TWENTY-FIVE POUNDS	BU
1994 50th Anniverary Normandy Landings gold	£175
1995 Queen Mother, gold, proof	£200
1996 Queen's 70th Birthday, gold, proof ...	£200
1996 European Football, gold, proof	£200
1997 Golden Wedding, gold, proof	£200
1988 Royal Air Force, gold, proof	£200
1999 Royal Wedding, gold, proof	£200
1999 Queen Mother, gold, proof	£200
1999 Churchill, gold, proof	£200
2000 Queen Mother, gold, proof	£200

TEN POUNDS
1997 Golden Wedding, silver, proof	£150
1999 Millennium, gold, proof	£350
2000 Century & Monarchy, silver, proof	£160

FIVE POUNDS
1995 Queen Mother, cu-ni	£7
1995 Queen Mother, silver, proof	£37
1996 Queen's 70th Birthday, cu-ni	£7
1996 Queen's 70th Birthday, silver, proof ...	£37
1996 European Football, cu-ni	£7
1996 European Football, silver, proof	£37
1997 Golden Wedding, cu-ni	£7
1997 Golden Wedding, silver, proof	£40
1997 Castle Cornet, silver, proof	£35
1997 Caernarfou Castle, silver, proof	£41
1997 Leeds Castle, silver, proof	£41
1997 Golden Wedding, gold, BU	£50
1998 Royal Air Force, silver, proof	£40
1999 Millennium, cu-ni	£10
1999 – silver, proof	£32
1999 – Royal Wedding, cu-ni	£10
1999 – silver, proof	£42
1999 Queen Mother, cu-ni	£10
1999 – silver, proof	£42
1999 Churchill, cu-ni	£10
1999 – silver, proof	£40
1999 Queen Mother, gold, BU	£50
2000 Centenary & Monarchy, cu-ni	£10
2000 – silver, proof	£40
2000 Queen Mother, cu-ni	£10
2000 – silver, proof	£40
2000 – gold, BU	£50

TWO POUNDS
1985 Liberation 40th Anniversary, crown size, in blister pack	£3.45
1985 – – silver, proof	£28.75
1986 Commonwealth Games, plastic case ...	£3.50
1986 – in presentation folder	£4
1986 – .500 silver, B. Unc	£15
1986 – .925 silver, proof	£28.75
1987 90th Anniversary of death of William the Conqueror, cu-ni, in presentation folder ...	£4
1987 gold, proof	£90
1987 – silver, proof	£28.75
1988 William the Second, cu-ni in presentation folder	£4
1988 – silver, proof	£28.75
1989 Accession of Henry I, cu-ni in	

presentation folder	£4.25
1989 – silver, proof	£28.75
1989 Royal Visit, cu-ni	£2
1989 – – in plastic case	£3.50
1989 – silver, proof	£28.75
1990 Queen Mother's 90th Birthday, cu-ni ...	£2
1990 – – in plastic case	£3.50
1990 – silver, proof	£28.75
1991 Henry II, cu-ni	£5
1991 – – silver, proof	£30
1993 40th Anniversary of the Coronation, silver, proof	£28.75
1994 Normandy Landings	f
1994 – silver, proof	£30
1995 50th Anniversary of Liberation, silver, proof	£35
1995 –, silver, piedfort, proof	£60
1995 – cu-ni	£5
1998 Bimetal	f

ONE POUND
1981 copper, zinc, nickel	£2
1981 gold, proof (8 grammes)	£85
1981 gold piedfort (16 grammes)	£250
1983 new specification, new reverse ...	f
1985 new designs (in folder)	£1.20
1995 Queen Mother, silver, proof	£22
1996 Queen's 70th Birthday, silver, proof ...	£22
1997 Golden Wedding, silver, proof	£22
1997 Tower of London, silver, proof	£22
1997 Golden Wedding, silver, BU	£10
1998 Royal Air Force, silver, proof	£22
1999 Millennium, gold plated, silver, proof ...	£27
1999 Royal Wedding, silver, proof	£22
1999 Queen Mother, silver, proof	£22
1999 Churchill, silver, proof	£20
2000 Queen Mother, silver, proof	£20

FIFTY PENCE
1969	£1
1970	£3
1971 proof (from set)	£5
1981	£1
1982	£1
1985 new designs	f
Other dates	f
2000 Battle of Britain, cu-ni	£3
2000 – silver, proof	£20
2000 – silver, piedfort	£45
2000 – gold, proof	£260

TWENTY-FIVE PENCE
1972 Silver Wedding (cupro-nickel)	£2
1972 – proof (silver)	£8
1977 Jubilee	£1.50
1977 – silver, proof	£10
1978 Royal Visit (cu-ni)	£1.50
1978 – silver, proof	£8
1980 Queen Mother's 80th birthday (cu-ni) ...	£1.25
1980 – silver	£10
1981 Royal Wedding (cu-ni)	£1
1981 – silver, proof	£10

OTHER DECIMAL COINAGE

120p, 10p, 5p, 1p, ½p. All issues face value only. *(The 5p and 10p were issued in a reduced size in 1992 and 1993 respectively.)*

COINS MARKET VALUES

SETS

1956 proof	... ...	£25
1966 proof	... ...	£8
1971 proof	... ...	£7.25
1929 proof	... ...	£8
1981 proof (including £1)	... ...	£10
1985 new designs, £1 to 1p (7 coins)	... ...	£6
1985 – £2 Liberation crown to 1p proof *9 coins)	£25
1986 BU set in folder, £1 to 1p (7 coins)	... ...	£6
1986 £2 Commonwealth Games to 1p,		
proof (8 coins)	... ...	£25
1987 BU set in folder, £1 to 1p (7 coins)	... ...	£6
1987 £2 William the Conqueror to 1p,		
proof (8 coins)	... ...	£25
1988 BU set in folder, £1 to 1p (7 coins)	... ...	£7
1988 £2 William the Second to 1p, proof (8 coins)	£25
1989 BU set in folder, £1 to 1p (7 coins)	... ...	£8
1989 £2 Henry I to 1p, proof (8 coins)	... ...	£26
1990 £2 Queen Mother's 90th Birthday to 1p,		
poroof (8 coins)	... ...	£28
1990 BU set as above (8 coins)	... ...	£10
1944 Normandy Landings, £100, £50, £25,		
£10 gold	... ...	£1000
1995 50th Anniversary of Liberation,		
£100, £50, £25, £10	... ...	£1000
1995 Queen Mother, £25 gold, £5 silver,		
£1 proof (3 coins)	... ...	£250
1996 Queen's 70th Birthday, £25 gold, £5 + £1		
silver, proof (3 coins)	... ...	£250
1997 Golden Wedding, £25 gold, £5 + £1 silver,		
proof (3 coins)	... ...	£250
1997 Three £5 + £1 silver, proof (4 coins)	...	£135
1998 Royal Air Force, £25 gold, £5 + £1 silver,		
proof (3 coins)	... ...	£250
1999 Royal Wedding, £25 gold, £5 + £1 silver,		
proof	... ...	£250
1999 Queen Mother, £25 gold, £5 + £1 silver,		
proof (3 coins)	... ...	£250

ALDERNEY

TWENTY-FIVE POUNDS

1993 Coronation, gold proof	... ...	£225
1997 Golden Wedding, gold, proof	... ...	£200
1999 Churchill, gold proof	... ...	£200
2000 Battle of Britain, gold, proof	... ...	£200

FIVE POUNDS

1995 Queen Mother, cu-ni	... ...	£7.50
1995 – silver, proof	... ...	£33
1995 – piedfort	... ...	£60
1995 – gold, proof	... ...	£800
1996 – Queen's 70th Birthday, cu-ni	... ...	£7.50
1996 – silver, proof	... ...	£35
1996 – piedfort	... ...	£60
1996 – gold, proof	... ...	£800
1999 Total Eclipse, cu-ni	... ...	£8
1999 – silver, proof	... ...	£39
1999 Churchill, cu-ni	... ...	£10
1999 – silver, proof	... ...	£38
1999 – gold, proof	... ...	£600
1999 Battle of Britain, cu-ni	... ...	£10
2000 – silver, proof	... ...	£38
2000 Queen Mother, silver, proof	... ...	£38

TWO POUNDS

1989 Royal Visit, cu-ni	... ...	£3
1989 – in plastic case	... ...	£5
1989 – silver, proof	... ...	£30
1989 – piedfort	... ...	£60
1989 gold, proof	... ...	£800
1990 Queen Mother's 90th birthday, cu-ni	... ...	£3
1990 – in plastic case	... ...	£5
1990 – silver, proof	... ...	£30
1990 – – – piedfort	... ...	£60
1990 – gold, proof	... ...	£800
1882 Accession, cu-ni	... ...	£3
1992 –, plastic case	... ...	£5
1992 –, silver, proof	... ...	£30
1992 –, piedfort	... ...	£60
1992 –, gold, proof	... ...	£800
1993 Coronation, cu-ni	... ...	£3
1993 – –, plastics case	... ...	£5
1993 – silver, proof	... ...	£35
1993 – –, piedfort	... ...	£60
1994 D-Day, cu-ni	... ...	£3
1994 –, card pack	... ...	£6
1994 –, silver proof	... ...	£35
1994 – –, piedfort	... ...	£60
1995 VE/Liberation, cu-ni	... ...	£3
1995 – –, plastic case	... ...	£5
1995 –, silver proof	... ...	£33
1995 – –, piedfort	... ...	£60
1995 –, gold proof	... ...	£800
1997 Golden Wedding, cu-ni	... ...	£3
1997 Golden Wedding, silver, proof	... ...	£38
1997 WWF, Puffin, cu-ni	... ...	£3
1997 WWF, Puffin, silver, proof	... ...	£32
1999 Total Eclipse, cu-ni	... ...	£4
1999 Total Eclipse, silver, proof	... ...	£34
1999 Total Eclipse, gold, proof	... ...	£800

ONE POUND

1993 Coronation, silver, proof	... ...	£30
1995 VE/Liberation, silver, proof	... ...	£22
1995 –, gold, proof	... ...	£300

SETS

1994 £100, £50, £25, £10, D-Day		
gold, proof (4 coins)	... ...	£1000
1994 £50, £25, £10, D-Day		
gold, proof (3 coins)	... ...	£500

JERSEY

CROWN	F	VF	EF	BU
1966	*	*	*	£1
1966 – proof	*	*	*	£3

1/4 OF A SHILLING				
1957	*	*	*	£2
1960 proof only	*	*	*	£5
1964	*	*	*	£0.30
1966	*	*	*	£0.75

1/2 OF A SHILLING				
1877 H	*	*	£7	£40
1881	*	*	£9	£50
1888	*	*	£8	£40
1894	*	*	£7	£30
1909	*	*	£8	£40
1911	*	*	£5	£25
1913	*	*	£5	£20
1923	*	*	£5	£25
1923 new type	*	*	£7	£20
1926	*	*	£5	£18
1931	*	*	£2	£10
1933	*	*	£3	£10
1935	*	*	£2	£10
1937	*	*	*	£5

ISLAND COINAGES

	F	VF	EF	BU
'1945' (George VI)[1] ...	*	*	*	£3
'1945' (Elizabeth II)[1] ...	*	*	*	£2
1946	*	*	*	£4
1947	*	*	*	£3
1957	*	*	*	£0.40
1960	*	*	*	£0.20
1964	*	*	*	£0.15
1966	*	*	*	£0.15

The date 1945 on one-twelfth shillings commemorates the year of liberation from German occupation. The coins were struck in 1949, 1950, 1952 and 1954.

1/13 OF A SHILLING

	F	VF	EF	BU
1841	*	*	£30	£100
1844	*	*	£35	£120
1851	*	*	£40	£100
1858	*	*	£35	£110
1861	*	*	£40	£100
1865 proof only	*	*	*	£350
1866	*	*	£20	£60
1870	*	*	£25	£60
1871	*	*	£25	£60

1/24 OF A SHILLING

	F	VF	EF	BU
1877 H	*	*	£4	£30
1888	*	*	£4	£25
1894	*	*	£4	£25
1909	*	*	£3	£20
1911	*	*	£3	£20
1913	*	*	£3	£20
1923	*	*	£2	£15
1923 new type	*	*	£2	£15
1926	*	*	£2	£15
1931	*	*	£1	£5
1933	*	*	£1	£5
1935	*	*	£1	£5
1937	*	*	£1	£5
1946	*	*	£1	£5
1947	*	*	£1	£5

1/26 OF A SHILLING

	F	VF	EF	BU
1841	*	*	£18	£75
1844	*	*	£18	£75
1851	*	*	£18	£75
1858	*	*	£18	£75
1861	*	*	£16	£65
1866	*	*	£15	£60
1870	*	*	£15	£50
1871	*	*	£18	£50

1/48 OF A SHILLING

	F	VF	EF	BU
1877 H	*	£8	£30	£75

1/52 OF A SHILLING

	F	VF	EF	BU
1841	*	£12	£50	£100
1841 proof	*	*	*	£300
1861 proof only	*	*	*	£400

DECIMAL COINAGE

f denotes face value

FIVE POUNDS
	BU
1990 50th Anniversary of the Battle of Britain, silver, proof	£85
1997 Golden Wedding, silver, proof	£38
1997 Golden Wedding, cu-ni	£8
1999 – 2000 Millennium, silver, proof	£40

TWO POUNDS
	BU
1981 Royal Wedding, nickel silver (crown size)	f

	BU
1981 – in presentation pack	£2.75
1981 – silver, proof	£15
1981 – gold, proof	£300
1985 40th anniversary of liberation, (crown size)	f
1985 – in presentation pack	£3.75
1985 – silver, frosted proof	£28.75
1985 – gold, frosted proof	£1000
1986 Commonwealth Games	£2
1986 – in presentation case	£3
1986 – .500 silver, B. Unc	£14.95
1986 – .925 silver, proof	£28.75
1987 World Wildlife Fund 25 years cu-ni in blister pack	£3.25
1987 – silver, proof	£30
1989 Royal Visit cu-ni in de luxe presentation case	£4
1989 – silver, proof	£28.75
1990 Queen Mother's 90 birthday, cu-ni	£4
1990 – silver, proof	£28.75
1990 – gold, proof	£402.50
1990 50th Anniversary of the Battle of Britain, silver, proof	£28.75
1993 40th Anniversary of the Coronation silver, proof	£30
1995 50th Anniversary of Liberation, silver, proof	£35
1995 –, silver, piedfort, proof	£60
1995 – cu-ni	£4
1996 Queen's 70th Birthday, cu-ni	£5
1996 – – – silver, proof	£33
1997 Bimetal, BU	£5
1997 – – – silver proof	£25
1998 – – – new portrait, BU	£5

ONE POUND
	BU
1981 cu-ni	£2.25
1981 silver, proof	£25
1981 gold, proof	£150

In 1983 Jersey issued a one pound coin with the specification changed to conform with that of the UK one pound coin. The reverse initially bore the emblem of St Helier Parish, but this was changed regularly to represent, in rotation, each of the 12 parishes of Jersey, the others being: St Saviour, St Brelade, St Clement, St Lawrence, St Peter, Grouville, St Martin, St Ouen, Trinity, St John and St Mary, in order of size of the population.

	BU
1983 new specification, new designs (both sides), on presentation card (St Helier)	£4
1983 silver, frosted proof, in case –	£23
1983 gold, frosted proof, in case –	£345
1984 in presentation wallet (St Saviour)	£4
1983 silver, frosted proof –	£23
1984 gold, frosted proof –	£345
1984 in presentation wallet (St Brelade)	£4
1984 silver, frosted proof –	£23
1984 gold, frosted proof –	£345
1985 in presentation wallet (St Clement)	£4
1985 silver, frosted proof –	£23
1985 gold, frosted proof –	£345
1985 in presentation wallet (St Lawrence)	£4
1985 silver, frosted proof –	£23
1985 gold, frosted proof –	£345
1986 in presentation wallet (St Peter)	£4
1986 silver, frosted proof –	£23
1986 gold, frosted proof –	£345
1986 in presentation wallet (Grouville)	£4
1986 silver, frosted proof –	£23
1986 gold, frosted proof –	£345
1987 in presentation wallet (St Martin)	£4
1987 silver, frosted proof –	£23

1987 gold, frosted proof –	**£345**	
1987 in presentation wallet (St Ouen) ...	**£4**	
1987 silver, frosted proof –	**£23**	
1987 gold, frosted proof –	**£345**	
1988 in presentation wallet (Trinity)	**£4**	
1988 silver, frosted proof –	**£23**	
1988 gold, frosted proof –	**£345**	
1988 in presentation wallet (St John) ...	**£4**	
1988 silver, frosted proof –	**£23**	
1988 gold, frosted proof –	**£345**	
1988 in presentation wallet (St Mary) ...	**£4**	
1988 silver, frosted proof –	**£23**	
1988 gold, frosted proof –	**£345**	

In 1991 Jersey launched a series of six coins featuring ships built on the island during the second half of the 19th century.

1991 Silver, frosted proof 'Tickler'	**£35**
1991 Gold, frosted proof 'Tickler'	**£352**
1991 Silver, frosted proof 'Percy Douglas'	**£25.80**
1991 Gold, frosted proof 'Percy Douglas'	**£352**
1992 Silver, proof 'The Hebe'	**£20**
1992 Gold, frosted proof 'The Hebe'	**£300**
1992 Silver, proof Coat of Arms	**£20**
1992 Gold, frosted proof Coat of Arms ...	**£300**
1992 Silver, proof 'The Gemini'	**£30**
1992 Silver, proof 'The Century'	**£30**
1992 Silver, proof 'The Resolute'	**£25**
1992 Gold, proof 'The Resolute'	**£360**

SOVEREIGN
2000 Millennium gold BU	**£70**
2000 Millennium gold proof	**£125**

FIFTY PENCE
1969	**£1**
1983 new obv, new rev...	**f**
1985 40th anniversary of liberation	**f**

TWENTY-FIVE PENCE
1977 Jubilee	**£1.50**
1977 – Silver, proof	**£17.50**

TWENTY PENCE
1982 date on rocks on rev (cased)	**£0.65**
1982, silver, proof, piedfort	**£35**
1983 new obv, with date, rev no date on rocks	**f**
Later dates	**f**

OTHER DECIMAL COINAGE
10p, 5p, 2p, 1p, ½p (to 1982). All face value only.
1983 10p, 5p, 2p, 1p: new obv and rev designs...	**f**
Later dates	**f**

SETS
	BU
1957	**£30**
1960	**£15**
1964	**£10**
1966 (4 coins) proof	**£4**
1966 (2 crowns)	**£7**
1968/7 1 decimal coins	**£2**
1972 Silver Wedding (5 gold, 4 silver coins)	**£400**
1972 – – proof	**£450**
1972 – – (4 silver coins)...	**£25**
1980 50p to ½p...	**£2**
1980 – frosted proof	**£15**
1981 £1 to ½p, in presentation pack	**£3**
1981 – base metal, proof	**£13.95**
1983 £1 to 1p (7 coins)	**£3.50**
1983 – silver frosted proof, in album	**£40**
1987 £1 to 1p, in folder (7 coins)	**£6**
1990 50th Anniversary of the Battle of Britain, gold coins with face values of £100, £50, £25 and £10 (4 coins)	**£1035**
1992 £1 to 1p (7 coins)	**£13**
1995 50th Anniversary of Liberation, £100, £50 £25 and £10 (4 coins)	**£1000**
1997 £2 to 1p incl. 2 x 50p (9 coins)	**£15**

ISLE OF MAN

Contemporary forgeries of several of the earlier Isle of Man coins exist.

COPPER AND BRONZE 1709-1839

Isle of Man, Penny, 1786

PENNIES
	F	VF	EF	Unc
1709	£15	£40	*	*
1733	£10	£30	£100	*
1733 proof	£20	£60	£120	£275
1733 silver	*	*	£200	£400
1758	£10	£20	£70	£200
1758 proof	*	*	*	*
1758 silver	*	*	£300	£500
1786	£10	£20	£80	£175
1786 plain edge proof	*	*	£150	£300
1798	£15	£40	£100	£200
1798 bronzed proof ...	*	*	£120	£200
1798 AE gilt proof ...	*	*	£300	*
1798 silver proof	*	*	*	*
1813	£10	£25	£95	*
1813 bronzed proof ...	*	*	£70	£175
1839	*	£15	£50	£100
1839 proof	*	*	*	*

Isle of Man, Halfpenny, proof in Silver, 1733

HALFPENNIES
	F	VF	EF	VAC
1709	£12	£30	*	*
1733	£8	£20	£50	£150
1733 proof	£10	£25	£80	£250
1733 silver	*	£60	£120	£300
1758	£8	£15	£50	£175
1758 proof	*	*	*	*
1786	£8	£15	£40	*
1786 plain edge proof	*	*	£110	£250
1798	£8	£15	£50	*
1798 proof	*	*	£65	£125
1798 AE gilt proof ...	*	*	*	*
1813	£8	£20	£40	£125
1813 proof	*	*	£65	£125
1839 proof	*	*	£15	£50

FARTHINGS
	F	VF	EF	VAC
1839	£10	£25	£50	*
1839 proof	*	*	*	*

ISSUES SINCE 1965

Prices for the gold series, £5 to half sovereign, plus 'angels', and platinum 'nobels' are directly goverened by day-to-day prices in their respective bullion markets, to which reference should be made for current valuations. Since 1973 there have been many changes to the designs of the circulating coins and these have often been accompanied by special sets in gold, platinum and silver. In addition there have been many commemorative crowns struck in base metal and in precious metal. A full list of the complete coinage is beyong the scope of this publication.

BNTA MEMBERS IN COUNTY ORDER
(Those members with retail premises are indicated with an *)

LONDON AREA
*A.H. Baldwin & Sons Ltd.
Beaver Coin Room
*W. & F.C. Bonham & Sons Ltd.
Chelsea Coins
*Philip Cohen Numismatics
Andre de Clermont
Michael Dickinson
*Dix Noonan Webb
Christopher Eimer
*Glendining's
Harrow Coin & Stamp Centre
Ian Jull
*Knightsbridge Coins
*Lennox Gallery
Lubbock & Son Ltd.
C.J. Martin Coins Ltd.
*Colin Narbeth & Son Ltd.
*Seaby Coins/C.N.G. Inc.
R.D. Shah
*Simmons Gallery
*Spink & Son Ltd.
Surena Ancient Art & Numismatic
*Vale Coins
Mark J. Vincenzi
BERKSHIRE
Frank Milward
BUCKINGHAMSHIRE
Europa Numismatics
CORNWALL
Michael Trenerry Ltd.
CUMBRIA
Patrick Finn
DORSET
*Dorset Coin Co. Ltd.
ESSEX
E.J. & C.A. Brooks
HAMPSHIRE
*SPM Jewellers
Raymond Sleet
Studio Coins
West Essex Coin Investments
HERTFORDSHIRE
K B Coins
David Miller

KENT
C.J. Denton
Stephen Lockett
*Peter Morris
LANCASHIRE
*B.J. Dawson (Coins)
*Colin de Rouffignac
*Peter Ireland Ltd.
Liverpool Medal Co.
*R & L Coins
LINCOLNSHIRE
Grantham Coins
NORFOLK
*Clive T. Dennett
Chris Rudd
NORTHUMBERLAND
*Corbitt Stamps Ltd.
OXFORDSHIRE
Simon R. Porter
SHROPSHIRE
*Collectors Gallery
SUFFOLK
*Lockdale Coins Ltd
Schwer Coins
SURREY
KMCC Ltd
Graeme & Linda Monk
Nigel Tooley Ltd
SUSSEX
*Brighton Coin Co.
WEST MIDLANDS
*Format of Birmingham Ltd.
Mint Coins Ltd
WARWICKSHIRE
*Warwick & Warwick Ltd
WORCESTERSHIRE
Whitmore
YORKSHIRE
Airedale Coins
Paul Clayton
Paul Davies Ltd.
*J. Smith

WALES
Lloyd Bennett
*North Wales Coins Ltd.
Colin Rumney

2000/2001

British Paper Money

THE prices listed here are only intended as a guide to values of English bank-notes. Notes of Queen Elixabeth II are generally available at a little above face value and previous to that notes tend to increase in value the older they are. Top condition is the most important factor in banknote pricing although it is quite possible to collevt a more attractive selection in lower grades; some notes for example are never seen in better then Very Fine. The proces quoted are for uncirculated and a premium can be expected on first class notes - this is especially relevant to notes of John Bradbury and to a lesser extent N.F. Warren Fisher.

We have not listed banknotes prior to 1914 as these are all scarce and only available in grades up to Very Fine. The past year has continued to show a healthy demand for material at every level, the emphasis still remaining on quality followed by rarity. The hobby continues to grow at a sensible pace, the shortage of good material being the only drawback.

Reference numbers are according to Vincent Duggleby's *English Paper Money*. The new (fourth) edition was published by Spink & Son Ltd in October 1990.

TREASURY NOTES

Signed by John Bradbury

First Issue

			VF	Unc
T9	10s	Red on white. Prefix 'No'	£140	£300
T8	10s	Red on white. Six digits	£300	£1000
T10	10s	Red on white. Five digits	£300	£1000
T1	£1	Black on white. Prefix large letters A., B. or C.	£300	£1200
T2	£1	Black on white. As previous but no full stop after serial letter	£800	£1800
T3	£1	Black on white. Six digits	£150	£600
T4	£1	Black on white. Large serial number, 'dot' and five digits	£400	£1400
T5	£1	Black on white. Large serial number, 'dash' and five digits	£350	£1200
T6	£1	Black on white. Double prefix letters	£300	£1250
T7	£1	Black on white. Small type face serial number	£450	£2000

(Serial number with prefix 'No' are referred to as 'dot' if 'No' is followed by a full stop and 'dash' when a dash is used).

Second issue

			VF	Unc
T13	10s	Red on white. Six digits	£45	£240
T12	10s	Red on white. Five digits	£45	£240
T11	£1	Black on white.	£60	£280
T15	10s	Red on white. Arabic overprint	£225	£900
T14	£1	Black on white. Arabic overprint	from £750	from £3500

Third issue

			VF	Unc
T20	10s	Green and brown on white Red serial no. with 'dash'	£50	£240

T19	10s	Green and brown on white Red serial no. with 'dot'	£50	£280
T17	10s	Green and brown on white. Black serial no. with 'dot'	£60	£280
T18	10s	Green and brown on white Black serial no. with 'dash'	£60	£240
T16	£1	Green and brown on white	£30	£80

Signed by Norman Fenwick Warren Fisher First issue (overall watermark)

T25	10s	Green and brown on white, 'dot'	£30	£140
T26	10s	Green and brown on white, 'dash'	£15	£90
T24	£1	Green and brown on white	£15	£45

Second issue (boxed watermark)

T30	10s	Green and brown on white	£20	£90
T31	£1	Green and brown on white	£12	£35
T32	£1	Green and brown on white, 'dash'	£15	£35

Third issue (Northern Ireland)

T33	10s	Green and brown on white	£25	£100
T34	£1	Green and brown on white, 'dot'	£15	£60
T35	£1	Green and brown on white, 'dash'	£20	£80

Unissued notes prepared during the Great War (all extremely rare)

T21	5s	Deep violet and green on white (Bradbury)	from £4000
T22	2s 6d	Olive-green and chocolate on white	from £2500
T23	1s	Green and brown on white	from £2250
T27	5s	Violet and green on white (Warren Fisher)	from £2250
T28	2s 6d	Olive-green and chocolate on white	from £2250
T29	1s	Green and brown on white	from £2250

BANK OF ENGLAND NOTES
Cyril Patrick Mahon 1925-29

B210	10s	Red-brown	£15	£90
B212	£1	Green	£10	£30
B215	£5	Black on white	£50	£220

Bank of England £1 serial no. 2 sold at auction by Spink and Son Ltd several years ago for £56,000.

John Bradbury 5 shillings.

Basil Gage Catterns 1929-34

B223	10s	Red-brown	£7	£35
B225	£1	Green (prefix: letter, number, number; e.g.E63)	£8	£20
B226	£1	Green (prefix: number, number, letter)	£10	£20
B228	£5	Black on white	£50	£170

Kenneth Oswald Peppiatt 1934-49

B236	10s	Red-brown (prefix: number, number, letter) 1st period	£3	£20
B251	10s	Mauve 2nd period	£7	£22
B256	10s	Red-brown (prefix: number, number, letter) 3rd period	£5	£15
B262	10s	Red-brown (metal filament) 4th period	£3	£12
B238	£1	Green (prefix: number, number, letter) 1st issue	£3	£7
B248	£1	Pale blue (prefix:A-D) 2nd issue	£6	£12
B249	£1	Blue (shades) 2nd issue	£1	£3
B258	£1	Green (prefix: number, number, letter) 3rd issue	£4	£6
B260	£1	Green (metal filament) 4th issue	£3	£5
B241	£5	Black on white, one straight edge, three deckled	£35	£120
B255	£5	Black on white, straight edges, metal filament, thick paper	£35	£100
B264	£5	Black on white, straight edges, metal filament, thin paper	£35	£100

Unissued notes of the 1939-45 War (very rare)

B253	5s	Olive-green on pale pink background	from £2400	*
B254	2s 6d	Black on pale blue background	from £1800	*

Percival Spencer Beale 1949-55

B266	10s	Red-brown (prefix: letter, number, number, letter)	£2	£8
B265	10s	Red-brown (prefix: number, number, letter)	£3	£10
B268	£1	Green	£2	£5
B270	£5	Black on white		

eslie Kenneth O'Brien 1955-62

271	10s	Red-brown (prefix: letter, number, number, letter)	£2	£4
272	10s	Red-brown (prefix: number, number, letter)	£15	£30
286	10s	Red-brown, Queen's portrait	£1	£5
273	£1	Green	£2	£4
281	£1	Green (prefix: letter, number, number) Queen's portrait	£2	£4
282	£1	Green (prefix: number, number, letter). Queen's portrait	£2	£4
284	£1	Green (prefix: letter, number, number, letter). Queen's portrait	£2	£4
283	£1	Green 'R' variety (letter R found in white space above lower BANK OF ENGLAND panel on reverse)	£100	£300
275	£5	Black on white	£30	£90
277	£5	Blue, pale green and orange (solid symbols)	£8	£25
279	£5	Blue, pale green and orange (symbols for £5 white)	£8	£25

asper Quintus Hollom 1962-66

295	10s	Red-brown (prefix: number, number, letter)	£2	£3
294	10s	Red-brown (prefix: letter, number, number, letter)	£1	£2
288	£1	Green	£1	£3
292	£1	Green, 'G' variety ('G' in same position as 'R' as B283)	£1	£1.50
297	£5	Blue	£5	£10
299	£10	Multicoloured	£12	£18

ohn Standish Fforde 1966-70

309	10s	Red-brown (prefix: number, number, letter)	£1	£2
310	10s	Red-brown (prefix: letter, number, number, letter)	£1	£2
311	10s	Red-brown (prefix: letter, number, number)	£2	£4
301	£1	Green	£1.50	£2
303	£1	Green 'G' variety	£1	£1.50
312	£5	Blue (prefix: letter, number, number)	£6	£8
314	£5	Blue (prefix: number, number, letter)	£6	£8
316	£10	Multicoloured	£11	£18
318	£10	Multicoloured	£22	£45

John Brangwyn Page 1970-1980

322	£1	Green (prefix: letter, letter, number, number)	f	£1.50
335	£1	Dark and light green, 1st series, AO1	f	£2
324	£5	Blue	f	£10
332	£5	Multicoloured (prefix: letter, number, number). 1st series	f	£7
334	£5	Multicoloured, L on reverse signifies lithographic printing	f	£6
326	£10	Multicoloured	f	£14

| B330 | £10 | Multicoloured A-series | f | £14 |
| B328 | £20 | Multicoloured | f | £40 |

David Henry Fitzroy Somerset 1980-1988

B341	£1	Green	£1.50	
B342	£5	Multicoloured	£6	
B344	£10	Multicoloured (prefix: letter, number, number)	£12	
B346	£10	Multicoloured (prefix: letter, letter, number, number)	£12	
B350	£20	Multicoloured	£30	
B352	£50	Olive green, brown, grey	£70	

George Malcolm Gill (1988-1991)

B353	£5	Blue	f	£8
B354	£10	Brown	f	f
B355	£20	Multicoloured	f	f
B356	£50	Multicoloured	f	f
B357	£5	Multicoloured (Series E) AO1	f	£16
		Presentation pair Series D and E £5	£200	
		Presentation pair Series D and E £20	£180	
		Presentation pair Series D and E £10	£120	
B358	£10	Multicoloured	f	f
B359	£20	Multicoloured	f	f
B360	£50	Multicoloured	f	f

G.E.A. Kentfield (1991-)

B-	£5	Multicoloured	f	f
B-	£10	Multicoloured	f	f
B-	£20	Multicoloured	f	f
B-	£50	Multicoloured	f	f

* Exist but no price can be quoted. f - still face value unless special prefix number, i.e. AD1.

A recently dicovered extraordinarily rare Bank of England £100 of 1790